AF539769

Advanced Educational Psychology

ADVANCED EDUCATIONAL PSYCHOLOGY

(For: B.Ed., M.Ed., M.A. Education, M.A. Psychology, M.Phil. Education and Psychology Students)

BY

B.N. PANDA

DISCOVERY PUBLISHING HOUSE

NEW DELHI-110 002

Reprinted - 2018

First Published - 1999

ISBN: 978-81-7141-500-7

Advanced Educational Psychology

Published by:

DISCOVERY PUBLISHING HOUSE PVT. LTD.
4383/4B, Ansari Road, Darya Ganj
New Delhi-110 002 (India)
Phone: +91-11-23279245, 43596064-65
Fax: +91-11-23253475
E-mail: discoverypublishinghouse@gmail.com
sales@discoverypublishinggroup.com
web: www.discoverypublishinggroup.com

Printed at:
Infinity Imaging Systems

FOREWORD

Though there are a large number of Educational Psychology books available for the graduate/postgraduate student of Education and Psychology yet there is a dearth of advanced level texts which are suitable to the educational framework and the teaching-learning situations prevalent in our country. The present book differs from many other Indian books not only because of its vast coverage of the topics, but 't gives the latest developments in the various areas of ational psychology and try to fill up the gap, deficiencies and lacunas of other books. Besides, the book is written in a very lucid manner with clarity of thought so as to assist the readers to grasp the subject better.

The indepth discussion of various chapters in the book along with illustrated examples facilitate the readers in understanding the topic more vividly. All the chapters are with uniformity in style, besides providing a summary for recollection of the topic, questions to understand the knowledge of the students and appropriate references have been given to enable the readers to understand deeper into the subject. The book shall certainly provoke wide-ranging interests and strive to draw the attention of students and teachers.

I congratulate my obedient student Dr. B.N. Panda and strongly feel that this volume will be a stepping stone and an additional book in the field of Educational Psychology.

I wish him all success in life.

C.L. Kundu

PREFACE

There have been countless new developments in the field of educational psychology. It is a fact that in recent years education has emerged as a professional subject knowledge of which is essential for an effective instruction. A teacher will be a failure in the class-rooms transaction if he/she has no ideas about his/her pupils, their development, their needs, their motives and their psycho-physical elements. Thus the teacher has to have a deep understanding of his/her pupils in order to make teaching effective and interesting in the class-room.

The present book begins with a discussion on the meaning, nature, scope, methods of studying human behaviour and views of different schools of psychology. The text then covers growth and development, heredity and environment, psychology of adolescence and individual difference. This is followed by an indepth discussion on the nature and theories of learning and their educational implications along with wide coverage of modern methods of learning. The cognitive and non-cognitive aspects, namely, intelligence, creativity, problem-solving, personality, adjustment, mental health and motivation have also been presented in a lucid style. The text concludes with an important chapter on gifted and slow learning exceptional children.

The utility of the book is further enhanced by the provision of number of exercises at the end of each chapter along with summary and references. Not only this the logistic and lucid presentation of the book will foster critical thinking and creative imagination in dealing with students. Thus it is hoped that this book will enable the teacher to perceive classroom situations with a deeper insight and also increase his/her professional competence.

I express my deep sense of gratitude to my esteemed teacher and supervisor Prof. C.L. Kundu, Vice-chancellor,

Himachal Pradesh University, Summer Hill, Shimla-5 who has written few valuable lines as a foreword of the book "Advance Educational Psychology", and always been a source of inspiration for my career development. I am especially grateful to him.

The author expresses his sincere gratitude to all the authors and publishers whose works have been consulted and quoted. I am grateful to many of my colleagues and friends who offered suggestions and criticisms to the improvement of the text. To all of these I owe my thanks.

I am extremely indebted to my wife who has inspired and helped me throughout in the preparation of the manuscript and was also a great source of encouragement for my vertical mobility.

At the end I am grateful to Discovery Publishing House, Darya Ganj, New Delhi-2, (India) who undertook the publication of this book and did it with great sincerity. All suggestions for improving the attempts will be accepted with thanks and acknowledged.

B. N. Panda
Regional Institute of Education,
(NCERT), Bhubaneswar -22
(India).

CONTENTS

EDUCATIONAL PSYCHOLOGY

Introduction

We are living in an age of science and technology and accordingly society has become bit complex. Life in the coming decades is likely to bring new tensions together with unprecedented opportunities. To enable the people to benefit in the new environment will require new designs of human resource development. Thus the coming generations should have the ability to internalise new ideas constantly and creatively and have to be imbued with a strong commitment to human values and to social justice. All this can be possible only through good quality education.

To achieve the above goal and to meet the situation in a gigantic way the teacher has to play a very vital role in the educational institutions and come into the limelight. He is really the backbone of the educational system, the maker of the mankind, the fountainhead of knowledge, the architect of the society and the potential guide to provide directive for the growth and development of students of today as the worthy citizens of tomorrow. He is the real principal agency who is ultimately to implement and interpret the plan and policies at various levels through teaching-learning processes. Good teaching, therefore, does not lie in the scholarly imparting of detailed information and knowledge of subject matter alone, but in creating a motivating learning environment in such a way as to facilitate independent thinking and self-learning curiosity on the part of the students. It has also been remarked by the Kothari Commission (1964-66) that "the destiny of the country is being shaped in her classrooms". Therefore, in order to be a good mediator, the teacher has to understand a great deal about the way in which people at various ages and stages of development perceive the world around them. To meet the 'new' challenges boldly and to play his/her role meaningfully, the teacher, besides imparting knowledge, has to help the students to understand the components of their conscious and unconscious personalities, the meaning of their dreams and aspirations and the nature of their relations with one another and with the community at large.

Under the above circumstances "Educational Psychology is a subject of study to equip the perspective teacher with the necessary skills and competencies to enable him to deal effectively with the teaching-learning problems of the class". As a result of its study, it describes and often formulates certain principles which are worthy of consideration in directing and fostering the programmes of school education on humanistic lines.

What is Educational Psychology? or Meaning and Definitions of Educational Psychology

Educational Psychology, what it is, really a straightforward question but there is no common agreement among educational psychologists to define it in a concrete form. Educational Psychology is concerned with the problems, processes and products of education, which is natural and heterogenous. It is the application of psychological principles, techniques and other resources of psychology in the field of education for the solution of educational problems like teaching, learning and class management, etc. When a person apply the knowledge of psychology in the field of education, study the human behaviour in relation to his environment and concern for the total growth and all round development of children in a scientific way is called educational psychology.

There are basically two different approaches to define the meaning of educational psychology, i.e., behaviourist and cognitive. The behaviourist approach involves determining the relationship between two factors—instructional manipulations and outcome performance. The instructional manipulations refers to the nature of the stimulus that is presented to the learners whereas outcome performance refers to the nature of the responses that the learner gives on tests.

In contrast, the cognitive approach involves determining the relationships among external factors, e.g. (instructional manipulations and outcome performance), and internal factors, e.g. (learning processes, learning outcomes, and the existing knowledge and skill of the learner). Thus, the cognitive approach attempts to understand how instructional manipulations affect cognitive processes such as paying attention, encoding, retrieving; how these processes result in the acquisition of new knowledge; and how new knowledge influences performance, such as on tests.

Educational psychology has been defined by various psychologists and scholars in their own way. The following are the meaning for the sake of understanding:

> *Skinner* (1958): Educational Psychology is that branch of psychology which deals with teaching and learning. It means psychology is applied in the field of education for improving the methods and products of the teaching-learning process.
>
> *Crow and Crow* (1973): Educational Psychology describes and explains the learning experiences of an individual from birth through old age. It means development of an individual in terms of learning achievement is judged through his life span. Therefore, what we do in the process of learning is the role of educational psychology.
>
> *Peel* (1956): Educational Psychology is the science of education. It means to help in realising the objectives of education in a scientific way as science and technology does. When our aims of education is to bring all round development of an individual, educational psychology supplies the necessary skills and expertise to achieve the same in the educational institution.
>
> *Anderson* (1949) : Educational Psychology is a subject to be studied, an area or field of knowledge, a set of applications of law and principles from a field of knowledge to a social process, a set of tools and techniques and a field of research for the development of an individual in an educational setting.

Thus, educational psychology is the application of the findings and theories of psychology in the field of education, a systematic story of educational growth, and an independent applied discipline that deals with the improvement in teaching and learning activity. In fact, it seeks to know the child's mind and how best the child can be motivated to learn in a desirable manner in the society. It is the empirical foundation of education and provides practical solution to educational problems with the help of sweet relation between the teacher and the taught.

Nature of Educational Psychology

The following are the nature of educational psychology.

1. Educational psychology is scientific in nature. In science collection of data, observation of facts and its verification of any phenomena are possible by any number of persons at any period of life. Similarly, educational psychology has also developed certain principles to collect data from human beings and predict his/her behaviour in a scientific manner.
2. Educational psychology is concerned with the study of behaviour of the learner in relation to his educational environment. Educational Psychology is constantly in search of the truth in the sense that the results of the study of human behaviour can be modified as per the latest findings in the field.
3. Educational psychology is a social science in the sense that it is like other social sciences to study the human beings and their sociability.
4. Educational psychology is concerned with 'what' and 'why' of happenings in the present rather than the past. It studies the problems of present behaviour of the learners and their causes rather than anything else.
5. Educational Psychology is a positive science rather than a normative science. It is not concerned with 'what ought to be' (why and what type of education to child, etc.), rather emphasises how, when and where of education.
6. Educational psychology is an applied psychology in the sense that it applies psychological principles in the field of education which are of specific significance to learning and teaching. It does not accept blindly the facts and principles of general psychology.
7. Educational psychology is narrower in nature because it deals with delimitation. Here the study of the behaviour is concerned in educational settings.
8. Educational psychology is a developing or growing science in the sense that the research findings

provide reliable data and insight into the child's nature and these can be used for predictions of the behaviour of a child in similar situations. Though it is not so perfect and developed as science like physics, chemistry and biology and absolute in nature, yet it follows the foot print of scientific investigation and considered as scientific.

Scope of Educational Psychology

The scope of educational psychology means the topics covered or the subject matters are included under the boundary of purview of the concerned paper. Lindgren emphasised that the focal areas of educational psychology are the learner, the learning process and the learning situation or the conditions under which learning takes place. This means educational psychology is concerned only or centred around to the study of human behaviour in educational situations, i.e., to help the teacher in his task of modifying the learners behaviour and bringing about an all round development of his personality.

A course in educational psychology must seek to enrich knowledge and develop competence in the following areas:

1. The process of growth and development of the learner in relation to infancy, childhood, adolescence and adulthood so that the teacher can formulate suitable plans for their development.
2. The process of learning, factors influencing learners, motivation in learning, problem solving, transfer of training and relation between teaching-learning will help the teacher to understand the child better and effective management of learning is possible.
3. The nature and development of personality, assessment of personality adjustment, mental health, etc., helps the teacher to guide the learner properly.
4. The psychology of individual differences, influences of heredity and environment, intelligence, creativity, aptitudes, interests, exceptional children, etc., will also help the teacher to understand the child better.
5. The measurement and evaluation in education, defects of essay type examination, objective type tests, characteristics of a good test and educational statistics, etc., provides answers to numerous questions arising in the educational institution.

Thus in the words of Crow and Crow 'the subject matter of educational psychology is concerned with the conditions that affect learning' or whatever touches the child in his/her class-room behaviour comes with the scope of educational psychology. Here the teacher not only acquire the theoretical knowledge but also give a practical shape to the theoretical knowledge acquired.

Educational Psychology being a science of education has to supply the necessary knowledge and skills for carrying out all the tasks of education. Education is not a constant entity rather it is dynamic and flexible in the sense that it has to be planned according to the changing circumstances and needs of a particular society. To meet the demands of the nation, educational psychology has to play a vital role and, therefore, scope of the subject is very extensive and broad based. The subject matter which help in knowing the learner; enabling the teacher to know his self, his strengths and limitations and acquire essential teacher-like traits; selection and organization of proper learning experiences suited to the various developmental stages of the learner; suggesting suitable methods and techniques for providing the desirable learning experiences; and in arranging proper learning situations, etc., should be given emphasis under the scope of educational psychology. Therefore, for better serving the cause of education, whatever contents are required must be included under the scope of educational psychology.

Need or Importance or Contribution or Utility of Educational Psychology

Though the knowledge of educational psychology do not guarantee good teaching yet without it, teaching becomes simply a case of rules of thumb, routine habits and trial and error procedures, many of which would be detrimental to the child. Its function is to promote greater understanding of the learning process, of the learning situation and of the learner and will put the teacher in a better position to decide the line of action. In addition to the above, it also enables the teacher to do more effective job by developing some of the insights, skills and attitudes to solve his professional problems and make the teaching-learning process more effective and brings improvement in the quality of instruction. Thus, the knowledge of educational psychology helps the teacher in the following ways:

1. To Understand the Stages of Development

Educational psychology helps the teacher to understand that human life is divided into different stages of development and each stage has special needs, abilities and characteristics. On the basis of this, the teacher gains better insight into the behaviour of his pupil and change his behaviour and methodology of teaching according to the child requirement in the class.

2. To Understand the Learner and its Characteristics

The child or the learner is the key factor in the teaching-learning process. Educational psychology helps the teacher to understand how children grow, develop, learn and adjust; his/her interest, attitude and innate potentialities; and likes and dislikes, level of aspiration and desires, etc., so that perfect guidance and help can be provided and positive attitude towards the learner can be formed.

3. To Understand the Nature of Classroom Learning

The classroom is hetrogeneous in nature. To deal with the groups effectively in the class the teacher must have the knowledge of the various approaches to the learning process, principles, laws and factors affecting it then only he/she can apply remedial measures in the learning situation.

4. To Understand the Individual Differences

It is a fact that no two individuals are alike so also no two students are equal in the class. Thus, psychology tells the teacher about the individual differences among the students in the class and the procedure, methodology and techniques to be adopted for them.

5. To Develop Necessary Skills and Interest in Teaching

Educational Psychology helps the teacher to develop necessary qualities and skills to deal with the problems created by the pupils, maintain a healthy atmosphere in the class-room and shows concern regarding the progress of the child. Not only this it helps in developing new strategies and different innovative approaches to tackle the problems of teaching in a sophisticated manner.

6. To Understand the Influence of Heredity and Environment on Child

Educational psychology help the teacher to know that the child is a bi-product of both heredity and environment. They are the two sides of a coin. While child is born with a number of hereditary qualities, environment helps them to be modified according to the requirements of the society.

7. To Make Wise and Correct Decisions in the Teaching-Learning

Educational Psychology helps a teacher to know about his/her own abilities and weaknesses and to bring about an improvement upon it so that decisions making in the teaching process will be accurate and exact.

8. To Understand the Efficient Class-room Management

Educational Psychology helps the teacher to maintain efficient classroom discipline by applying new principles of learning. The teacher can overcome the classroom problem and manage it very effectively by knowing the psychology of students.

9. To Understand the Mental Health

Educational Psychology helps the teacher to know what are the factors responsible for the mental ill-health and maladjustment of a student and suggests improvement thereof. Besides this, it also provides the teacher with necessary insight to improve his own mental status to cope up with the situation.

10. To Understand the Group Behaviour

Human beings cannot live in isolation. He needs company. Similarly, we all of us are members of certain social group and depend upon others. In this situation, psychology tells a teacher how a group life modifies the individual and vice-versa and provide information how to handle groups and modify their behaviour.

11. To Understand the Procedure of Curriculum Construction

Curriculum is an integral part of the teaching-learning process. Curriculum should be child-centred and fulfil the motives and psychological needs of the individual because child capacities differ from stage to stage. Educational psychology helps the teacher to suggest ways and means to curriculum framer to prepare sound and balanced curriculum for the children.

12. To Provide Guidance and Counselling

Today guidance to a child at every stage of life is needed because psychological abilities, interests and learning styles differ from person to person. Similarly, what courses of study the child should undertake in future is also a vital question. All these can be answered well if the teacher knows the psychology of children.

13. To Understand the Principles of Evaluation

Evaluation is an integral part of the teaching-learning process. How to test the potentialities of the child depends upon the evaluation techniques. The development of the different types of psychological tests for the evaluation of the individual is a distinct contribution of educational psychology.

14. Educational Psychology and Research

Educational Psychologists conduct research to improve the behaviour of human beings in the educational situation. For this purpose it helps in developing tools and devices to measure the performance and suggest remedial measures thereof.

15. Educational Psychology Helps in Professional Growth, Changing Attitude and Innovative Thinking

Inside the classroom, educational psychology has enabled the teacher to achieve proper conditioning of pupils by achieving and directing classroom programmes on human lives. Not only this, educational psychologists are busy in finding out innovations in the field of education. These innovations will being about professional growth of the teacher.

Difference between General Psychology and Educational Psychology

Psychology is the positive science of behaviour. It aims at the study of the facts of behaviour, their collection, classification and comparison and find out general hypothesis based upon them. Thus, psychology studies man's overt and covert behaviour and physical, social and mental activities.

The aim of psychology is not only theoretical but also practical in the sense that the theoretical studies aim at finding out general laws regarding behaviour whereas it can be used in other applied branches for better human activities.

With the help of psychology, man today is able to control many phenomena, which were out of his hold previously. It has changed man's approach towards life and world to understand himself and his fellow beings. The study of individual differences and their capacities has helped in the planned economy of modern nations.

Psychology has made revolutionised and reform in the field of education, syllabi and methods of education so that the relationship between the teacher and the taught has been strengthened.

Psychology has been very helpful in understanding the causes of crimes and their cures; helped the sociologists and the social reformers to solve various problems of society; helped in minimising the fatigue and using human capacities with utmost efficiency; helped man to form his character, and to change his habits to adjust himself to new situations; helps the parents to understand the child and the teacher to understand the taught; helped the leaders to understand masses and control them; and not only in the time of war but also in the time of peace psychology has its own importance.

Psychology is a science and applies scientific methods to study the human behaviour, i.e., the child, adolescents, adult and the old. It studies the man from the cradle to the grave and animal behaviour also.

Psychology studies the facts of behaviour and finds out cause-effect relationships in them, i.e., why and in what circumstances a child becomes a delinquent. Similarly, on the basis of psychological tests prediction of human behaviour is possible. Thus its subject matter is what people do and how and why they do.

An appropriate description and quantification of behaviour is possible through psychology. On the basis of the above characteristics, it may be established beyond doubt that psychology is scientific and emphasizes the search for truth.

On the otherhand, *Educational Psychology* is that branch of psychology which deals with teaching and learning; applying psychological principles and laws in the field of education and studying the child behaviour in educational settings. It is an applied science. It explains the nature and characteristics of the learner, nature of learning process and learning outcome. It is narrower in scope and professional in nature. It studies heredity, growth and maturation, environmental influences, intelligence and process of socialization in relation to group and many other related areas for enabling the teacher and learners to do their jobs as satisfactorily as possible. Educational Psychology is concerned with 'what', 'who', 'why', 'how', 'when' and 'where' of education. Educational Psychology suggest ways and means of improving the processes and products of education.

Educational Psychology has simplified the tasks and developed the efficiency of the teacher by supplying them necessary skills to improve the teaching-learning process. Thus, without the knowledge of psychology education will be non-psychological and lack romantic and human background.

To sum up, psychology of education gives us the ends to be achieved whereas educational psychology gives us the means to achieve those ends. An understanding of educational psychology will put the teacher in a better position to decide the line of action and solve the professional problems effectively and to make the teaching-learning process viable, effective and changing her attitude towards the growing child. The educational psychologists find out how best the child can be motivated to learn. How this aspiration can be increased? What methods of teaching would be most effective? How learning materials can be sequenced and delivered? What are the conditions of positive transfer? How education can be directed towards socialisation of the child? Therefore, it develops the insight into the teaching-learning process. In fact, its use furnishes the teacher with the basic psychological understandings, skills and sophistication which he can apply to improve his classroom teaching.

In the concluding remarks it can be said that the purpose of general psychology is to build up a body of principle of behaviour which are general in nature and basically academic minded. But the purpose of educational psychology is to find out practical solutions to educational problems and helps to adopt a professional point of view by developing useful professional practices in the field of education.

Methods of Educational Psychology

Educational Psychology is the scientific study of the human behaviour of the learner in relation to educational setting. To study the behaviour of the learner, there are different approaches or methods used. While some psychologists are in favour of subjective methods others are in objective methods. Though the methods used by educational psychologists are many and varied yet their main purpose is to investigate the behaviour of a learner. Thus the knowledge of methods used to gather psychological data is beneficial to develop insight into the nature, source and techniques of psychological understanding of a learner.

The following are the various methods of studying human behaviour. These are:

I. *Introspection Method*

When psychology was defined as the science of consciousness the method of introspection was considered as vital one and widely used to study the human behaviour. It is the oldest known method of psychology and psycho-analysis school has widely utilised this method. The propounder of this method is structuralists.

The term introspection is originated from the two Latin words, intro means "within" or "inward" and spection means "looking" or "observing". Hence, introspection means looking within or looking inward. It is a method which helps the individual to analyse and report his own mental feelings. It is otherwise known as internal perception or self-observation method. For example, if a man goes to see a picture and returns after seeing it, it is only through introspection that he can tell others how he feels about it. Thus, in the field of feelings, emotions, sentiments, prejudices and various types of internal experiences, e.g., love, hate, pleasure, pain and fear, a man can know them only by introspective analysis. It is a process of examining one's own mental process of thought, feelings and motives. No man can know the covert or internal behaviour or mental feelings of other person from outside. Thus, introspection is a developed form of self-consciousness. It is also called the subjective method because the subject is alone capable of introspecting his own mind.

This method is important in the sense that in introspection the individual himself systematically observes his inner mental processes and feelings which cannot be known as external observation.

Advantages of introspection method

1. Introspection enables us to understand one's own

mental status or what is going on in the mind without involving any extra expenditure of material or apparatus. One can introspect while walking, travelling, sitting or at the time of gossiping.
2. It is simplest, economical and readily available method.
3. Introspection provides adequate knowledge to know about internal behaviour of an individual or actual facts of mental activities are understood properly.
4. It leads to better understanding of one's own self and help to improve one's own styles of functioning.

Disadvantages or Limitations

1. It is true that the mental processes can be directly observed through introspection but the collected data is subjective, unscientific and personal in nature and verification cannot be possible of the collected data.
2. Introspection can only be applied to adult normal human beings. This method cannot be applied to children, animals and mad or defective persons because they are unable to perceive their mental feelings judiciously.
3. Here the observer and observed are the same. Hence, biasness of data can be possible.
4. By introspection one cannot know the experience of others. Hence, comparison of one's own experience with others is not possible.
5. Mental processes are psychic and abstract. Hence, it is not easy to attend the mental processes without practice.
6. Mental processes are changeable and followed with constant fluctuation. The thoughts, feelings, desires, etc., are constantly changing. If a person wants to know his mental state in fear, it is likely that fear may disappear as soon as he looks at it or introspects. They cannot be detained like stocks and stones so that we can observe them.
7. Reliability, validity and objectivity of this method is questionable.

So we can come to the conclusion that introspection, in spite of its criticism, is quite practicable method of psychology to study the mental process of an individual. Though this method is entirely useless in many situations, e.g., in the study of the psychology of the children, insanes and abnormals, patients and animals yet from the practical point of view introspection method cannot be eliminated from the field of psychology. Its value stands unquestioned in its own field.

II. The Observation Method

To study the human behaviour the observation method is a very popular one. It is a method of measurement without instruments or looking outside oneself. Hence, visual procedure is followed to see the mental processes and behaviour of others or how a person reacts in a given situation. Through this method the individual's behaviour is observed by somebody other than the person himself and make certain generalisations about human behaviour. The outer manifestations or external behaviour or overt behaviour of the individual is observed objectively by this method so that it gives indirectly clue to the understanding of the mental conditions of the individual. In fact it is an indirect approach to study the mental process.

The observation may be of two types: direct and indirect or natural and artificial, or scheduled and unscheduled, or participant and non-participant, or controlled and uncontrolled or free observation.

In natural or unscheduled or non-participant or uncontrolled or indirect observation the observer observes the actual behavioural characteristics of the subject or children without giving any hints or clue that their behaviour is observed. This observation can be done either in playground or in any other social situation where students are not conscious about their behaviour. Hence, the individual cannot know the presence of observer and he performs behaviour in a natural fashion.

On the otherhand, artificial or scheduled or participant or controlled or direct observation, the observer mingles or establishes proper rapport with the subjects first so that they are not able to know that their behaviour is observed. Here the observer becomes the part of the group to find out the hidden ideas or actual behaviour in such a manner so that the subjects may not hide their internal feelings while expressing their ideas. In this form of observation the observer actually becomes an active participant in children's activities to elicit actual behaviour.

Steps of Observation method

Roughly speaking, various steps in the method of observation are as follows:

(a) Observation of behaviour
(b) Noting of behaviour
(c) Interpretation and analysis of behaviour
(d) Generalisation

The observation of behaviour is the first step of this method. Here the observer perceives everything objectively. If some one has to observe the social behaviour of monkeys, then he should go where the monkeys are assembled and observe their behaviour.

The second step of observation method is noting down the observed behaviour. In the examples of the study of the social behaviour of the monkeys, the observer should carefully note down their various activities.

The third step is interpretation and analysis of behaviour. The recorded data of behaviour is analysed point by point to express the internal conditions of the person.

Lastly, generalisation is made and general principles are formed on the basis of observation, noting, analysis and interpretation.

In addition to the above steps the following fundamental principles/rules may be followed to make the observation method systematic in order:

1. Objective of the observation must be specified
2. Make a plan how to proceed and what are the points to be observed
3. Decision of the time, hour and place must be decided earlier
4. What type of devices, i.e., movie, camera, tape recorder, etc., are to be used must be planned beforehand
5. Instruction regarding observation must be clear
6. Who is to observe and what type of competencies, aptitude or training, etc., are needed must be clear
7. How to observe precisely, concretely and unambiguiously must be known to the observer.

Advantages and limitations of observation method

1. This method is very helpful to study the individual and group behaviour easily because no tools and techniques are required to study the behaviour
2. It is more objective, reliable, systematic, flexible, economical and verifiable method
3. It helps in finding out remedial measures for abnormal person after observing him under natural conditions of his day to day life
4. Observation can be made for children as well as animals
5. Observation method help in improving teaching process by studying the developmental characteristics of children in the classroom.

Difficulties/Drawbacks of observation method

1. The behaviour of the individual is interpreted wrongly due to personal interests, biasness of the observer and prejudices based on colour, sex and religion, etc. Subjectivity affect the results of observation
2. It requires trained and technical observers otherwise unnecessary huge data can be collected and leads to wastage of time, money and energy
3. There is every possibility that false, misleading and artificial data can be collected if we make the subjects conscious or whom we are observing
4. It is difficult to replicate each natural situation to collect data
5. The internal or covert behaviour of the individual cannot be studied through this method.

III. **The Experimental Method**

Out of all the methods of psychology, experimental method is the most important one because it is this method which has the credit of bringing psychology to the level of an exact science. It was Wilhlem Wundt, a German Psychologist who for the first time set up a psychological laboratory at Leipzig in 1879 for the successful implementation of this method. This is the method which is considered as most scientific and objective in nature to study the human behaviour.

What is Experimental Method

The experimental method of psychology means the

method of scientifically studying mental processes. In this method, the observation of mental status/processes is held in certain predetermined conditions. Thus experiment is a controlled observation. It is the observation of the behaviour or activity in fixed circumstances. Experiment is nothing but a set of systematic enquiry or asking questions. In experiment, the experimenter has a problem before him and find solution to this problem. Thus for the success of this method the following ideal conditions must be ensured.

Essentials of Experimental Method

1. Either laboratory setup or outside the laboratory setup. If the experiment is to be conducted in outside system then there is a need of some specific experimental designs like one group or single group design, control-group design, one group pre test-post test design, two group design, multi-group design, and designs involving rotation, etc.
2. The person who is going to conduct the experiment, i.e., the experimenter(s)
3. The subject or the person whose behaviour is to be observed
4. Controlling the effect of variables. This means we can control or eliminate irrelevant conditions or variables and isolate the relevant ones. For example, if we wanted to study the effect of SES on academic achievement by this method, then causative relation between the two phenomena (variables) are to be studied. Here SES is independent variable because the effect of which is studied and the other is dependent variable. Thus the independent variable stands for the cause and the dependent variable is the effect of that cause. Similarly, the other variables like IQ, sex, environment, personality and education of parents, etc., also affect ones academic achievement. These variables are called intervening variables. In experimentation all such intervening variables are to be controlled by making the group constant or equalized and the effect of only one independent variable, i.e., SES is studied.

How to conduct experiment

The following are the procedure or various steps involved in planning and conducting the experiments:

1. Statement of the problem: The first step in an experiment is the raising of the problem either through discussion or reviewing the past literature. In this way, problem for the experiment is selected.
2. Formulation of hypothesis: The second step in experimental method is the formulation of a hypothesis. It is a intellectual guessing or hunch which suggest answer to a problem. The experimenter either writes the hypothesis in a declarative, or null or question form to testify the proposed problem and find solution of it.
3. To distinguish independent and dependent variable: The third step in experimental method is the distinction between independent and dependent variables. When the experimenter interested to manipulate or to see the effect of some variable or object upon others is called independent and dependent is the *effect* of that cause.
4. Controlling the environment or situation: The fourth and the most important step in the experimental method is controlling the conditions of experiment. Here, the experimenter should see that there is a balance or homogeneity in the group or both the experimental and control groups are uniform as far as possible by controlling or eliminating the intervening factors or variables, otherwise the results would have been influenced. As per the selection of the problem, the experimenter either choose one group, two groups, multi-groups or factorial design for the experiment.
5. Analysis of the results: The fifth important step in the experimental method is the analysis of the results. The experimenter analysed the collected data by applying different statistical techniques as per the design and requirement. After that he can come to the conclusion.
6. Verification or confirmation of the hypothesis by the result of experiment: After analysis the experimenter exhibits whether the hypothesis was right or wrong. It also suggest the ways to see and verify the findings of experiment by repeating it.

Merits of Experimental Method

1. Experiments can be conducted as many times as

possible to verify the results of finding.
2. It is a systematic, reliable and objective method of psychology.
3. The experimenter can control and manipulate the effects of independent variable on dependent one.
4. It provides sufficient knowledge of information to the teacher experimenter to improve the qualitative development of teaching and learning process.
5. It suggests precise information about the problems and new ideas for further investigation.

Demerits of Experimental Method

1. Artificial situation of laboratory experiment may not give correct information about the covert behaviour.
2. As mental processes are not static and fluctuating in nature it cannot be detained for the purpose of experimental study.
3. It is not always easy to control the attitude of subjects specially when they are children or students. This makes the result of the experiment unreliable.
4. Experimental method requires active cooperation of the subject, but sometime it is not possible.
5. There are some mental processes like emotion which are difficult to experiment upon. Thus all problems of educational psychology cannot be studied.
6. It is time consuming, costly, and difficult to control all the intervening variables.

IV. **The Clinical Method or the Case-study Method**

Individuals differ from one to another. While some of them are normal others are abnormal. When the individuals are abnormal and suffering from truancy, stealing, worries, anxieties, fears and show deviant and maladjusted behaviour, that time this method is appropriate. To find out the causes and sources of the unsocial behaviour and suggesting remedial measures is the main purpose of this method. Hence intensive investigation of the particular case or cases of groups are done to detect and diagnose their specific problems and to suggest therapeutic measures to rehabilitate them in their environment (Sawney and Telford).

The basic factors in this method are the diagnosis and treatment of the individual. Under this method the past and present experiences, conditions in home, parent views, school and society, etc., are collected from all sources in an orderly fashion in order to solve the problems of an individual. In addition to that, the techniques of clinical interview, questionnaire, physical examination, psychological testing and case history are followed to diagnose the problem. The anecdotal cummulative record cards also, if maintained in schools would also give many clues regarding the child.

There are two approaches under this method. First one is case history or the clinical case study and other one is developmental case study. Under the first category the psychologist or the teacher collect detailed information on the problem of maladjustment from the following sources like preliminary information, past history, present condition either through clinical interview or direct observation or using tests and measuring devices to understand the root causes of maladjustment so that the treatment of a behavioural problem can be made and ultimately changes in the behaviour and normal mental health can be restored. After collection or diagnosis of the facts the method of treatment are to be followed up. Hereafter the analysis either the individual may be removed from his existing situation to another (if required), the attitude of the parents, teachers and others towards him may be changed, or the situation like more recreational facilities, better living conditions and facilities to fulfil his repressed desires may be provided to restore the normalcy. Other techniques like therapies of various types, guidance and psycho-analysis can also be provided.

On the other hand, the second method is developmental case study or genetic method. Here two approaches are generally followed to collect the data. These are longitudinal and cross sectional approach. In the longitudinal approach a child is studied from birth to maturity or up to any specific age level continuously from year to year. Whereas in the cross-sectional approach the sample from different age levels are collected to study specific aspect of development. Whatever may be the procedure of collecting data the main purpose is to find out or to discover the real causes of mental abnormalities and suggested recommendation thereof.

Merits of clinical method

1. It is a useful method to study the problems of behaviour and suggest suitable treatment or remedial measures.
2. It is the only method dealing with a particular person and intensive study involving all possible details

regarding individual behaviour is followed.

3. This method is useful in the problem of reading disability, emotional disturbance and anti-social behaviour.

Demerits of clinical method

1. It is subjectivity in nature, time consuming and costly method.
2. It needs technically trained person to collect and study human behaviour.
3. The results cannot be generalised and restricted in scope.
4. It is difficult to know the whole history of an individual and arrive at a particular diagnosis and treatment.

V. **The Differential or Survey Method**

The method which is used to study individual difference among the students is called as differential or survey method. The investigator first has to choose the population according to certain criteria, and then he measures the variables which he wants to investigate.

Thus, obtaining the objective and quantitative measurement of individual differences is the chief characteristics of differential method. By using this method it is possible to know why differences exist among the individuals. Since the data is collected from the field and statistical techniques is applied to analyse it this method is otherwise known as field survey or statistical method.

In this method various steps like selection of the problem, selection of the procedure, selection of a sample, collection of data and their interpretation, main findings and drawing conclusion, etc., are followed. This method makes use of various techniques of collecting data such as tests, questionnaire, observation, interview and use of statistics in analysing the data.

Generally four types of approaches are followed to study the individual differences. These are: correlational approach, field survey approach, longitudinal and cross-sectional approach.

Under the correlational approach various relationships and associations between two variables are studied by using the statistical technique of correlation.

In the field survey approach, the differences with regard to a particular trait or various characteristics among the individuals are studied on the basis of conducting field survey.

In the longitudinal approach, the differences among the individuals or the differences in an individual are studied over a long span of time. The longitudinal method is more intensive and involves a series of planned and systematic observations of behaviour over a considerable period of time.

Similarly, under the cross-sectional approach different individuals of varying age groups are studied or we take many individuals and study them simultaneously at a particular age level. Because of the practical difficulty of following up the same individual over a period of time, this method help the investigators to collect sample of different age groups available at the same time.

Thus, through this method the educational problems of local, state, national or international problems can be studied. It provides useful information to the solution of local problems and collect what exists, what we want and how to get there.

Advantage of survey method

1. This method helps in solving individual problems and contribute advancement of knowledge and insight for future solution of the problem.
2. Longitudinal and cross-sectional approaches have become very important for the purpose of prediction of behaviour.

Disadvantages of survey method

1. Sampling error and reliability of the data is questionable because there is a doubt to collect acurate information through this method.
2. Lack of cooperation of the subjects and manipulation of data is possible through this method.
3. More planned and systematic observation of behaviour over a considerable period of time is required in case of longitudinal approach.

VI. **The Psycho-Physical Method**

This is a method of the combination of psychological and physical devices for the study of the behaviour of an individual. In this method, physical devices are used for the scientific measurement of some psychological experiences like sensations of weight, brightness, loudness and other such dimensions like sleep or span of memory, etc.

German Physiologist and Physicist Gustav Fechner (1801-87) was the father of this method and developed three procedures to be studied in this method. These are:

1. The method of minimal changes or methods of limits
2. The method of constant stimuli or the method of right and wrong responses
3. The method of average or mean error.

These methods are employed to measure the absolute threshold (the minimum value of a physical stimulus that reliably produces sensation, i.e., separate the sounds we can hear from those we cannot and the brightness of the light we can see from that which we cannot and so on) and the difference threshold (the minimum difference in value between two stimuli which enable perceived by the subject, i.e., when one experiences a particular weight put in one's hand, how much minimum weight has to be added to it so that the total becomes just distinguishable as different from the first).

To find out the absolute and difference threshold in the first method of minimal changes or methods of limits the following procedure has been followed. Suppose a child is asked to see an object which is lying at a particular place. If he is unable to see it then the distance is gradually decreased until the subject is able to see it. Suppose at a distance of 50 cm. he says no and at the distance of 49 cm. he says yes, then both these values will be noted. In the next trial, the object is shown to the child from a very near place. Then the distance is gradually increased till the subject says that he is not able to see it. The successive values from yes to no is noted. This process is repeated many times. After the completion of several ascending and descending series, the researcher computes the average of all these minimal values (50+49+48+49=49 cm) as a minimal value of the distance at which the subject may be able to see the experimental object.

In the second category, i.e., the method of constant stimuli or the method of right and wrong responses the sensory stimuli of varying intensity are presented to the subject at random and asked to indicate whether or not he detects each of these randomly presented stimuli. The responses of yes or no are noted. All the values related with the yes responses are averaged to give the required threshold.

In the method of average error the subject is presented with some stimulus of a standard intensity. He may then be asked to adjust a variable stimulus to this standard by making a number of attempts. The average of errors while making adjustment may be noted down and either added or subtracted to the standard value for absolute threshold of sensitivity to the stimulus.

Thus all these psycho-physical methods are primarily employed to measure the absolute and the difference threshold to see the sensitivity of the subject.

Schools of Educational Psychology

It has been said that "Psychology is the science of the mental activities of the organisms". Thus to study or to understand the child behaviour different psychologists have given different approaches and styles but the target is the same. It is very difficult to say that one school is better than other schools of psychology. Therefore, educationists do not believe in any particular schools of psychology rather takes the help of all schools while studying behaviour. The following are the different schools of psychology:

(i) Structuralism
(ii) Functionalism
(iii) Behaviourism
(iv) Gestalt
(v) Psycho-analysis
(vi) Humanistic
(vii) Hormic

I. *Structuralism*

Wilhelm Wundt (1832-1920), a German Psychologist was the father of this school. Here the main purpose is systematic study of the mind. For this conscious experience (one's own thoughts, feelings, sensations, perceptions and ideas) of the individual is studied through introspection or self-observation by asking them to analyse what they were experiencing at the moment when they were exposed to stimuli such as sound, colour, or an object, etc. Thus it can be concluded that structuralists concentrate on mental conditions rather than on behaviour.

Contributions of Structuralism

The most important contribution is introspection method of studying behaviour. It is because of structuralists now psychology is considered as a independent discipline and stress on scientific study of personality is given emphasis. Similarly they have also established first psychological laboratory and it is because of education and psychology department have laboratory setup in their respective institutions to study the human behaviour. These are the hints and positive contribution of the school of structuralism.

Limitations of structuralism

The greatest lacuna's of this school is giving maximum emphasis on introspection method to study the human behaviour although they have understood that it is not the scientific way to verify the fact which will be collected. Thus its scope is limited and lacking the objectivity, reliability and validity of the data.

II. Functionalism

The functionalist school of Psychology was developed in America by William James, who is considered as pioneer or propounder with a strong objection to structuralism. The propagonists and their followers believe that mental process are not static rather it is dynamic and changeable. Functionalist attempt to give accurate and systematic answer to question like what do men do and why they do it. They laid stress on function of mind and intelligence and found that it is possible to solve many problems of the human society. As soon as a particular thing finishes another thing starts. It is like a constant flow of water. Angel advocated that all psychological activities are the result of the combined action of the body and the mind. It believes that in the study of the man the background of his environment must be studied then only correct ideas about man and his mental faculties are known. They further elaborated that habits are nothing but it is the functions of the nervous system. When we repeat an activity a number of times, our nervous system are altered so that the next time we engage in it, we do it automatically without much conscious thought.

Contribution of Functionalism to Education

1. Functionalists believe that curriculum of the child should be such which can help him to apply in everyday life.
2. This school propagated the views of child-centred approaches in the teaching-learning process along

with emphasis on needs of the students rather than subject matter.

3. Functionalists widened the scope of studying the human behaviour by developing new methods and devices for the objective description of behaviour.
4. The study of the problems of the individual (normal as well as abnormal) were incorporated in the subject matter of psychology and educational psychology due to functionalism.
5. Functionalists emphasise environment in the process of learning.

III. Behaviourism

J.B. Watson, who was the founder of behaviourism believes that the study of human behaviour is not possible scientifically through consciousness or on the basis of mentalistic notions like soul, mind and mental life, etc. The other exponents were Tolman, Hall, and Skinner. This school realises that study of human/animal behaviour depends upon the overt or observable activities of an organism. They also believe that the things that cannot stand the test to reality have no values for them. This means they are concerned with behaviour and not with consciousness. It does not recognise the existence of any secret between body and the mind. The basic principle of behaviourism is to use the word stimulus—response and learning and habit which indicate some behaviour. Watson while experimenting an 11 month old child could be able to condition his behaviour to fear a rat by substituting the rat for a loud sudden noise. Thus it can be concluded that behaviour is merely the result of a response to some environmental stimulus. How we behave and why we so behave can be successfully demonstrated through habit formation or conditioning. Therefore, behaviour of an individual is controlled by environmental forces rather than innate endoments. To strengthen this view Pavlov's experiment on a dog is an important one and can be cited here.

While Watson emphasized stimulus response bond and environmental influences on behaviour he asserted that "Give me a dozen of healthy infants, well informed and my own specified world to bring them up in and I will guarantee to take any one at random and train him to become any type of specialist. I might select—doctor, lawyer, artist, merchant chief, and yes, even beggar—man and thief, regardless of his talents, tendencies, abilities, vocations and race of his ancestors.

Contribution of Behaviourism to Education

1. It brought psychology out from the controversy of mentalistic-mechanistic approach to human behaviour.
2. Its emphasis on environment and its impact on human growth and development.
3. The introduction of scientific method of studying behaviour by replacing introspective measures.
4. Behaviourism advocated the use of reinforcement and rewards in the learning rather than punishment to have desirable behaviour.
5. Because of behaviourists new innovative ideas in the learning has emerged, i.e., programmed learning, computer-assisted instruction and individualised self instructional programmes.

IV. *Gestalt School of Psychology*

Gestalt school of Psychology was originated in Germany as a protest against structuralism, functionalism and behaviourism. Max Werthimer, Kurt Koffka, Wolfgang Kohlar and Kurt Lewin were the founders of this school.

This school believes that the psychology should study patterns or whole of behaviour or experience. According to them an individual perceives the thing as a whole and not as a mere collection of its constituents or elements.

The word Gestalt means 'form' 'pattern', 'figure' and 'configuration'. This school regards man as a unitary whole and insists that the discovery of behaviour can be successful only to the extent that it emphasizes the entire reacting organism and not merely its parts. They asserted that there exists a bond between stimulus and response but these bonds helps in forming a new gestalt or an organised whole while observing the objects. This means when we look at a tree we perceive whole of it as a tree even though a tree consists of colour, brightness and a form but when perceived by the mind all these components become a pattern or a gestalt. Thus, Gestalt psychologists used the term 'insight' to describe the human behaviour and summarised the process by saying that the perception of the situation as a whole is first step while judging the relationships between various factors involved in the situation is second one and taking an immediate decision and behave accordingly is the final stage of human behaviour.

Contribution of Gestalt Psychology to Education

1. Gestaltists laid stress on principle of unity or integrity and environment while studying human behaviour.
2. This school made a valuable contribution to the field of sensation and perception by saying that teachers and parents should give emphasis on the whole (overall aspect of learning) in the class and at home.
3. This school suggests the construction of curricula by the principle of Gestalt, i.e., the concerned subject matter of a particular subject is always organised or a whole and the curriculum comprising different subjects and activities is so framed as to reflect unity and cohesiveness among them. It means inter-disciplinary approach may be followed.
4. This school suggests experimental procedure to study human behaviour.
5. They realised that for successful teaching-learning process in school there is a need of integration of teachers, students and principal. If there is a proper coordination among the subjects and work as a organised whole then improvement in teaching-learning process in school is inevitable.
6. Kohler on the basis of his experiment on monkey and chimpanzi laid down the principle that in order to learn certain things it is necessary to organise the field of the action and activity so that the mutual relationship between different objects and ideas that form the basis of learning could be made clear. Thus emphasis on 'insight' was given due importance in Gestalt school.

V. **Psycho-analysis School of Psychology**

Sigmund Freud, a Viennese physician was the propounder and father of this school. He has given altogether new ideas through which abnormals may be properly treated. In spite of that this school studied the totality of human behaviour including the topography of mind, i.e., the conscious, sub-conscious and unconscious behaviour, structure of the psyche (i.e., Id, ego and super ego), the concept of repression, the psycho-sexual development, etc., for study of the human behaviour.

Freud claimed that greater part of our personality lies in unconscious and the conscious part occupies only the one-tenth portion of the total mental life. There are repressed desires, thoughts, feelings, drives and motives related to sex and aggression and remain in unconscious and continually influence our behaviour. According to him these are very much responsible for several of our behaviours though our unfulfilled desires go into our unconscious mind and remain there hidden.

Freud has given a good deal of importance to the sex instinct in his psycho-analytical school of psychology. According to him all our actions are guided by our sex desires. When the sex desires move towards wrong direction they result into several sex delinquencies and wrong acts.

Later the two very close associates of Freud had established their own schools. Alfred Adler's school was known as 'Individual Psychology". He opposed the view of Freud on 'sex' and pointed out that the human behaviour as the creative power, the aggressive drive, inferiority complex and style of life, etc. Similarly, Carl C. Jung established his own school of 'Analytical Psychology'. He replaced the sex urge with the more comprehensive term 'libido' or the life urge. Later on many notable neo-Freudians like Erich Fromm, Erik Erickson, etc., pointed out the role of society by replacing the role of sex while studying human behaviour.

Contribution of the Psycho-analytical School to Education

1. 'Child-centred education' is one of the important contribution of this school. This school uses 'clinical-method' for studying maladjusted and abnormal human behaviour and treatment thereof.
2. This school laid stress on the importance of the child and his early experiences in the process of education. Therefore love, affection, sympathy, etc., may be provided in early childhood so that positive attitudes among the learners will be developed.
3. This school finds out unconscious motivation which plays an important role in the process of learning. Therefore opportunities should be provided to express emotions and motives freely in class for effective learning.
4. Curricular activities should be given due importance in such a manner so that monotonous and pentup feelings may be released.
5. As far as possible, freedom in education may be provided and see that development of whole personality is noticed.

6. Psycho-analytic school helps in knowing the causes of the unhealthy attitudes and bad habits and help him to change it in orderly manner.
7. Training of instinct in proper direction and help them to grow into useful citizens is the contribution of psycho-analytic school of psychology.

VI. Humanistic School of Psychology

This school of psychology was developed by Abraham Maslow, Carl Rogers, Arthur Combs, and Gordon Allport. This school gives more value to the human being by not considering him as a sophisticated machine or a victim of the conflict between the ego and the id. He is a purposeful being and is free to choose and to determine his action and capable of adapting himself to his environment and choosing his own course of action in order to achieve the goals which he has selected for himself. Consequently, each person is responsible for his action and cannot blame the environment, his parents or circumstances for what he does.

Every person has a basic need to develop his potential to the fullest, to progress beyond what he is now. He may not know which path leads to growth, and he may be blocked by all kinds of environmental and cultural obstacles, but his natural tendency is towards actualisation of his potential. The humanistic psychologists concerned with changing society's priorities to place more emphasis on improving inter-personal relationships and providing conditions that promote the development of mans potential for constructive and cooperative actions.

Thus, humanistic psychology emphasises such distinctly human aspects of personality as the existence of free will and freedom of choice and man's search for unique goals and values to guide his behaviour and to give a personal meaning to his existence.

Thus it can be said that humanistic school give emphasis on human qualities and self-actualisation which distinguish man from the animals. The humanistic school rejects the concept of man as a mechanism controlled by external stimuli or by conscious instincts. Rather humanist prefer to see man as an "actor" capable of controlling his own destiny and changing the world around him.

Limitation of Educational Psychology

Every subject has advantages and disadvantages. While

some of the aspects are facilitating and fulfilling the national objectives others are hindering the path of the same subject. So, educational psychology is no way exception to it. On account of these limitations, a number of difficulties are encountered when we make an attempt to apply psychological principles and facts to the solution of educational problems. These are as follows:

1. *Educational Psychology/Psychology is not an exact science like the Physical Science*: In which way physical scientists determine the exactness of the effect of one object upon another the psychologist cannot exactly determine the effect of praise/blame or reward/punishment or other incentives on the learner in the similar manner. No psychologist can provide a formula for developing interest in the classroom. If some thing help improve the learning in one situation this may not be applicable in another situation. Moreover, psychologist cannot derive any magic box to study the living individuals behaviour or predicting it exactly. However, it gives the teacher general principles that will guide him in interpreting and predicting the behaviour of the learner.
2. *Educational psychology/psychology is a positive but not a normative science*: Educational psychologists are concerned with the discovery of techniques and methodologies for the solution of problems of the classroom but not decide the aims of education. This means they are interested in the study of behaviours but not its moral worth and the intensity of happiness or sorrowness.
3. *The problems of individual differences*: Individuals differ from one to another. The emotions, perception, feelings and reasoning, etc., are not the same in everybody though there are some qualities which all human beings have in common. In the same age levels there are differences. It is very difficult to generalise the facts unless it is to be studied with great care and caution.
4. Educational psychology borrowed the principles of laboratories experiments which is generally conducted on animals. Sometimes these findings are not suitable to the classroom situation. Hence, psychological results are less reliable.

5. What educational psychology tells us theoretically may not be applicable in day-to-day classroom situations. Different interpretations of the same facts have led to a great deal of confusion.
6. Psychology does not provide readymade solutions or explanations why people behave in certain ways. This situation create lot of difficulties in the teaching-learning process.
7. An individual's behaviour cannot be controlled. In the physical sciences it is possible to repeat an experiment on a number of occasions by controlling external factors. But in educational psychology there is no guarantee that the individual may behave in the same manner even though external factors are controlled.

Conclusions

Whatever may be the limitations of educational psychology the study of this subject will help the teacher to enhance and enrich the quality of instruction. In addition to that it also ensures the teacher with scientific and practical insights into the various aspects of the teaching-learning process.

Summary

Educational Psychology is designated as science of education. It is that branch of psychology which helps the teacher to study the behaviour of the learner in relation to his educational environment. It applies the psychological principles and techniques in the educational setting. It suggest ways and means of improving the process and products of education.

The nature of educational psychology are the following:

1. It is scientific in nature.
2. It is concerned with the study of behaviour of the learner in relation to his educational situation.
3. It is a social science.
4. It is concerned with what, why and how of present situation of the learner's behaviour.
5. It is a positive science rather than normative.
6. It is an applied psychology.
7. It is narrower in nature.
8. It is not so perfect a science rather defined as a developing positive science of the learner's behaviour.

The scope of educational psychology is both limited and extensive. It is limited in the sense that it is concerned with the learners behaviour in the educational environment. But it is extensive because whatever comes to improve the teaching-learning process are included under its scope. The topics like growth and development, learning process, learning environment and the teacher are the central theme of the educational psychology.

Since the process of education is dynamic, it is difficult to delimit its boundary because what is needed for better serving the cause of education should be included under educational psychology.

The aims and objectives or relevance or utility of educational psychology is to equip the prospective teacher with necessary skill and competencies to deal with the teaching-learning process effectively. The following are the essential features of educational psychology:

1. To understand the behaviour of this students.
2. To develop scientific attitude towards them.
3. To provide suitable guidance programmes.
4. To help in the evaluation of the outcome of the educational process.
5. To understand the learning process, to find out the individual differences and make wise decisions in the teaching-learning process.
6. To provide ways and means for maintaining sound mental health and prevent maladjustment.
7. To suggest good time-table, utility of audio-visual aids in teaching and better child-centred approach curriculum.
8. To understand the group behaviour and group dynamics effectively.

The difference between general psychology and educational psychology is that general psychology is basically academically oriented and consists of general principles of behaviour. Whereas educational psychology is professionally oriented and interested in finding out practical solution to educational problems.

Thus it can be concluded that educational psychology helps the teacher and shows the right path to remove the darkness of difficulties in teaching-learning process. But due to too many varieties of topics it has little relevance to classroom teaching.

On Methods of Psychology

The knowledge of psychological methods are essential for developing scientific attitude for solving the problems of the behaviour. The following are methods of educational psychology.

In introspection method the individual is to perceive, analyse and report his own feelings. It is a sort of self-observation or looking within his ownself while he is to report about a mental act. It is unscientific method to study human behaviour.

The method of observation indicate that the behaviour of an individual will be observed by another individual either in a natural or artificial created condition. Data regarding the individual can be collected through indirect or direct manner but it also suffers from limitation that it is not objective, reliable and valid for studying human behaviour.

Experimental method consists of objective observation under controlled conditions to study human behaviour. It is employed to understand cause-effect relationship regarding human behaviour by performing experiments. Manipulation of independent variable is an important attribute of experimentation. Here independent variable stands for the cause and dependent for the effect of that cause is studied. The other conditions or factors that influence the cause and effect relationship are called intervening variables. In an experiment all such variables are controlled. To study the behaviour through this method various experimental designs have been devised.

Clinical method is used to study one individual in depth when he is facing some adjustment problem. It helps in diagnosis and suggest therapeutic measures or treatment of the problem of an individual. The physical checkup, case-history, interview, observation and tests are used in diagnosis whereas the techniques of psycho-analysis and counselling are therapeutic in nature.

Differential or survey method is used to study individual differences. Here several individuals are studied to findout the relative differences or psychological differences in group conditions which determine these differences and how these differences manifest themselves. With the help of statistical techniques the data is described and inferences are drawn.

Psycho-physical methods employ physical devices for the scientific measurement of some psychological experiences like sensations. The popular methods of this techniques are the method of minimal changes or the method of limits, the method of constant stimuli or the method of right and wrong responses and the method of average or mean error. These methods are employed to measure the absolute threshold and the difference threshold.

Summary on Schools of Psychology

Different psychologists have expressed their ideas and thought at different times. The following are the different schools of psychology:

Structuralism was propagated by Wilhelm Wundt (1832-1920) followed by E.B. Titchener. This school emphasized the systematic study of the mind through introspection. This school also separated psychology from Philosophy and metaphysics and because of their effort now psychology is considered as a independent discipline.

Functionalism was developed by William James (1842-1910) followed by John Dewey, James Angele, E.L. Thorndike and R.S. Woodworth. This school gives emphasis on functional aspects of the mind and suggested functional curricula, methods and techniques of learning and for describing human behaviour they have given emphasis on introspection as well as observation method.

J.B. Watson (1878-1958) is the exponent of Behaviourism and the other followers are Ivan Pavlov, Tolman, Hull and Skinner. This school believes that the behaviour of the individual can be observed through observation method and considers environment is the sole factor in shaping one's personality and influencing one's behaviour. The main contribution to education is the use of reinforcement and programmed learning.

Gestalt School was originated by Max Werthimer, Koffka, Wolfgang Kohlar (1887-1967) and Kurt Lewin. They emphasized to study the whole of things rather than parts. Through perception and insight one can understand the whole and solve the problem. This school suggests the ways for organising the subject matter from whole to parts, etc., in the learning areas.

Psycho-analysis was propagated by Sigmund Freud (1856-1939). He put forth the ideas of unconscious and subconscious mind, the concept of repression and catharis, psycho-sexual development and sex as an urge is responsible for all types of behaviour. This school believes that these factors are responsible for individual behaviour and therefore, in early years better education should be provided to them.

Similarly humanistic school was developed by Abraham Maslow, Carl Rogers, Arthur Combs and Gordon Allport. This school believes that man is a purposeful being and free to choose and to determine his action to achieve the goals which he has selected for himself. He is responsible for his action and cannot blame the environment for his failure.

Questions

1. What is educational psychology? Describe its nature and scope?
2. What is the nature of educational psychology? How can it be useful for classroom teacher?
3. What is the relation between psychology and educational psychology? How does psychology help in understanding the concept of child-centred education?
4. Why is a course in educational psychology made compulsory in a teacher education programme? How does it help a teacher to become a good teacher?
5. Explain what are the uses of educational psychology to a teacher? Would you suggest any improvement in the course?
6. What do you mean by educational psychology? What are its aims and objectives?
7. Why should a teacher know the knowledge of psychology? What significant changes can be done after knowing the psychology?
8. What are the various methods of studying children's behaviour? Discuss any two methods with their advantages and limitations?
9. What is observation method? What procedure you would adopt in studying the overt behaviour of your students?
10. What is experimental method? What are its steps. Discuss the merits and limitations of this method.
11. When is the clinical method to be used? What is the role of the teacher in this method?
12. What is survey method? In which situation it will be applied.
13. What are the different schools of psychology? Explain any one school in detail.
14. What is structuralism? What are the contributions of this school to education.

15. How is functionalism different from structuralism? Describe the main contribution of functionalism.
16. What is the main idea of behaviourism? What are its contribution to education?
17. Discuss the essential features of psycho-analytic school of psychology. What are its contributions to education?
18. Gestalt school of psychologists give emphasis on configuration or whole. Explain why and describe the contribution to education.

References

Andrews, T.G. (Ed.) (1968): *Methods of Psychology*, Wiley, New York.

Ausubel, D.P. (1968) : *Educational Psychology—A Cognitive View*, Holt, Rinhart and Winston Inc., New York.

Bigge, M.L. and Hunt, M.P. (1968) : *Psychological Foundation of Education*, Harper and Row, New York.

Chauhan, S.S. (1988) : *Advanced Educational Psychology*, Vikas Pub. House, New Delhi.

Commins, W.D. (1937) : *Principles of Educational Psychology*, The Ronald Press Company, New York.

Crow, L.D. and Crow, H (1973) : *Educational Psychology*, Eurasia Publishing House, New Delhi.

Douglas, O.B. and Holland, B.F. (1958) : *Educational Psychology*, Macmillan, New York.

Dubois, N.F. *et al.* (1979) : *Educational Psychology and Instructional Decisions*, The Dorsey Press, Ontario.

Dutta, N.K. (1974) : *Psychological Foundation of Education*, Doaba House, Delhi.

Gates, A.I. *et al.* (1964) : *Educational Psychology*, The Macmillan Company, New York.

Guthri, E.R. and Powers, F. (1950) *Educational Psychology*, The Ronald Press Co., New York.

Heidbreder, E. (1971) : *Seven Psychologist*, Kalyani Publishers, Ludhiana.

Jordan, A.M. (1942) : *Educational Psychology*, Henry Holt & Company, New York.

Kuppuswami, B. (1974) : *Educational Psychology*, Sterling Pub. Ltd., New Delhi.

Kundu, C.L. and Tutoo, D.N. (1980) : *Educational Psychology*, Sterling Publisher Ltd., New Delhi.

Lindgren, H.C. (1967): *Educational Psychology in the Classroom*, John Wiley and Sons Inc., New York.

Mathis, B.C. *et al.* (1970) : *Psychological Foundations of Education, Learning and Teaching*, Academic Press, New York.

Mathur, S.S. (1977) : *Educational Psychology*, Vinod Pustak Mandir, Agra.

Mayer, R.E. (1987) : *Educational Psychology: A Cognitive Approach*, Little, Brown & Company, Canada.

Morris, E.E. (1972) : *Psychological Foundation of Education*; Holt, Rinehart and Winston, New York.

Peel, E.A. (1956) : *The Psychological Basis of Education*, Oliver and Boyd Pub., London.

Rastogi, K.C. (1983) : *Educational Psychology*, Rastogi Pub., Meerut.

Skinner, C.E. (Ed.) (1958) : *Essentials of Educational Psychology*, Prentice-Hall: Englewood Cliffs, New Jersey.

Sorenson, H. (1964) : *Psychology in Education*, McGraw-Hill Book Company, New York.

Travers, J.F. (1982) : *Educational Psychology*, Harper & Row, New York.

Travers, R.M. (1973) : *Educational Psychology*, Macmillan, New York.

Woodworth, R.S. (1948) : *Contemporary School of Psychology*, Methuen, London.

GROWTH AND DEVELOPMENT

Introduction

The education of a child starts since his birth, though in an informal manner. A person to some extent shapes the pattern of his life by the choices and decisions he makes at successive stages. A teacher's main concern in the classroom is the development of the child but he cannot fully understand such basic processes as perception, motivation and emotion, etc., without knowing something about their development. If a teacher is interested to educate the child in a balanced and integrated manner then he is to understand the child fully and understand the characteristics of a child at various age levels. Therefore, it is essential for the teacher to study the growth and development of different periods of life.

Meaning of Growth and Development

Growth refers to quantitative changes in physical development, i.e., increase in size, height and weight. We speak of the growth of heart, nerves, muscles and body in general. Thus growth is observable and can be measured. Crow and Crow suggest that growth refers to structural and physiological changes. Frank said growth as the multiplication of cells, i.e., growth in height and weight or it may be changes in the particular aspects of the body or it means increase and enlargement of the body or some part of the body.

The term development refers to change in structure, form or shape and improvement in functioning. When qualitative changes occur in behavioural characteristics of the child is called development. According to Peary, development means the whole sequence of life from conception to death. Frank said that development may imply the change in organism as a whole. Hurlock said it is progressive series of changes in an orderly coherent pattern. The changes are directional leading forward rather than backward and results in new characteristics and new abilities on the part of the individual. Thus development is progressive, orderly and coherent means that there is a definite relationship between each stage in an sequential manner and is a continuous process. Development is more comprehensive which includes physical, social, intellectual, emotional and moral aspects of an individual.

DIFFERENCE BETWEEN GROWTH AND DEVELOPMENT

Growth	*Development*
1. Growth may be limited to the changes in the quantitative aspects, i.e., increase in size, length, height, weight and expansion of vocabulary, etc.	1. Development implies the overall changes occurring in both quantitative and qualitative aspects. It is the changes in structure, form or shape and improvement in functioning and behaviour as a whole.
2. Growth is used in a narrower sense such as increase in size, weight, etc.	2. Development is a wider and comprehensive term, related to all types of changes both physical and psychological.
3. Growth is physical and external in nature.	3. Development is internal and can be physical, social, emotional and intellectual, etc.
4. Growth stops after sometime. Maturity is the end point of growth.	4. Development is continuous. Starting right from conception it does not end with the attainment of maturity but continues throughout the entire life span of an individual.
5. Growth is measureable because the quantitative changes are very specific and it can be directly measured.	5. Development is observable because the results of development are quite complex and difficult as far as their actual assessment and measurement is concerned.
6. Growth is always systematic and follows a definite pattern It is very rapid in infancy and later on it becomes slow and becomes rapid during the period of early adolescence.	6. Development is always from general to specific.

Principles/Patterns or Characteristics of Growth and Development

Studies in genetics have shown that behavioural development follows a pattern even though there is individual difference among children. The various principles of development are given below:

1. Principle of uniform developmental pattern:

Development occurs in orderly manner and follows a certain sequence and a regular step by step process. All the developmental direction and sequences are almost the same for all children, but each child follows his own time schedule of growth. For example—the baby creeps before he crawls and crawls before he walks.

2. Principle of continuous:

Human beings are constantly changing. One is not the same today as one was yesterday and one will be different from what one is now. Thus the process of growth and development continues from birth to death in some or other form and a never-ending process.

3. Principle of lack of uniformity in the developmental rate:

Although the human developmental sequence is uniform and continuous, it does not exhibit uniformity in the developmental periods and stages of life. It is this variation in individual development that makes it impossible to predict how an individual will react to a particular stimulus.

4. Principle of developmental speed variation:

It is observed that growth and development becomes very rapid in infancy and early adolescence and latter the speed decreases.

5. Principle of cephalocaudal and proximodstal sequence:

The growth and development has got its own direction. It follows cephalocaudal sequence, which means that the human beings grow from head downwards that is in the direction of the longitudinal axis (head to foot) or head is developed in the embroynic stage than the development of body and legs occur. It is also known as principle from the head-tailward.

Proximodistal sequence indicate that the development takes place from centre to peripheri. The spinal cord of the child develops first and then the outward development of heart and chest, etc., takes place.

6. Principle of proceeding from general to specific:

This is true of all phases of development. The new born baby moves his body as a whole and slowly he learns to control his full hand and later he tries to control on the movement of his hand fingers.

7. Principle of integration/ total development:

Development involves a movement from the whole to parts and from the parts to the whole in the areas of both physical and psychological aspects and are interrelated and interdependent.

8. Principle of orderly and proceeds by stages:

Human development follows a known sequence. Each child stands before he walks and babbles before he talks. Physical development occurs in a head to foot direction and proceeds from the central parts to more distant ones. Thus each stage has certain unique characteristics and behavioural patterns.

9. Principle of individual difference:

Every organism is a distinct creation in itself. Therefore the development which it undergoes in terms of the rate and outcome in various dimensions is quite unique and specific and varies from child to child.

10. Principle of learning and maturation:

Every development has got their own limits. The child may be matured for something and may not be matured for others. Therefore it can be said that development emphasis on the factor of maturation. Unless the child gets proper maturation the efforts of coaching, etc., to accelerate learning are not desirable.

11. Principle of cumulative:

In the course of development, a single experience matters a lot and it does not go unnoticed and unaccounted because it has been found out that subsequent behaviour is the result of previous experiences. The day a child utters his first word, the appearance of his first tooth, his first shave, etc., are turning point in life. Thus the development pattern represent sequential advancement rather than series of mere additions and did not reach abruptly.

12. Principle of predictability:

Due to uniformity of the pattern and sequence of development, forecast of the general nature and behaviour of the child in one or more aspects of any particular stage of its growth and development can be predicted. For example, with the knowledge of the development of the physical structure of a child it is possible to predict his adult structure and size.

13. Principle of heredity and environment (Interaction):

The process of development involves active interaction between the forces within the individual and the forces belonging to his environment. The child gets the body structure and many mental and personal qualities due to heredity factor but these qualities are influenced by the environment. The two work hand in hand from the very conception. Thus, at any stage of growth and development, the individual behaviour is the constant interaction between his heredity endowment and environmental make-up.

Factors Influencing Development

It is a fact that the child development depends on certain factors. These factors are the following:

(a) Genetic factor or Heredity,
(b) Environmental factor, and
(c) Physiological factor or maturation.

The study of heredity leads to the suitable answers of the questions like how does the child come into this world? What powers and tendencies he brings with him for his growth and why does he want to keep his existence after coming into this world, etc. So, the study of heredity shows how potentialities or characteristics (biological and mental), etc., are inherited from parents to their children or from one generation to another. (For more details please see the heredity and environment chapter of this book.)

The child, when he comes to this world, finds himself surrounded by innumerable objects and circumstances which influence him. In fact, everything that is externally operated either consciously or unconsciously by parents, teachers, community and others to influence or help the child to develop in a desirable manner is called the impact of environment. (For details please see the environment chapter of this book.)

The third factor which influence the child is called maturation. It refers to the development of physiological and anatomical structures of the body. Thus, whatever training we provide to an infant will be in vain/vague, if the infant is not mature to do so. For example, a baby of six month cannot walk unless his body is mature to do it. This indicates that maturation brings changes in behavioural patterns.

Now it can be concluded that genetic factor determine the base, physiological factors determine the time, sequence or order of development and environmental factors influence the pace and limit of development. Thus, growth and development are the result of interaction and interplay of genetic, physiological and environmental factors.

Educational Implications of the Principle of Growth and Development

1. The principle of growth and development has contributed to the knowledge of individual differences. To fulfil the individual needs and aspirations it is better to have diversified courses in the educational institutions so that the development of specific talent, abilities and interests of the child can be enhanced. In addition to the existing co-curricular activities it is better to have improved need based co-curricular activities according to the modern demand of the society.
2. The ideas of growth and development help the teacher and parents to know what children are capable of and what potentialities they possess. Thus this knowledge help us to provide suitable opportunities and favourable environmental facilities which are conducive to the maximum growth of children.
3. Each stage of growth has its possibilities and limitations. This implies that teachers and parents should not expect from pupils or from their children what is beyond to their stage of growth. Thus with

the help of this knowledge, the teacher should be in a position to know what is to be done for a child at a particular stage.

4. The principles like "proceeding from general to specific" and "integration" help the teacher to plan the learning process and arrange suitable learning experiences so as to achieve maximum gains in terms of growth and development.
5. The principle of growth and development gives the ideas of physical growth and intellectual attainment of the child. Thus for physical growth the students may be advised to take suitable food at different stages of development and arrange educational programmes in such a manner so that they will not feel frustrations and nervousness in the educational institutions.
6. The importance of the role of heredity and environment must be understood by the teacher, then only, he/she can help to eliminate evil behaviour of the children in the institution.
7. The principle of cephalocaudal and proximodistal tendencies help us to arrange the learning experiences and environmental set-up according to the need of the child so that it helps the child to grow smoothly.
8. The principle of growth and development help the teacher to mobilise for all round development of the child rather than development of a particular aspect in the institution.
9. The ideas of growth and development have indicated that each developmental phase has certain traits or characteristics which are usually found at that age. Thus by looking into the stage of development and their readiness the teacher should treat each child and plan the programme accordingly.
10. The principle of prediction give the ideas that within which period the mature development of the child is likely to fall. Thus it helps the teacher to control the behaviour and helps the child to inculcate good habits and save him/her from going the wrong way.

Stages of Development

Psychologists have attempted to divide the whole life span of the individual into distinct stages on the basis of certain common developmental characteristics. As the human organism passes through a number of stages from conception to death the characteristics and behaviour of one stage is different from the other, hence, teacher should have knowledge of these stages for better teaching-learning process. The various stages of development are:

(1) Pre-natal	-	conception to birth
(2) Infancy	-	Birth to 5 years
(3) Childhood	-	6 to 11/12 years
(4) Adolescence	-	12 years to 20/21 years
(5) Adulthood	-	From 22 years and beyond

Similarly, Kolesnic has given the classification of the stages of growth and development in the following manner.

I. Prenatal stage	-	from 0 (conception) to 280 or 300 days (birth)
(a) Germinal period	-	from 0 to 2 weeks
(b) Embryonic	-	from 2 weeks to 10 weeks
(c) Foetal	-	from 10 weeks to birth
II. Infancy	-	Birth to 5 years
(a) Neonatal	-	Birth to 8 weeks
(b) Early infancy	-	2 months to 30 months
(c) Late infancy	-	30 months to 60 months
III. Childhood	-	6 years to 12 years
(a) Early childhood	-	6 to 9 years
(b) Late childhood	-	9 to 12 years
IV. Adolescence	-	12 years to 21 years
(a) Early Adolescence	-	12 to 15 years
(b) Middle Adolescence	-	15 to 18 years
(c) Late Adolescence	-	18 to 21 years
V. Adulthood	-	22 years and beyond

(1) Pre-natal Stage (Conception to Birth):

Ruch (1970) pointed out that prenatal stage is from conception to birth which passes through a series of developmental stages. These are:

(i) Germinal period which lasts for the first two weeks. During this stage the fertilized egg develops by a process of cell-division into a hollow sphere of cells about one-fifth of an inch in diameter.

(ii) Embryonic period starts after two weeks and continue up to 10 weeks. The primitive structures of the new individual slowly begin to form, the internal organs have begun to take shape and the external physical characteristics have assumed definite form even though the embryonic period is only about 1¼ th inches long.

(iii) Foetal period is from 10 weeks to birth.

This pre-natal period normally lasts for about 40 weeks. The scientific study of the pre-natal growth of the organism in the womb is that head is about half the size of the whole body during the second month and in the 10th month it is only about one-quarter. By the end of sixth month, the movements of the foetus become very powerful and complex. Thus, it is found that before birth, the organism is capable of reacting to the internal as well as external stimuli in the appropriate environment.

(II) Infancy Stage of the Pre-school Period (0-5 years)

This period ranges from birth to five years of age. These years are of tremendous importance from the point of view of development. This stage has a prolonged period of dependency on parents but quite independent as regards to the basic function of the body like respiration, digestion, circulation, and maintaining constant temperature are concerned. After birth the child is called neonate (the first four weeks of life). In Hindu scriptures Infancy is called "Kumaravastha". According to Freud, the child by the age of 4-5 years, becomes, what he has to grow in the coming life. Hurlock called the infancy age as a period of "Appealing Age". Strang writes, "infancy" is a period of foundation for his future". Thus the environment of the family and parental activities has a direct bearing and affect the future thinking, reasoning, development and style of his life.

Characteristics

1. The child has a very small world
2. Egocentric and more self love
3. Behaviour is instructive

4. Imagination is identical
5. The child cannot distinguish the differences in the world
6. More playing and repeating performances.

Development During Infancy

(a) Physical and Motor Development

During infancy, the following development within the body of the child takes place, i.e., height and weight, respiration and circulation, muscular and motor development. These development takes the following shapes:

(1) The entire structure of the body starts functioning and a sort of balance comes in the various organs of the body.

(2) Growth is very rapid, the brain develops very fast, change is seen in shape of the child, increase in arms and legs, and the sense organs rapidly develop.

(3)

entire weight of body, coordination between the mind and the body of the child starts at the age of three, and speed of the nervous system is quite fast and quick.

(4) At the age of five a child will be about 35 to 40 inches tall and will weigh about 35 pounds.

(5) Almost all the organs of the body start functioning during this period and so there is a balance and co-ordination in the action and activities during this period.

(6) The process of muscle maturation is very slow and motor skills are acquired very slowly. The psychologists have studied the development of various motor skills in children which are given below:

DEVELOPMENT OF MOTOR ABILITIES

Age in months	*Development*
1. One month	Chin up
2. 2 months	Chest up
3. 3 months	Reach and Miss
4. 4 months	Sits with support
5. (a) 5 months	Sit on lap, Grasp object, Turns from back to side

{cont.}...

(b) 5.4 months	Effort to sit
6. (a) 6 months	Sit High chair, Grasp Dangling object
(b) 6.2 months	Sits alone for thirty seconds or more
7. (a) 7 months	Sits alone
(b) 7.3 months	Rolls from back to stomach
8. (a) 8 months	Stands with help
(b) 8.6 months	Babbles
9. 9 months	Stand holding furniture
10. (a) 10 months	Creeps
(b) 10.6 months	Stands up
11. (a) 11 months	Walk when led
(b) 11.6 months	or walk with help
12. (a) 12 months	Pull to stand by furniture
(b) 12.5 months	Sit down
13. 13 months	Climb a staircase
14. 14 months	Stand alone
15. 15 months	Walk alone

Thus it can be said that physical development here includes height and weight of the child (length 16 to 18 inches and weight 6 to 8 pounds at the time of birth to 35 to 40 inches tall and weight about 35 pound at age 5), respiration and circulation (lungs develop rapidly and breathing capacity is increased and heart grows in size but developmental rate of the heart varies with children); Muscular development (slow development and proceeds from bigger to smaller muscles) and motor development (motor skills are acquired very slowly, to grasp an object an infant will exhibit several unnecessary movements of the shoulders, upper arms and elbows, and action refined in advances in age and greater speed in movements). Thus motor growth is the development of strength, speed and precision in the use of arms.

(b) Intellectual development in relation to perception, Imagination, concept formation and language development:

(1) A new born child perceptions are vague and diffused. Gradually the child is able to discriminate between differences in brightness and colour. The sense of taste develops and sensitivity to pain become keener. The child can distinguish between heat and cold and is able to be aware of his biological need between the age of three years. Between 3 and 6 years, colour

attracts more attention and by the age of 5 a child is able to differentiate between letter and number forms. Self-concept is, however, hardly developed but the ability to perceive the shape of objects develops.

(2) Imagination and memory are very active and strong. Children at this stage love repetition and love nursery rhymes and songs, fairy tales and fantasy.

(3) Child's concepts are concrete and determined by immediate perception but not acquired the concept of conservation. Concept formation is difficult in relation to the difference between day and night.

(4) The period from 3 to 5 years is the phase of rapid mental development. Vocabulary develop and child talks incessantly. The how and why questions are more predominant. Abstract thinking is not proper but the child learns by trial and error. The concept of time develop gradually but the concept of quantity is cleaner, able to count in small series.

(5) According to Burt—The child may concentrate 4-5 minutes at the age of 3 and 5 to 6 minutes at the age of 4 and learn things as a whole rather than by parts.

(6) During this stage development of rote memory and unsystematic planning is found out whereas curiousity and self-assertion are quite strong and shows much self-consciousness.

(c) Language development :

Regarding language development it can be said that the first word is uttered around the child's first birthday. After few months of the Ist year dramatic improvements occur. Development of growth of vocabulary are presented below approximately:

Age in Years and months	*Average no.of words*	*Age in years and months*	*Average No. of words*
0-8 months	0	2 years 6 months	446
0-10 months	1	3 years	896
1 Year	03	3 years 6 months	1222
13 months	19	4 years	1540
16 months	22	4 years 6 months	1870
19 months	118	5 years	2072
2 years	272	6 years	2562

Thus, the development of language helps the child to differentiate between objects of his environment and increases his self-identity.

(d) Emotional Development:

Woodworth says that emotion is stirred up state of an organism. Gate and others defined emotion denotes episodes of anger, fear, joy, sorrow, jealousy and resentment in which an individual is moved. M.C. Dougal says emotion involves feelings, inner drives, impulses and physiological reaction in the organism which can be observed and measured. Thus, it influences the individuals character, adjustment habits, nature and temperament, etc. The following are the emotional development during infancy.

(1) Emotional response of the new born is undifferentiated excitement. As the child grows in age he expreses distress and delight, anger and fear, elation and affection. Jealousy appears by about 18 months of age and joy further differentiates from elation and affection.

(2) In early infancy any sudden or intense stimulus such as a flash of light or loud noise, etc., produce fear. Physical injury and other bodily discomforts, strange objects, dogs, doctor, blood, ghosts, death, lighting, dark places and loneliness develop fear.

(3) Anger is aroused and cause violent kicking, yelling and even rolling on the floor. Happiness is expressed when parents or elder brother or sister plays with him by clapping his hands and jumping up and down at the age of 4.

(4) Gradually child uses language to express his emotions rather than violent reactions. Infants show fear, anger, love and hate from the beginning of life and the emotions are spontaneous.

(5) The emotions of the child are intense and common emotions of children during infancy are Fear, Anger and Jealousy.

(e) Moral Development :

Moral behaviour means behaviour in conformity with moral code of the social group. In Kohlberg's view moral development takes place through three levels, namely: (a) The pre-moral level, (b) The level of conventional morality, (c) The level of morality of self-accepted principles which followed with two stages in each level of development. Thus there are six stages of moral development. In addition to the above categories it is a well known fact that during infancy the moral development of the child has not taken place and so he is not able to distinguish between right and wrong. He is guided by the advice and directions of his elders and parents. Thus, Hurlock have the opinion that since the infant has no conscience, what is told to him by parents is taken by him either as bad or good according to their direction.

(f) Social Development:

Social development means acquisition or the ability to behave in accordance with social expectations or attaining of maturity in social relationship (Hurlock, 1950), Freud says that the first two years determine most of the basic social attitudes of the individual. He learns to be social. The following are the social behaviour during infancy.

(1) Smilling is the first social behaviour that appears at the third month. He imitates the speech sound of others at the 9th month. From 15th month the baby shows increasing interest in adults and a desire to be with them. The child start imitating each other during the second year and adjust and cooperate in play by the time they become three years old.

(2) The mother is the first company of the infant and early socialisation develops between the infant and the mother is called attachment. Hurlock called it a security blanket of the child. The child is self-centred in his social behaviour. Quarrelling, negativism and aggression, etc., found out with children. With the increase in age the child becomes increasingly anxious to win the approval of others and choose company from members of the same sex and become increasingly aware of themselves as people.

(3) During pre-school years children develop new interpersonal relationship and he begins to show preferences in playmates. Thus, early nursery training has been found to be very helpful in the socialisation of the child because the child gets opportunities at a very early age to associate and live with others.

(g) Educational Importance of Infancy:

(i) During this period the children are too young to cope up with the work of the primary school but they are mature enough to start preparing for it. Thus, Kindergarten training is very important to expose the child to get the first experiences of school life. He gets accustomed to being separated from his mother and learns to adjust to a fixed schedule. Hence, learning atmosphere of the nursery school should be lively, interesting and joyful.

(ii) Activity must form an integral part of nursery training. As the children are acquiring new motor skills, they have an innate urge to practise them. Thus activity based teaching like action song and games like running, skipping and jumping and repetition type of work can be practised for effective training in the nursery school.

(iii) As eye movements and hand to eye co-ordination are not perfect during infancy, reading and writing must not be given undue emphasis.

(iv) The immediate problem of the new school entrant is separation from his mother. Sometime the child may require special attention, but the teacher must neither be too harsh nor should she be over-indulgent.

(v) During the first 3/4 years, the child is the centre of attention at home. But due to training in nursery school the child changes in his attitude and learns that he cannot have his own way in everything. Thus, teachers of Kindergarten schools should give more emphasis on social and emotional development of the child rather than rigid type of cognitive development through teaching of the three R's only.

(III) Childhood Stage (6 to 11/12 years)

This is the period extending from six to twelve years. At this stage the youngster is still a child, but he is more mature than the Infancy stage. This period is known as intervening stage between infancy and adolescence. This stage is known as stage of varied experience of objects and persons and called pre-adolescence period. This is the period beginning with the entry into school and ending in the advent of puberty. It is otherwise the stage of latency period, the period of excellence and pseudo-maturity.

Characteristics of childhood stage:

(i) Childhood is a period of pseudo-maturity, mental stability and seriousness in behaviour set in.
(ii) Ripening of the gregarious instinct and formation of group activities.
(iii) Development of outward look or becomes naturally an extrovert.

Development during Childhood :

(a) Physical and Motor Development:

It includes height and weight, stature, respiration and circulation, muscular and motor development.

(1) Physical development at this stage is relatively stable, and his sense organs, muscles, brain are more or less mature enough. The body of the child develops at a fast speed in early stages and goes slow in later stages.
(2) The teeth of the child start growing permanently. An average six year old is about three feet tall and thirty-five to forty pounds in weight. The most significant physical change occurring during this period is the lengthening of the limbs, the legs grow very fast and generally look healthy.
(3) The lungs continue to grow and the breathing capacity increases. Almost all the organs and parts of the body start growing. Muscle tissue increases and co-ordination improves but digestive organs of the child are very tender.
(4) The innocence of the infant starts lessening and signs of maturity appear on the child.
(5) Children between the ages of six and nine have a reasonably good mastery over the basic motor skills of standing, walking and simple figure manipulation. Improving muscle coordination helps the child to acquire new skills and improves the already acquired ones. By the age twelve muscle coordination is almost perfect.
(6) The children at this stage are healthy and full of energy. There are skills in self-feeding, self-dressing, writing, climbing, jumping, etc., are fairly developed.

(b) Mental development:

(1) By age six, a child is ready for school and his brain has attained 80% of its total development, his vocabulary has increased and is able to form simple concepts. He is capable of both inductive and deductive reasoning. There is increased ability to generalize and to explain things in terms of cause and effect relationship.

(2) The instincts of curiosity, constructiveness and acquisition and the innate tendency of play work wonders at this stage. The child is imaginative and interested in both fanciful and factual literature, like stories having a surprise element, interested in comics, excitement, humour, mystery, suspense, creative and productive work.

(3) Imitation and make-believe are also at the climax during this stage. The span of attention becomes longer. The children between nine and twelve years are willing learners (if motivation is stronger or if a reward is announced and enjoy learning.

(4) Interests start widening and go beyond his immediate surroundings, capable of forming concepts (on concrete objects) but difficult in abstract concepts like justice, kindness or honesty. The child is able to see the similarities and differences between objects but children are found to be quite immature and their concepts are native and shallow.

(5) The critical attitude is not yet developed at the age of nine but at about twelve years, child's self-concept starts growing and gradually he comes critical of all his elders. He begins to admire things and peoples around him. He begins to imitate the manners and behaviour of those people whom he admires.

(c) Language Development :

Language is a tool of both thinking and communication. It helps for social communication and for better understanding among individuals and groups. During childhood stage there is rapid increase in vocabulary and words are combined into coherent phases and sentences, and simple thoughts are communicated with ease.

The child shows a keen desire to learn meanings of nev words and he tries to use them in his conversation, thou often quite awkwardly. Grammatical errors are also slowly eliminated. Studies by Terman, Thorndike and many other investigators have shown that there is a continuous increase in the size of one's vocabulary. It was found out from the findings of Seashore that the child is able to learn 26,000 basic words at the age of eight and 34,000 basic words at the age of ten.

(d) Moral Development :

As the child approaches middle childhood his capacity to understand relationship increases. His concepts of right and wrong is different but related situations emerge. By the time a child is eight or nine years old his concept become more generalised.

The child tries to understand his duties and rights as a member of the group or the gang whose member he is. During the last part of this stage, moral behaviour is oriented towards authority, law, duty and maintaining the status quo which is assumed to be a primary value.

(e) Emotional Development :

Due to influence of maturation and training the expression of emotions is refined. He does experience intense emotional feeling of love, hate, fear and these endure for long periods of time along with pleasant emotions.

Generally, it is at this stage that the sentiments and the complexes are formed. This period is known as a period of stability and control. Emotional behaviour starts getting its rational. Does not like to be kissed at this stage and called by nicknames. Starts telling lie and does not like unfairness of teachers and parents, etc., and express anger or fear in a refined way.

(f) Social Development :

During this period the process of socialization takes place as a fast speed and qualities of self-consciousness, socialization and co-ordination, etc., takes place. He becomes well-adjusted, co-operative and stable. The child is no longer in need of close parental supervision. He spends most of his time in playing, exploring his world and learning about people and things. This new challenges and opportunities help him to develop a desire of popularity. He is interested in peer group interactions and a sense of belongingness is developed.

It is found out that the child at this stage acts and dresses like rest of the gang, ready for widening of social contacts, have keen sense of right and wrong, want some social approval from parents, try many experiments and want to show their independence. He develops the feelings of sacrifice and co-operation and development of team spirit and group-affinity increases in later childhood stage. Gregarious instincts ripens at this stage and the self-centred behaviour sometimes give rise to jealousies, quarrels and aggression. But this period is undoubtedly calm as compared to the storm and stress of adolescence.

(g) Educational Implications of Childhood Stage :

(1) Children between age six and nine years have a keen desire to read and write. But their muscle coordination is still imperfect. Hence, the teacher must not over-emphasize reading and writing but between age nine and twelve reading can be encouraged.

(2) As children between six and nine years have very short span of attention, text books must not have long words. As the child grows older, the span of attention lengthens and longer words can be gradually introduced.

(3) For conceptual clarification of the classroom teaching it is better to use pictures at this stage. Not only it will make the lesson interesting but also it will help the learner to make the concept clear.

(4) During the stage of childhood interests are centred round his close associates and surroundings. Hence, lessons in personal hygiene, cleanliness and behaviour with elders is more meaningful than lessons dealing with the people and customs of a foreign country.

(5) Since abstract reasoning is not developed, teacher should give them enough opportunities to solve problems of a concrete nature. Thus more realistic concept of daily living may be given for better intellectual development.

(6) Since the time concept is of a crude nature, it is of no use of introducing 250 B.C. or 410 B.C. in front of the child. As far as possible teacher should avoid inconsistency in their behaviour, otherwise their image will be devalued.

(7) Because of muscular development, children are very active and sometimes they exert themselves too much, which may cause harm to their health. Teachers should see that games and other exercises are taken under proper guidance.

(8) Since the concepts of time, space, weight, length, etc., are crude, teachers should provide learning experiences which will help children to develop these concepts. Practical training regarding length, weight, and volume, etc., be demonstrated and ask them to practice to develop these concepts.

Summary

Education, in order to be effective, must be adopted to the course of child's development. Children differ in their behaviour since early childhood and development depends both on maturation and learning and requires careful guidance. Growth refers to structural and physiological changes and development refers to change in organism as a whole.

Important characteristics of development are: principle of continuous, uniform, developmental speed variation, cephalocaudal and proximodistal sequence, proceeding from general to specific principle of integration, orderly, cumulative and predictability. Thus, there is interaction between different aspects of development and it is found out that development is more rapid at certain stages than others. Not only this, there are factors like heredity, environment and maturation, etc., affects the speed of development. All these principles have direct bearing on educational process for effective teaching and learning.

Psychologists have demarcated five stages of growth, i.e., prenatal, infancy, childhood, adolescence and adulthood. All these stages have followed with varieties of development, i.e., physical and motor, mental, language, moral, emotional and social development and different from one to another. Because of differences in growth and development it has direct bearing on education.

Questions

1. Explain the meaning of growth and development. How does the study of development help a teacher?
2. Describe the main stages of development along with their main characteristics.

3. "Development is a result of both maturation and learning" Discuss the statement with suitable examples.
4. Discuss the general principles of the growth and development and their educational implications.
5. Discuss the various development stages during the infancy and their educational implications.
6. Differentiate between growth and development. State four reasons why a teacher should be familiar with growth and development of children.
7. What are the main characteristics of physical, mental, emotional and social development of children during childhood?
8. How does the education of a pre-school child differ from that of child of 6-12 age group?
9. Describe briefly the development of the child during infancy and childhood. What should be the pattern and form of education during these periods.
10. Discuss the psychological consequences of physical and mental factors on behaviour.

References

1. Crow, L.D. and Crow, A (1962): *Child Development and Adjustment*, The Macmillan Company, New York.
2. Cruze, W.W. (1942): *Educational Psychology*, the Ronald Press Company, New York.
3. Garrett, H.E. (1996): *General Psychology*, 6th reprint, S. Chand and Company Ltd., New Delhi.
4. Garrison, K.C. (1959) : Growth and Development, Longmans Green and Company, New York.
5. Gates, A.I., *et al.* (1948): *Educational Psychology*, The Macmillan Company, New York.
6. Gesell, A. (1948): *Infancy and Human Growth,* The Macmillan Co., New York.
7. Gesell, A.L. and Thompson, H (1938): *The Psychology of Early Growth*, The Macmillan Company, New York.
8. Hurlock, E.B. (1968): *Child Growth and Development*, McGraw Hill Book Company, New York.
9. Hurlock, E.B. and Schwartz (1956): Child Development, McGraw Hill Book Company, New York.
10. Jersild, A.T (1954): *Child Psychology*, 4th edition, Prentice Hall Inc., New York.
11. Lindgren, H.C. (1956): *Educational Psychology in the Classroom*, Wiley, New York.
12. Prescott, D.A (1957): *The Child in the Educative Process*, McGraw-Hill Comp. Inc, New York.

13. Skinner, C.E. (1984): *Educational Psychology*, 4th Edition, Prentice Hall International, Inc, Englewood Cliffs New Jersey.

14. Stolt, L.H. (1967) : *Child Development: An Introduction*, Holt, Rinehart and Winston, New York.

15. Watson, E.H. *et al.* (1954): *Growth and Development of Children,* 2nd Ed., Year-book Publisher, Chicago.

DEVELOPMENT OF BEHAVIOUR DURING ADOLESCENCE

Introduction

Psychologists recognize that many options for change remain open throughout life. Understanding human behaviour over the life span is a major focus of developmental psychology. With the coming of adolescence, physiological changes accelerate, sexual maturity arrives, social relationship become more intense and new cognitive capacities emerge. Although psychological maturity does not occur quite so rapidly the teenage years are a time of dramatically speeded up development. When we speak of the adolescent as 'growing up' we mean that the youth has leaving behind the phase of protective childhood and is becoming independent, capable of going out to fend for himself. Let us now discuss the above period in details.

Meaning of Adolescence

The term 'adolescence' is derived from the Latin verb "adolescere" which means to grow to maturity or to grow-up. This period is most critical period of individual development which begins from 12-13 years and ends at 21/22 years. During this period the establishment of the childhood goes away and a revolutionary change starts. Thus this period is known as revolutionary period of human life during which the child develops into a man or woman. It is characterized by the change in physiological, psychological and sociological aspects of individuals. During these years, one is neither a child nor an adult and generally referred as the period of life from puberty to maturity.

The period of adolescence is defined in several ways. These are the following:

1. According to A.T. Jersild "Adolescence is that span of years during which boys and girls move from childhood to adulthood mentally, emotionally, socially and physically".
2. From biological point of view this is a period of rapid growth. The period of adolescence begins when the individual shows the first signs of making the transition to sexual maturity and ends when physical growth almost ceases at about the age of 21.
3. According to Hadfield "when we speak of adolescent as 'growing up' we mean that the youth is leaving behind the phase of protective childhood and is becoming independent, capable of going out to fend for himself".
4. In a purely psychological sense, Hamachek defined "Adolescence means a state of mind, an attitude, a style of existence that begins with puberty and ends when one is relatively independent of parental control.
5. Ross defined "Adolescence is best regarded as a recapitulation of the first period of life, as second turn of the spiral of development".
6. Mead defined "Adolescence is the period from the beginning of sexual maturity (puberty) to the completion of growth".
7. According to Hall "Adolescence is that period of human life where an individual is capable of producing of offsprings of same kind".
8. Medinnus and Johnson view that "Adolescence begins when signs of sexual maturity begin to occur in both physical and social development, and ends when the individual has assumed adult roles and is accepted in most ways as an adult by his reference group".
9. According to sociological interpretation of the word adolescence, "it is a transitional period between childhood and adulthood when a child moves from

dependency to independency in his behaviour".

10. Dorothy defined "Adolescence is not a separate period but a continuous process of growth".
11. According to Anderson, "Adolescence extends from puberty to the attainment of full height and weight and cessation of growth. It is the period in which the person moves out of the home circle and becomes physically and mentally independent".
12. Erikson defined, "Adolescence is a period of rapid change—Physiological, Psychological, moral and social, a time when all sameness and continuities relied upon earlier one more or less questioned again".
13. Jean Piaget said that "Adolescence is the age of great ideals and the beginning of theories as well as the time of simple present adaptation to reality".
14. Hurlock defined "Adolescence as the years extend from the time the child becomes sexually mature and includes mental, emotional and social as well as physical maturity".
15. Hollingshead defined as "Adolescent years, a period in life when the society in which he functions ceases to regard him as a child and does not accord him full adult status, roles and functions".
16. Schulz defines "Adolescence is a period of normative crisis when the young adult is permitted to experiment with various adult roles without having to pay the consequences of full public responsibility".
17. Ausubel defines "Adolescence is a distinctive stage in personality development precipitated by significant changes in the bio-social status of the child".
18. Eisenberg defined "Adolescence is a critical period of human development manifested at the biological, psychological and social skills of interaction of variable onset and duration but marking the end of childhood and setting the foundation for maturity".
19. Strang (1957) defines that "Adolescence is usually described as the developmental stage beginning with puberty—the period when sexual maturity occurs and the attainment of the emotional, social, and other aspects of adult maturity".
20. Ambron (1975) defined "Adolescence is the bridge between childhood and adulthood. It is a time of rapid development of growing to sexual maturity,

discovering one's real self, defining personal values, and finding one's vocational and social directions. It is also a time of testing of pushing against one's capacities and the limitations as posed by adults".

21. Piaget Inhelder (1969) defined "Adolescence is the age of great ideals and the beginning of theories, as well as the time of simple present adaptation to reality".
22. Kennedy (1975) defined "Adolescence is the transitional years between puberty and adulthood in human development, usually covers the teens".
23. Landis (1945) states that "Adolescence comprises that period in life when the individual is in the process of transfer from the dependent, irresponsible age of childhood to the self-reliant, responsible age of adulthood. The maturing child seeks new freedom and becomes accountable to society".

In fact, the child takes a new birth in adolescence. It is more or less like a jump from one stage to the other. Thus, with this period various adjectives are attached. These are the following:

(a) Adolescence is a period of "spring of life".
(b) Adolescence is called "attractive age" but "uneven and strange in life".
(c) Adolescence is the period of "Stress and strain" and "storm and strife" (Stanley Hall).
(d) Adolescence a "Phenomenon" which happens once in life time.
(e) Adolescence is a period of "teen age".
(f) Adolescence is a period of "youth".
(g) Adolescence is the period of "transition from childhood to adulthood".
(h) Adolescence is called the "revolutionary period" of human life.
(i) Adolescence is called a "sharp and distinct critical period" in development.
(j) Adolescence is a "period of second birth" (Hall's).
(k) Adolescence may be called "sensitive" period in development.
(l) Adolescence begins in "biology and ends in culture".

(m) Adolescence is a "complex and difficult" period in development.
(n) Adolescence is a period where "hero worship starts".
(o) Adolescence is a "awkward, exciting and crucial" period in the life cycle.
(p) Adolescence is a period of "peak in human growth and change".
(q) Adolescence is a time "when all is questioned again".
(r) Adolescence is "the age of great ideals".
(s) Adolescence is a period of a "normative crisis".

Needs of the Study of Adolescence Period

Adolescence is the most important period in human development about which poets, writers, historians have made references. It is a period of transition and a turning point in the life of the individual. The following are the needs to study the psychology of adolescence.

1. *Understanding developmental characteristics*

To study the adolescence period means to understand the growth and development in almost all dimensions of the above period. It helps the parents, teacher and all others who are responsible for proper development of the adolescents and guide him/her to adjust in a better way in the society.

2. *Adjustment to responsibilities*

The study of adolescence period helps the teachers and parents to know the responsibilities of the adolescents and guide them to live harmoniously without any emotional tension.

3. *Maintenance of mental health*

The study of adolescence helps the parents and teachers to prevent, cure and improve the deteriorating trends in mental health of adolescents.

4. *Planning Curriculum and Education*

The study of adolescence period help the teacher, curriculum workers and guidance personnel to plan curricular and co-curricular activities according to the needs, interests and aptitudes, etc., of adolescence.

5. ***To study the maturity and curiosity***

The knowledge of the psychology of adolescence help the teacher and parents to understand the maturity level, behavioural characteristics and their curiosity in relation to the larger interest of the society.

Characteristics of Adolescence Period

Hurlock in her book 'Developmental Psychology' outlines the following characteristics of the adolescence period.

(1) ***Adolescence is an important period***

Adolescence is a complex and often difficult period in development both for adolescents and for their families. Because of rapid physical, physiological and cognitive changes, and by an accelerating succession of urgent societal demands, adolescents face formidable challenges in the essential task of deciding who they are, what they are going to be, and how they are going to get these. Thus this is an important period of the human life.

(2) ***Adolescence is a transitional period***

Adolescence is a period of transition and rapid change. Neither the person is called a child nor an adult because the individual has crossed the childhood and yet to react the stage of adulthood. Thus the status of the individual is vague and diffused and there is a confusion about the roles he/she is going to play. Sometimes his innocent behaviour is either called "childish" or "too big for his age".

(3) ***Adolescence is a period of change***

It is a general characteristics of the adolescence period. During this stage there is a change in physical, psychological and sociological aspects of individuals along with values, attitudes, interests, and behaviours. Thus consistency and inconsistency is found out in the life cycle.

(4) Adolescence is a period of ego centric and problem age

The sudden and rapid changes of physical and psychological aspects during this stage create problem for the adolescents. Adolescent youth are interested to solve their problems independently and try to achieve independence from parents, establish co-operative and workable relationships with peers and prepare for a meaningful vocation. But sometime they do not have the capacity nor the experience to solve their problems, which itself create a problem for them.

(5) Adolescence is a time of search for identity

Each of the periods has its own problems which must be solved if the individuals are to enter the next period without handicap. Adolescence is perhaps no more important a stage of development then any other, but it is the last stage before adulthood, and it therefore, offers to both parents and teachers the last opportunity to educate a child for his adult responsibilities. During this period adolescents begin to search for their identity and try to develop individuality in their own way which sometimes lead to identity crisis in some adolescents.

(6) Adolescence is a period of unrealism

During this period the aspirations, thoughts and achievement, etc., are more idealistic rather than realistic. The young boys and girls think more unrealistic, false and absurd ideas which sometime hurt and disappoint them in life. It is found out that this false idealistic ideas disappears gradually and adolescent see their life, family and friends more realistically.

(7) **Adolescence is a period of Hero-Worship and sexual maturity**

During this period the boys and girls consider themselves they are the hero and heroine of the life cycle. They think they can do and undo everything during their life span without understanding the reality of the life. The above feelings take place due to the sudden sexual development on the part of the boys and girls.

(8) **Adolescence is a period of intensely emotional**

During this period the youth often resulting in intense excitement and deep depression. Sometimes he/she may exhibit a "know-it-all" attitude. Boys like to be thought big, strong and healthy. Girls desire prettiness. In both the sexes there is interest in and emphasis on physical attractiveness and good grooming.

(9) ***Adolescence is a period of sexual delinquency***

During this period sexual manifestation may cause self consciousness and desire for other ties. It is a period of mutual liking, thus homosexual and hetrosexual feelings create confusion among the adolescents.

(10) ***Adolescence is a period of high moral values and sacrifice***

During this period high moral values is seen. The adolescents youth likes to serve in the fairs, festivals, social gatherings, etc., and sacrifice their own conveniences for social service due to their high moral feelings.

Stages Of Adolescence and Objectives of the Adolescence Period

E.B. Hurlock lists the entire range of adolescence period as follows :

(1) Pre-adolescence—1 1to 13 years (girls): 13 to 15 years (boys)
(2) Early-adolescence—13 to 15 years (girls); 15 to 17 years (boys)
(3) Middle-adolescence—15 to 18 years (girls); 17 to 19 years (boys)
(4) Late-adolescence—18 to 21 years (girls) : 19 to 21 years (boys)

It is understood that one does not automatically pass from one of these periods to another on a given birthday. One level of development help the other. In order to pass from childhood to adulthood the child is to pass through the adolescence period which is full of problems. During this period hetro-sexual interests, free from home supervision, make new emotional and social adjustments to reality, began to evolve a philosophy of life, achieve economic and intellectual independence, and learn how to use his/her leisure time profitably, etc., are developed. If he fails in any of these achievements, he fails to gain full maturity. Let us now discuss in detail in terms of change from a childish towards an adult level.

TABLE - 3.1
GOALS OF THE ADOLESCENCE PERIOD

A. *General Emotional Maturity :*			
From	1. Destructive expressions of emotion 2. Subjective interpretation of situation. 3. Childish fears and motives 4. Habits of escaping from conflicts.	towards	1. Harmless or constructive 2. Objective interpretations of situations. 3. Adult stimuli to emotions. 4. Habits of facing and solving conflicts.
B. ***Establishment of Hetrosexual Interests :***			
From	1. Exclusive interest in members of same sex. 2. Experience with many possible mates. 3. Acute awareness of sexual development.	towards	1. Normal interest in members of opposite sex. 2. Selection of one mate. 3. Causal acceptance of sexual maturity.
C. General Social Maturity :			
From	1. Feelings of uncertainty of acceptance by peers. 2. Social awkwardness 3. Social intolerance 4. Slavish imitation of peers.	towards	1. Feelings of secure acceptance by peers. 2. Social poise 3. Social tolerance 4. Freedom from slavish imitation
D. *Emancipation from Home control:*			
From	1. Close parental control 2. Reliance upon parents for security. 3. Identification with parents as models.	towards	1. Self-control 2. Reliance upon self for security 3. Attitude towards parents as friends.
E. *Intellectual Maturity:*			
From	1. Blind acceptance of truth on the basis of authority. 2. Desire for facts.	towards	1. Demand for evidence before acceptance 2. Desire for explanations of facts

	3. Many temporary interest		3. Few stable interest

F. *Selection of an Occupation:*

From	1. Interests in glamorous occupations 2. Interest in many occupations 3. Over or under-estimation of one's own abilities 4. Irrelevance of Interests to abilities	towards	1. Interest in practicable occupations 2. Interest in one occupation 3. Reasonably accurate estimate of one's own abilities 4. Reconciliation of interest and abilities

G. *Uses of Leisure:*

From	1. Interest in vigorous unorganized games. 2. Interest in individual powers. 3. Participation in games 4. Interest in many hobbies 5. Membership in many clubs.	towards	1. Interest in team games and intellectual contests 2. Interest in success of team. 3. Spectator interest in games. 4. Interest in one or two hobbies 5. Membership in few clubs.

H. *Philosophy of Life:*

From	1. Indifference toward general principles 2. Behaviour dependent upon specific, learned habits 3. Behaviour based upon gaining pleasure and avoiding pain	towards	1. Interest in and understanding of general principles 2. Behaviour guided by moral principles 3. Behaviour based upon conscience and duty

I. *Identification of self:*

From	1. Little or no perception of self 2. Little idea of other peoples perception of self 3. Identification of self with impossible goals	towards	1. Moderately accurate perception of self 2. Good idea of other peoples perception of self 3. Identification of self with possible goals

Growth and Development during Adolescence

Adolescence begins in biology and ends in culture. It is a period of growth which is characterised by rapid physical, emotional, social, moral and intellectual developments. The following are the developments during adolescence.

(a) *Physical growth/changes in Adolescence*

(i) *Height and Weight (size) and bodily development:*

Adolescence is a period of rapid physical growth and dramatic bodily changes. There is a sudden change in height and weight due to hyper activity of endocrine glands. The girls are about two years ahead of the boys in the early adolescence in almost all the physical growth and maturity but boys are able to compensate it in the later part of the adolescence period. The glands become active and there is increased production of hormones. Arms and heart also grow in length and size. There is growth in bones and muscles and as a consequence adolescent become conscious and comes to acquire great energy and power.

(ii) *Appearance and voices*

There is a change in appearance, face is more angular, sound is hoarse and high-pitched and sweeter in case of girls. Many boys begin to shave, though most of them have little reason to do so. Slowly not only face whiskers but also hair comes on the forearms, and legs and chest begin to appear in a goodshape. In case of females, the face takes on a softer look, the lips become fuller and the breast start filling out.

(iii) *Change in body functions:*

With the secretion of hormones from ductless glands there is change in body functions. The muscles hardens, menstruation starts in girls and night emissions in boys. The sensory and motor organs assume their complete development during this period. Cole said 'Adolescence is a period of growth in all systems of the body to the fullest and greatest possible extent. Stanley Hall pointed out that "not only motor activity increases but there is also a great development in the motor power".

Thus adolescence is a period of growth. In the course of a few years the individual undergoes changes in both size and proportion—changes that take him/her from a childish to a mature level. The rapidity, variety, and force of these developments are alike bewildering, even though they are sometimes exciting and satisfactory. The alternations are indeed so extensive that some people have regarded adolescence as a sort of second birth. Usually there is some degree of mal co-ordination to be seen during the period. It is therefore essential that teachers should keep in mind the physical background of adolescence so that effective learning can takes place.

The most characteristic developments during adolescence are the lengthening of all the long bones and the final articulation of all the bones at their respective joints, changes which underlie the increases in height and strength. The wisdom teeth appear, causing some trouble, the face changes a great deal and loses its childish contours by the end of adolescence period.

(b) ***Sexual development***

Puberty, the 'centring event' of adolescence, refers to the beginning of sexual maturity. The maturity of the sex glands is the most important single development of the adolescent years. In case of the males the penis, growth of pubic hair, prostate gland and seminal vesicles begin to work. Similarly in females gradual enlargement of the reproductive organs, change in ovaries and uterus, development of breasts, pelvic area and menstruation starts. All girls become self-conscious about this type of change. Both boys and girls develop attraction towards the opposite sex. Members of both sexes display a variety of attitudes towards the changes in their bodily functions and these attitudes influence their personalities, their school work, and their general adjustment to life.

(c) ***Mental Development during Adolescence***

During the adolescence the capacity to acquire and to utilise knowledge reaches its peak efficiency. Adolescent becomes capable of accomplishing more easily, more quickly and more efficiently intellectual tasks and he or she is able to define problems and to give reason about them. Thus there is a marked growth in mental power. He can apply logical thought to all classes of problems. Problem solving behaviour also appears at this stage. The adolescent can plan carefully, design an experiment appropriately, observe the results accurately and draw conclusions rightly.

In simple sense we can say that adolescents may

concentrate for longer time, think abstractly, development of permanent memory starts, imagination power increases, development of logic, more curious to ask questions, become critical to everything, start thinking about their future vocations, marked increase in vocabulary and matures mentally.

He has a greater ability to form concepts, the concept of time gradually gains in clarity and tendency to over-generalise the concept is still present. The adolescent shows an increased interest in national and international affairs and is seriously concerned about his place in society and his success in his role.

He is more introspective and analytical and Piaget called it formal operation period of cognitive development. This period of intellectual development is the ability to "see through" situations of all kinds to their inner meaning.

(d) *Religious beliefs and Moral Development during Adolescence*

An interest in or a revolt against religion is an integral part of adolescence. In spite of a small minority of highly verbal cynics, religion continues to play a part in human existence and is of special value during the adolescent years in formulating ideals and standards of conduct.

By the time the child reaches adolescence, his moral conduct is fairly well informed and he is capable of understanding what is right and what is wrong. The desire to reform the world and to do some good work during life time is very strong. Most young people want to find a satisfactory philosophy of life and his values are influenced by peer group than by parental values system.

(e) *Emotional Development during Adolescence*

Emotional life of adolescence concerns loyalties to the group, aggression and affection. Peel has commented that "the adolescent is beset by problems of divided loyalties, accentuated by the lack of adult privileges and responsibilities. He thus appears excessively aggressive and then excessively shy, excessively affectionate and then quite suddenly detached and cool because of bodily changes." Thus, sometimes he is "hillarious" but on the otherhand he is extremely "melancholy". He is also very sensitive and does not welcome any criticism or attack on his prestige.

Strange feelings capture the minds of adolescents. Sex-consciousness raises the feelings of curiosity, secretiveness and guilt. He has a strong group feelings and loves adventure, travel and wandering. Emotions become realistic and some time he is over-joyed by his success but at the sametime he is extremely depressed and sad by imagining the problems of finding a job. Adolescents may be termed as moody because their emotions fluctuate too rapidly.

The onset of sexual maturity also contributes to adolescent fears and anxiety. Emotions become intensed like hate some one strongly and love passionately. If they suffer from inferiority complex and do not get their dues they may think to run out from the house (to do some better work) and also to commit suicide, if it becomes more perplexed.

(f) *Social Development during Adolescence*

Adolescents are tremendously sensitive to social stimuli. They react faster and more deeply to the influence of their age-mates than to that of adults. Adolescents strive for psychological separation from their parents. Gregarious instinct plays an important role in this period. He continues to be a member of a gang or group. Adolescents often act in very inconsistent ways. Peer group relationship established according to their sex, interests, abilities and attitudes.

During the teenage years, hetrosexual relationships emerge. Development of conscience and "peer culture", the sum total of spontaneous social manifestations among age-mates, is most influential during the adolescence. Self consciousness increases, want to be praised by others and want social approval of their mode of behaviour, development of leadership qualities and love social service and like to serve in the fairs, festivals, social gatherings, etc. During this period adolescents follow adult culture patterns in their behaviour. Loyalty to group is strengthened and develop insight into social human relation. They often come into conflict with adults on social problems and tradition of the community.

Need and Problems of Adolescence

Adolescence is a period of rapid changes. The peculiar and unusual changes that take place during this stage create problems for the adolescent boys and girls. Similarly the need of adolescents are really different from earlier stages of life cycle. If the need of adolescents are not properly gratified the adolescent becomes a problem youth. The basic need and problems of the adolescent boys and girls are as follows.

(A) *Need of Adolescence*

(i) Sex need:

The maturing of the sex glands is the most important single development of the adolescent years. The sexual instinct which was dormant takes a strong turn and develops into hetro-sexuality (attachment towards the opposite sex). Development and sudden functioning of the sex organs create worries, anxieties and tension among the adolescent boys and girls. Members of both sexes display a variety of attitudes towards the changes in their bodily functions, and these attitudes influence their personalities, their school work, interest and their general adjustment to life. Thus to channelise the sex desire of an adolescent youth in a right track, varieties of programmes like creative activities, athletics, moral and sex education can be introduced in the school.

(ii) Security Need:

The adolescent is on the boundary line of childhood and adulthood. So he is typically a person who needs security, guidance and protection like a child and independent views, maturity of opinion and self support like an adult. This need can be fulfilled if the adolescent is given an opportunity of studying the biography of greatmen like Gandhi, Tagore, Vivekananda, Kabir, Nanak, Dayananda, Laxmibai and Sarojini Naidu, etc.

(iii) Gregarious Need:

It is a fact that instincts of the adolescents assumes greater strength and importance at this stage. The adolescents have the enormous power and desire to do many activities to sublimate the animal instincts, which may be desirable or undesirable. Without this sublimation, his intellectual, social, moral and intellectual aspects of the personality cannot be properly trained. Thus adolescents should be provided opportunity to satisfy their basic need through group formation as scouting, NCC, Social service, and community activities otherwise they may indulge themselves into the activities of pick-pocketing, truancy and robbery which are unsocial activities to satisfy their gregarious feelings.

(iv) Adventurous Need:

The feeling of adventure is maximum during

adolescence. In the absence of proper direction it takes the form of aimless wandering and unsocial activities. In order to satisfy the anxiety of adolescents excursions, picnic and educational tours, etc., should be organised. Thus providing an opportunity to the adolescents during this period can fulfil their physical needs vis-a-vis adventurous qualities.

(v) Social Need:

An adolescent, in almost all the activities, wants recognition in the form of a praise or a reward or a prize for social approval. He is ambitious of achieving success and getting public recognition. Thus during this stage an adolescent youth requires a good deal of sympathy. If their success or achievement is not recognised at home or in the school they begin to lose interest in such activities and may turn into violent and unrealistic ways.

(vi) Self-awareness Need:

Adolescence is a age of self-decoration. Both boys and girls pay more attention towards their dress, make-up, manner of talking, walking, eating, etc., and desires that he/she should be a centre of attraction for the opposite sex and recognised by the peer group and elders. So, if their need of self-awareness is not looked into then the adolescents become either aggressive or withdrawn type depending upon the circumstances.

(vii) Need for Status:

Although adolescence is a stage of transition and period of rapid change yet their behaviour and thinking are not accepted by the society easily. If their need for status is not met satisfactorily in the family or in the school it may lead to confusion, ambiguity and disappointment in them. Thus their status in the society must be understood by parents and teachers and accordingly opportunity for participating in all decision making programmes in home, school and the community should be provided.

(viii) Need for Independence:

Adolescents youth need economic and emotional independence. They do not like to depend upon their parents regarding money matter and no longer want to be treated as a child. They want to be self sufficient but they are inexperienced and incapable of taking responsibility for their security and comforts which leads to confusion, anxiety and frustration in them.

(ix) Need for Recreation Activities:

Adolescents are interested to spend their recreation time in useful ways. If their need for recreation is not utilised in proper order then their study is hampered. Thus parents and teachers should guide them properly to utilise their recreation time in a fruitful manner.

(x) Vocational Need:

The strong desire of adolescents is to achieve self-sufficiency and make himself/herself quite independent like an adult member of the soceity. They prefer to earn himself/herself independently and follow a suitable vocation. Thus during this stage proper care should be taken while educating them as well as an idea about selection of the various vocations as occupation must be informed.

(B) ***Problems of Adolescents***

Adolescence is a period of rapid changes in all demensions of development. When the needs of adolescents are not satisfied problems occur in behavioural characteristics. Thus problems of adolescents are either due to himself/herself or due to the conditions of the society in which he/she lives. Lay Cock and other psychologists grouped the problems of adolescent as under:

- (i) Problems of adjustment due to changing physical growth and physiological development.
- (ii) Becoming emancipated from family and free from emotional dependence on parents.
- (iii) Accepting own characteristics of sex-role and making adjustment to the opposite sex.
- (iv) Finding and ensuring on a suitable vocation.
- (v) Developing a sound philosophy of life which will give meaning and purpose to life.
- (vi) Adjustment to personal, social, health and home life-relationship.
- (vii) Adjustment difficulties with parents and the community.
- (viii) Adjustment difficulties in relation to finance, employment, marriage life and future educational and vocational adjustment.

In addition to the above, the problems frequently reported by the adolescents are given in details:

I. *Problem of Sex*

The period of adolescence is known as a period of stress and strain. It is the most difficult and the awkward period. The period marks the re-awakening of repressed sex-impulse. Thus to help an adolescent sex-education may be introduced in the syllabus as a compulsory subject.

II. *Problems related to Education*

During the period of adolescence the specific problems related to education are dislike for study, fear of failure, restlessness in class, low grade in the examination, fear of speaking in the class, too much work, dislike for school, partial behaviour of teachers and groupism on the basis of caste, creed and religion. This situation frustrate the mental state of the adolescents.

III. *Problems of adjustment at Home*

It is a fact that Indian parents have not changed their traditional attitude towards their adolescent sons and daughters. Sometimes parents in majority of the cases are responsible for the problems like imposing restriction on their freedom misunderstanding between parents and adolescents at home, treating adolescent as a small child and not providing facilities when he is in need, etc., are the causes of adjustment problems of adolescents.

IV. *Problems related to emotion*

The abnormal functioning of the nervous system and the endocrine glands are mainly responsible for emotional problem. Adolescents have both the extreme emotions, i.e., positive and negative. What is required is to help him/her in emotional control. His/her various needs must be satisfied and guided properly.

V. *Adjustment difficulties with school and the community*

A rigid discipline, an over-crowded school, an unhealthy atmosphere, and lack of activities in the school, etc., may create problems of adjustment. Adolescents like to go out, mix with friends and to do some social service but the society has some restrictions. Thus an adolescent must be dealt with sympathy and engaged in work according to their ability in the school.

VI. Problems of Economic Independence

It has been reported by a number of studies that the adolescent does not like to depend upon their parents regarding money matter. He/She prefers to earn for himself/herself and follow a suitable vocation. But due to inadequate experiences and incapable of taking responsibilities for their security and comforts they feel frustration. Thus proper guidance may be given to adolescents by the parents and teacher.

VII. *Problems of Vocational Adjustment*

Adolescents are very much concerned about their future vocation. The problems lie with the selection of a vocational preference and preparation for it. Thus proper care should be taken in the school that while educating him/her an idea about the availability of different vocations and its selection procedure, etc., must be informed.

IX. *Problems of choosing right philosophy of life*

Adolescence is a period of wider social contacts, increased mental ability and understanding, and excessive physiological development which create problems and bother adolescents too much. Which philosophy of life they have to follow is difficult and complex on their part to decide. Thus, opportunity must be provided to the adolescent to take a decision to govern their future life in a positive manner.

Developmental Tasks of Adolescents

The concept of developmental task was developed by an American Psychologist, Robert Havinghurst on the basis of his extensive researches and proposed a list of development tasks right from infancy to old age. He defined "a developmental task is a task which arises at or about a certain period in the life of the individual, successful achievement of which leads to happiness and success with later tasks while failure leads to unhappiness in the individual, disapproval by the society and difficulty with later tasks". Thus it can be said that in each stage of development there are certain tasks or activities, skills, understanding and attitudes that must be met before a person can move on to a higher level of development.

The developmental tasks of adolescence are given below:

I. *Achieving new and more mature relationships with age-mates of both sexes*

When a child enters adolescence, the society expects that he should be able to establish healthy relationship with the members of both the sexes. But generally, we do not permit free mixing of adolescent boys and girls in our society. Therefore it can be suggested that one should not always think negatively rather an adolescent should be allowed to communicate freely about the quality of social life and occupational choice with his/her peer group for better social dealings.

II. *Achieving a masculine or feminine role*

During this transitional period, adolescents should be provided guidance and counselling as regards to their sex-role in the society which they are going to perform as man or woman.

III. *Accepting one's physique and using the body effectively*

During adolescence, physical and physiological changes occur at a very rapid speed. Thus he/she must be guided properly so that they can make proper use of their physical strength for the benefits of the society.

IV. *Achieving emotional independence of parents and other adults*

Sometimes it is noticed that parents treat their adolescent son and daughter as child and behave accordingly. But due to mature development, adolescents rebel against the rigid attitude of parents. So, it is suggested that they may be guided properly and parents should understand their problems and difficulties sympathetically.

V. *Preparing for family and marriage life*

During this period an adolescent needs proper education regarding the preparation for family and marriage life otherwise successful achievement of life may be hindered.

VI. *Preparation for an economic career*

During adolescence organization and planning of future life can be strengthened in such a way that one can enter a career of his/her own choice and can justify it. Thus guidance must be provided in the educational institution so that development of courage and confidence can be strengthened among the adolescents.

VII. *Acquiring a set of values and an ethical system as a guide to behaviour*

What should be the values and ethical system (religion) that one will eventually adopt in life depends upon the society and the system where he/she lives in. Therefore, varieties of values and beliefs of the society must be put forth before the adolescent to facilitate to draw conclusions according to the demands of the society.

VII. *Desire to achieve socially responsible behaviour*

The main objective of this task is to include the development of social ideology which allows the adolescent to be a responsible participant in the development and progress of his/her community and country. Therefore it is said that to be a responsible adult and a responsible citizen demands that one takes into account of the values of society in one's personal behaviour.

Role of the Teacher and Educational Importance of the Adolescence Period

(1) Adolescents worry a great deal about the physiological changes that occur in them. Thus honest replies to their queries could help to eliminate much of the fear and anxiety that the adolescent experiences.

(2) It is a known fact that teenaged boys and girls are growing into adult men and women. Therefore, school library and work rooms must be adequately equipped in order to cater to the needs of the adolescent.

(3) Adolescence is a critical period. They feel happy if they are asked to help or to give their ideas and resent adult attempts to impose views on them. Hence parents should discuss the matter with them and leave them free to accept or reject the view.

(4) Adolescents demand independence. Hence the teacher must provide opportunities for self-study and

freedom to select their courses and hobbies in their day-to-day life.

(5) Teachers must be patient and tactful in all their dealings with adolescents. Sincerity and a friendly attitude help the adolescent from destructive tendencies in them.

(6) Teachers should not adopt double standards while dealing with adolescents. They should set a good example of good conduct and display his/her own emotional stability.

(7) The teacher should make a thorough understanding of the general characteristics of the period of adolescence, its stress and strains, urges, charges and problems so that proper information about sex and vocational guidance can be provided.

(8) If the parents and teachers expect respect and trust from the adolescent they must first give it on the basis of clear and correct information to them.

(9) Teacher should redirect the energies of the adolescents into fruitful channels through games, sports and other creative recreational activities. Even some programme of moral and religious teaching should be organised in the school.

(10) Adolescents try to establish link with their peer groups to maintain social relationship. Hence the adolescent can be given scope in this direction by allowing them to participate and take leadership in different activities organised in the school.

(11) Since the adolescent is attaining intellectual maturity the school curriculum must be varied to meet his intellectual curiosity. Hence suitable books on adventures, travels and biography must be provided to them so that good reading habits and noble ideas can be developed in them.

(12) Parent-teacher associations should be strengthened and joint efforts should be made to understand the problems of an adolescent and necessary remedies should be provided.

Summary

Adolescence is a period of growth and of maturation. It is a period of transition from childhood to adulthood. There is growth spurt during adolescence resulting changes in body and voice, physical energy and sexual maturity. Emotional life of adolescence concerns loyalties to the peer group, shyness, self-consciousness, sensitivity, intense hero-worship. Social relationship is marked by changing relationship with the parents and attachment with the peer group. In order to get freedom from adult control, they form group and establish friendship among themselves.

Hurlock described adolescence as a period of change, sexual delinquency, transition, ego-centric, search for identity, unrealism and high moral values. These are the special characteristics of the above period.

There are many problems and needs of adolescents. If their needs are not gratified then they become problem youth. The problems of the adolescents are sex development, education, emotion, difficulties with school and community, economic independence, vocational choices, and selecting right philosophy of life. There are also different developmental tasks of the adolescents. Thus the basic psychological and physiological problems of the adolescents can be studied by the teacher and parents to help him/her to develop harmonious personalities and maintain a balance in the society.

Questions

1. What is adolescence? Discuss the stress and strains experienced by adolescents? How can the teacher help adolescents to tide over these difficulties?
2. What peculiar characteristics mark the period of adolescence? Discuss their educational implications.
3. Enumerate some of the main problems faced by adolescents in our country.
4. What are the needs and problems of an adolescent? How can you as a teacher help to overcome the difficulties of adolescence?
5. Why is adolescent period called a period of storm and strain? Explain what can the teacher do to help the adolescents?
6. Describe briefly the physical and psychological characteristics of the boys and girls during the period of adolescence. What should be the pattern of education at this stage?
7. Discuss the basic needs and problems of adolescents with special reference to their developmental tasks.
8. Discuss the emotional and social characteristics of adolescents. How do these influence their behaviour?

9. Define adolescence. Describe the importance and needs of psychology of adolescence.
10. Discuss the developmental tasks for adolescents as suggested by Havinghurst?

References

1. Adams, J.F (1979): *Understanding Adolescence*, Allyn and Bacon, Boston.
2. Ausubel, D.P. (1954) : *Theory and Problems of Adolescent Development*, Grune and Stratton, Inc, New York.
3. Blos, P. (1962) : *On Adolescence*, Free Press, New York.

   3(B).Berzonsty M.D. (1981): *Adolescent Development*, Macmillan Publishing Co., New York.
4. Cole, L (1946) : *Psychology of Adolescence* (5th Ed.), Holt, Rinehart and Winston, New York.
5. Coleman, J.S (1961) : *The Adolescent Society*, Free Press, New York.
6. Conger, J.J. (1977) : Adolescence and Youth (2nd ed.) Harper and Row Pub. New York.
7. Douvan, E.A. and Adelson, J (1966): *The Adolescent Experience*, Wiley, New York.
8. Gold, M. and Douvan, E (1969): *Adolescent Development*, Allyn and Bacon, Boston.
9. Grinder, R.E. (1973) : *Adolescence*, John Willey and Sons, New York.
10. Havinghurst, R.J. (1972) : *Developmental Tasks and Education*, MCkay, New York.
11. Hurlock, E.B. (1973) : *Adolescent Development* (4th ed.) McGraw Hill Book Company, New York.
12. Jersild, A.T. (1963) : Psychology of Adolescence (2nd ed.), The Macmillan Company, New York.
13. Kuhlen, R.G. (1952): *The Psychology of Adolescent Development*, Harper and Row Brothers, New York.
14. Malm, M. and O.G. Jamison (1952) : *Adolescence*, McGraw Hill Book Company, New York.
15. Manaster, G.J. (1977): *Adolescent Development*, Allyn and Bacon, Boston
16. Rogers, D (1981) : Adolescents and Youth (4th ed,) Prentice Hall International, Inc, Englewood Cliffs, New Jersey.
17. Weiner, J.B. (1970) : *Psychological Disturbance in Adolescence*, Wiley Interscience, New York.
18. Staton, T.F. (1963) : *Dynamics of Adolescent Adjustment*, The Macmillan Co, New York.

HEREDITY AND ENVIRONMENT

Introduction

Man is the best creation of nature in the earth. Not only he is unique but also he is different in physical, mental, social, psychic, cognitive, moral, language and ancestral traits from other individuals in the society. Thus these natural characteristics or innate tendencies which we possess have come or transmitted to us from ancestral stock through parents. Because of this situation an individual is a unique creation. After coming to this world with certain characteristics, we the human beings come into contact with the environment and social surroundings. Then the debate of heredity and environment come into the limelight. While some of the scholars are in favour of former one the others lay emphasis on the latter concept. Any way it can be said that to understand the development of the human personality it is necessary to study the actions and reactions of heredity and environment. Psychologically one cannot exist without the other. Heredity provides raw materials and how the materials are moulded depends upon the environment.

In our day to day observation it is noticed that the individuals are different from one to another. It is a fact that some of the children learn their lessons very rapidly while some others may not be able to master the concept even after repeated attempts. Whether such differences in learning ability are due to the differences in innate capacity or due to social and cultural environment, are answered in this chapter.

It is often pointed out that we cannot get grapes from thorns or figs from thistles. The farmer ploughs the field and sows the seeds in it. The seed which lands on the stone does not sprout while the other one which lands on hard land does so with difficulty. The seed away from water sprouts but does not grow because it dries up due to lack of water. If the farmer fails to look after the crops, wild animals and birds would destroy it. The absence of fertilizers would restrict the proper growth of plants. Thus, the mere sowing of seeds will not allow one to reap it. It is essential that the crop be given manure, water, etc., at the proper time and it be protected from other destructive elements. Does it mean that the seed has no importance? Let us now discuss about heredity and environment so as to get answers what exactly they mean and what is their role in personality formation.

Heredity: Meaning and Nature

Heredity is defined by different psychologists in different ways. Heredity involves all those physiological and psychological peculiarities which a person inherits from his parents. It is the minute seed which a child receives from his parents or ancestors. It is all the factors that were present in the organism at birth or it is the sum-total of inborn individual traits or unique sum of the inherent qualities transmitted to an individual by his parents at the moment the child is conceived. Heredity thus contributes something in the form of inheritance just as we inherit law, money and assets or liabilities from our parents and forefathers. From the genetic angle this transmission occurs at the time of conception of the child in the womb of the mother. Conception of life is in fact a beginning of a new life. Hence, heredity includes all likeness and dislikeness between parents and off-springs. It forms a foundation and the whole of later behaviour depends on heredity.

Cuber, J.F. said: "Heredity consists of all those traits and characteristics, which a person possesses because he is a specimen of the homo-sapiens".

Woodworth said : "Heredity covers all the factors that were present in the individual when he began life, not at birth but at the time of conception about nine months before birth".

Ruch defined: "Heredity as the totality of biologically transmitted factors that influence the structure of the body".

Peterson said: "Heredity may be defined as what gets from his ancestral stock through his parents".

Benedict defined: "Heredity is the transmission of traits from parents to offspring".

Beals and Hoijer defined: "Heredity means the tendency of things to produce their ownkind". It is heredity which determines the structure, colour of the skin, the hair structure, height, facial features, nasal index, cephalic index, etc.

Heredity has two aspects—biological and psychological. When the sum total of biological traits are present in the fertilised ovum and the traits like innate tendencies and traits that resemble between the parents and the child is otherwise known as biological and psychological heredity. Heredity, therefore, can be defined as the sum total of traits potentially present in the fertilized ovum.

Mechanism of Heredity

How life begins

The mechanism by which heredity is passed on to a person begins with conception. The first step for this is mating or intercourse between male and female so that the ovum of the female unites with the sperm of the male to form a zygote. Due to coitus, the male germ cells millions in number usually come in contact with the female germ cells. When the male germ cells are deposited at the mouth of the uterus and try to make contact with the single ovum out of so many sperm, only one sperm (single male cell) is able to contact with the ovum (single female cell) situated in the ovarian duct of the female and makes it fertile. Thus the transmission of characteristics from one generation to another takes place by means of germ cells of the parents. In the nucleus of the germ cells, life chromosomes are the material basis of heredity. There are 23 pairs of chromosomes in the human sex cell. Each chromosome consists of string of minute particles called the genes. The genes are the true careers of heredity. Each chromosome bears a large number of genes. The chromosome can be seen under the microscope but genes are too small actually to be observed visually. Recent work has placed the number of genes in man somewhere between 30,000 to 40,000. Once the ovum is fertilized it is technically called zygote. Growth and development takes place by the multiplication of the fertilized cell through continuous division.

Why there is a variation in behaviour

The determination of the traits in the individual is caused by the pairing of genes. Some of the genes are dominant while some are recessive. The gene is never found single because both the parents contribute one gene each for making pair. If these two genes are similar then the child inherits that quality, but if the two are dissimilar it is the dominant of the two genes which gives its qualities to the child but the recessive genes will be carried by him which may show up in trait in his offspring. Thus the genes determine the characteristics in an individual. For example, if both mother and father are not fair, and their genes are of a fair colour, the children may be probably fair. If the gene of one of the parents is fair while that of the other is dark the qualities that the child inherits will come from the more prominent or dominant of the two, though it is not inevitable that the child will be fair if the parents are both fair. Thus it comes about that heredity does not necessarily make a child resemble his two parents entirely. He may resemble one more than the other, depending upon from which one he draws more dominant genes or he may resemble neither and look like his grand or great grand parents. Heredity does not depend on the immediate parents but it goes very far. It may go up to animal level. According to Galton, if heredity

parents, i.e., father and mother. One fourth is due to grand parents, i.e., parental grandfather and mother and maternal grand father and mother. Similarly, one-eight (1/8) of heredity depends on the father and mother or grand fathers and mothers. The same series goes on and its sum total is never equal to one or unity, and, therefore, heredity is very old. That is why even members of the same family differ in heredity constitution so that in real sense each person is unique.

How sex of the offspring is determined

Whether the offspring will be a boy or a girl is a matter of chance and the chance is 50%. Sex chromosome determine the sex of an individual. When the two cells (sperm and ovum) unite it is then and there the sex of the offspring is determined whether this fertilization will be a male or female. If any thing is added after the egg is fertilized to change the sex it will be in vain. After fertilization the fertilized egg or the zygote divides into two cells. One is known as germ cell and the other as body-cell. Galton and Weisemann showed that the germ cell is reserved unchanged for the formation of germ cell of the following generation. So, the sex cells which form the generation are separated from the rest of the body at a very early period of embryological development. The second part, i.e., egg zygote or the body cells divides quickly to form the various parts of the body.

There are two different types of sex chromosomes, i.e., X and Y. According to geneticists X is big and Y is small. Male is the carrier of X and Y and female is only X and X chromosomes. So the mother's role in the determination of sex of the child is quite neutral. Only at the time of conception she can contribute X chromosomes. If it is XX combination (X is from male and X is from female) then the offspring is a female or daughter and if it is XY combination (X is from female and Y is from male) then the result is a son or male. So in the sex determination male individual plays a vital role whether the offspring will be a son or daughter. Therefore one should not blame the female that she has not given birth to a son.

The twins mechanism

Twins are of two kinds, i.e., identical and fraternal. Identical twins are the result of the germination of one ovum. Fraternal twins arise from the germination of two separate ovum. In a normal case when a single ovum is fertilized by sperm cell of the male, it results in the birth of single offspring. But in some cases normal function of the cell division is disturbed.

After fertilization of the ovum by sperm, the ovum is made to split into two parts. In the normal cases these parts are again united. But sometimes these two parts fail to unite together. So, each part develops into a complete individual and twin is identical because of the indentical nature of the genetic material.

Similarly, in each menstrual cycle, the female ovaries produce a single ovum that can be fertilized by the sperm cell. In an exceptional case two ovum may be produced simultaneously and be fertilized at the same time by two different sperm. Because of different combination of chromosomes and genes either the child may be similar or opposite sex.

Laws of Heredity

There are three laws of heredity. These are law of similarity, law of variation and law of regression.

The law of similarity indicates the principle of 'like begets like'. It means human beings give birth to human babies, cats give birth to kittens, dogs to puppies, and cows to calves, etc. No way it can be a exception. In case of individual the germ-cell is handed over from generation to generation and the individual is the custodian of it. Thus it can be said that each species transmits its own code of heredity so that out of it, only that species develops.

The second law of inheritance is the law of variation. It means though all the members of a family resemble one another in some degree, yet there is a great deal of variation because of the various combinations of genes structure. No body is perfect exactly like their parents. The cause of variation is still a mystery and because of the peculiar combination of genes in each individual no two beings are equal although they appear to be similar.

The law of regression indicates the principle of moving back. It means, sometime the bright parents may have the children of average intelligence and tall man may have a short child or some individual possess a characteristic to an extreme extent, i.e., very tall people, very short people or very intelligent people, etc. This situation may be due to transmission of genes from many generations and the principles of dominant and recessive traits on the part of the species. Thus, the teacher must know these laws to understand the nature and quality of the raw material pupil at his disposal.

Significance/Importance/Effects Implications of Heredity on Human Life

A number of studies have been conducted regarding the influence of heredity on human life. These are the following:

1. ***Franz Baos and Yarkes study on physical appearances and Intelligence***

To study the effect of heredity on physical appearances, children of many varied races were compared with their parents. From these experiments it was concluded that it is heredity which determines physical appearance. Similarly, Yarkes, while experimenting upon Negroes and White soldiers in connection with their intelligence, he concluded that due to heredity, there is a difference of intelligence between the two.

2. *Study of Commonsense Variety*

In our day to day observation it is noticed that the children who have come from good families at least try to maintain their reputation and enhance family credibility though there are few exceptions to it. It can also be referred that the doctor who is working in a mental hospital and a jailor with prisoners did not affect in any way in their behaviour. Thus, we can come to the conclusion that heredity is influencing the development of personality of an individual.

3. *Biographies of Great Men*

By reading autobiography of great men it can be indicated that exceptionality of greatness was found from the very beginning of their life. The great men like Issac Newton, Francis Galton, Darwin, Macaulay, John Stuart Mill and in India Sankaracharya, Ramanujam, Vivekananda and J. Nehru, etc., were geniuses from the very beginning because of their inner potentialities. Thus heredity is playing a dominant role for shaping the human behaviour in proper fashion.

4. *Study on Family History*

(i) Francis Galton, while analysing the data of 977 eminent men he summarised that 536 were found to have close blood relationship are famous. On the other hand he also studied 977 common individuals out of which only he could notice 4 near relatives who were famous.

(ii) Winship studied Edward's family and concluded that natural abilities are inherited. Edward was married to two women one is intelligent and high status and their descendents were in high position in the society. Whereas the descendents of ordinary women side were poor and not having any status.

(iii) The Study of Goddard: Goddard studied Kallikak family. Kallikak, a soldier had married two women—one was an intelligent girl and the other one was abnormal and feeble minded girl. From the descendents of the former one it was noticed that except (5 to 10 out of 496) few others were normal and talented and placed in a high position in the society whereas in later cases it was noticed that all the descendents (except 46 out of 480) were abnormal and involved in antisocial activities.

(iv) The study of Dugdale : Dugdale conducted a study on Juke's family. Juke was a fisherman and corrupt. He married a woman of degenerate family. About 1000 persons were born in 5 generations out of which 300 died in infancy, 310 were orphans, 130 were criminals and rest 120 were somewhat normal. Thus, the family inherited certain physical and mental traits from generation to generation and because of this they might have involved in antisocial activities. This situation might have occurred because of heredity, he argued.

(v) The Study of Nunn: Nunn made a study of the family history of 'Lukes' in USA. Lukes had married a degenerated woman. Ii was found out that most of their off-springs in the five generations suffered from crime and other social ills may be due to influence of heredity.

5. Tryon conducted some experiments on rats, dogs, and monkeys, etc., to understand the inheritance of traits and its impact on them. He selected high and low mouse and studied up to eight successive generations. Lastly he concluded that intelligent mouse were having intelligent generation.

6. Study of the Twins

Psychologists have made studies of identical twins who develop, from the same fertilized eggs and fraternal twins arise from germination of two separate ovum. The identical twins not only possess physical resemblance but also identical heredity. Psychologists like Freeman, Thorndike, and Wingfield, etc., found out that twins are having correlation of .5 to .8 and it is because of heredity.

7. Racial difference studies have been conducted to compare the intellectual capacity of negro and white children. It is found out that negro children were poor in intelligence as compared to their counterparts may be due to heredity.

8. Similarly, Decandolle studied 1000 men of Europe to find out their greatness. Lastly he concluded that greatness is due to heredity.

On the basis of above arguments one can come to the

conclusion that heredity plays an important role in the formation of basic necessity of an individual to run the balanced personality in future.

Environment: Meaning and Nature

Environment is otherwise known as nurture. It has broad significance in the formation of balanced personality. The influence of environment start from the time of conception in the mother's womb and almost continues till the very death. Western scholars called the influence of environment as social heredity. Environment is everything, other than heredity, that influences an individual's growth and development. Thus, environment means sum total of the forces and stimulations (i.e., social, moral, economic, political, physical and intellectual factors), which the individual receives from the conception until death. Whatever is found around the individual, may be covered by the term environment. It has been defined by various psychologists as follows:

1. J.B. Watson, the behaviourist psychologist, believed that environment is important for a person and not heredity in the sense that it determines human behaviour. Environment is everything that affects the individual except his genes.
2. Boring, Longfield and Welle defines that "A person's environment consists of the sum total of the stimulation which he receives from his conception until his death".
3. P.Gisburt defines "the environment is anything immediately surrounding an object and exerting a direct influence on it".
4. Douglas and Holland say "the term environment is used to describe, in the aggregate, all the external forces, influences and conditions which affect the life, nature, behaviour and the growth, development and maturity of living organisms".
5. E.J. Ross says "Environment is an external force which influences us".
6. Elliot says "the field of effective stimulation and interaction for any unit of living matter is called environment".
7. Woodworth says "Environment covers all the outside factors that have acted on the individual since he

began life". Thus, after the conception the game of environment affect the individual.

8. According to Ruch "Environment refers not only to the physical surroundings but even to the thoughts and attitudes of others which exert an influence on the individual.

Thus it can be concluded that the child, when he comes to this world, finds himself surrounded by innumerable objects and circumstances which influence him. This is otherwise known as environment.

Environment: Type/Classification

Basically there are three types of environment:

(i) *Natural/physical/geographical*

It consists of all outer physical surroundings both animate and inanimate objects which have to be manipulated for individual living. It includes all the natural things, i.e., food, water, air, climate, mountains, moon, sun and all the geographical features that have an effect on the individual.

(ii) *Social/Psychological Environment*

Social environment refers to all forces and influences that enumerate from the environment. It includes all types of activities—social, cultural, spiritual intellectual and economic which, in all their totality, affect development. Under this category the influence of home, neighbourhood, school, church and the social surroundings, laws, customs, etc., which affect the individual, constitute the social environment. Thus it is much more important for determining behaviour as far as man is concerned. If social environment is very stimulating and enriching, it will create favourable impression in the person on his/her development and if dull, negative.

(iii) *Cultural Environment*

Every individual inherits the cultural traits from the social environment. It includes the cultural atmosphere of the society with its ingredients as religion, folklore, literature, art, music, social rules/conventions and political organisation and traditions, etc. These influence the personality of an individual.

In addition to the above three types of environment the

other school of thought has given emphasis on the following types:

(i) *Free or restricted and poor or rich environment:* Children born in a free or restricted environment follow a distinctive pattern of development. The behaviour and manner of thinking in students of restricted is hostile than the other one. Rich cultural life produces personality with rich experiences and the environment where there are conflicting cultural forces changes the personality of people and create a sense of shallow outlook and mundane attitude in people.

It his also been found that poor environment produce serious maladjustment in a person. In this environment needs are not properly gratified and tends to develop destroying tendencies and delinquency acts, etc. Bloom suggested that 50% of the development of intelligence occurs in the first four years. So early deprivation of facilities is very serious and can produce negativity.

(ii) *Mental Environment*: It is that environment where the child learns new experiences for the mental development. Thus the intellectual atmosphere at the home, the atmosphere at school, the library, the recreation room and laboratories, etc., must be congenial so that it will help the child to learn more and more new things.

Importance or Effect of Environment on Human Life

In the opinion of Sigmund Freud the personality of a person is fashioned in the first seven years, the rest of the life being an expression of those tendencies. Whether all thinkers agree with Freud's opinion or not, all have agreed with regard to the effect of the environment or the family upon the character, nature, mental tendencies, habits and behaviour of the individual. Let us now discuss some of the results of various studies which provide clue of the influence of environment on human life.

1. *Studies on the Influence of Mental and Social Environment on Children*

Woodworth found out that giving stimulating environment to children means increasing his IQ. In his experiment he found out that good nursery schools have been stimulating the intellectual growth of children irrespective of heredity background.

Freeman and his associates report that foster children when placed in superior homes, gained 5 to 10 IQ points after four years.

Monroe in his developmental study of children also found that quality of home environment was positively related with IQ changes. It is the home and family environment which lays down motivational patterns for the child and is responsible to a great extent for his language development.

Gordon studied the intelligence of gypsy children and found that their IQ is only 70 due to their isolation from normal social life.

Sherman also reported that children living in the mountain hollows of Virginia, were found to be mentally inferior due to their primitive way of life and poor environment.

Terman and Merrill found out that the children of professional men and executives obtain the highest scores and those of unskilled labourers the lowest scores in an intelligence test.

Candoel made a study of 552 persons of eminence and found that development of IQ depends on environment. Good environment leads to better IQ and the poor is related to lower IQ.

Gesell in his study revealed that the serious retardation may be due to poor environment.

Robert Owen says that the development of men is influenced by environment and not by heredity. He says that we are made by the society. We receive the means of improvement by the society and education is the main amongst them. It means that good education can make a man good in character and intelligence.

Hayward opposed the views of Galton that man's personality is determined by heredity only. Though "the child is endowed with some inherited tendencies but they are so plastic that they can be moulded almost in any way according to educators desires".

Huxley says that the environment is everything in the development of the child.

2. ***Study of Fly and Edith:***

These two identical female twins were separated in childhood. One of them was married to a business man and the other to a farmer. The behaviour, IQ and in many other psychological areas there were lot of differences between the two in the latter part of their life.

3. *Study of James and Reece*

These two twins reared in a hill and a village respectively. When their intelligence was marked, the difference of 19 point was found. This indicates the influence of environment.

4. *Study on Amla and Kamala*

These two girls were found in the forest of Midnapur (West Bengal) by J.A.L. Singh. They were taken by a wolf in their early infancy stage. They adopted all the characteristics of the wolf and ran swiftly like the wolf and ate raw meat. While they were taken care of in the hospital the younger died within a year but the older one lived for nine years, but never became a perfect human being.

5. *Study on Donald and Gua*

Kellog and Kellog conducted a study on a human infant (Donald) and a Chimpanzee (Gua). They were reared together and treated equally like two infants. At last after 9 months of experiment it was noticed that Gua made excellent progress in learning to eat with a spoon, drink water in a glass and understood over 50 words. By this study we can conclude that heredity sets limits for the development and the environment works within that limit.

6. Watson believes that it is environment which has an upper hand in the development of an individual. He said that "Give me any child and I will make him what you want".

7. *Study on Ramu—the Wolf boy*

Ramu, a human infant was taken by wolf in early infancy to the jungle and reared in the company of wolves and developed all the qualities of wolves. After 14 years of treatment in the hospital he could not stand up right and unable to behave like a human being. He has conditioned the habits of walking on four legs and eating raw flesh, etc. It may be said that an individual is more a product of environment.

8. Cattell conducted a study on scientists to find out the role of

heredity, environment and achievement. He concluded that there exists a close link between the environmental quality and the production of scientists.

9. MacIver has said that the direction of man's development is determined by the environment. In reality, to be good or bad of the child, depends on the environment. He further said that environment directs or diverts and stimulates or depresses man's energies and moulds his speech. Environment is present from the beginning of life even in the germ cells. Thus the responsibility of the development of personality of the student lies on teaching and good environment is the means, the vehicle of life.

In this connection, Landis and Landis correctly said "Heredity explains man the animal, environment man the human being". Thus, environment moulds and influences the behaviour of a person from time to time and changes the shape of a raw material just as a potter does while making toys from mud. Two individuals born with the same biological heritage may differ in personality because of difference in environment.

D. *Relative Importance of Heredity and Environment (Nature and Nurture)*

There has long been a controversy about whether heredity or environment is more important for the growth and development of an individual. While Galton and others strongly supported that heredity influences and shapes an individual the other environmentalists like Watson, Locke and others believe that environment is solely responsible for what an individual becomes. It is very difficult to separate both of them from one to another for the development of an individual. Parker, a biologist said 9/10th traits are born and 1/10th is acquired and a race of genius cannot be made out of idiots. Similarly, Watson, a behaviourist said "Everything can be made out of anything". He further said "Give me a dozen of infants, I will guarantee to take any one at random and train him to become any type of specialist, regardless of ancestral traits. Considering the bulk of evidence available, it may be stated that there is a definite operation between heredity and environment. There is a constant interaction between the two forces on an individual and they operate in an integrated and collective manner. Both are potent factors in the development of an individual.

The relationship of the two forces are complementary

to each other like seed and soil, ship and current, warp and roof, bed and steam, etc. Heredity is the raw material out of which the object is to be prepared and environment is the technique for the manufacture. While heredity determines the level, environment determines the functions of these abilities.

Nunn concludes that the human organism (body and mind) is a centre of creative energy that uses endowments and environment as its working material, so that the elements, it receives from nature and nurture, do not make it what it becomes. Both heredity and environment is essential for the smooth development of personality. As it is not possible to demarcate the dividing line between the two, both should be given equal importance.

Landis and Land said that "heredity gives us the capacities to be developed but opportunity for the development of these capacities is with environment". Heredity gives us our working capital, environment gives us opportunity to invest the working capital. Thus, the individual is a byproduct of both heredity and environment.

E. *Educational Implications of Heredity and Environment*

Now it is clear that both heredity and environment or nature and nurture jointly shape a person's abilities, skills and personality characteristics. While heredity deals the cards environment play them. Inheritance or potentialities are given by nature and its proper shape is given by nurture.

To understand the child and enrich his/her learning, the teacher must know his/her biological organism (family history) and social and psychological environment of the child. It is clear that the level of mental development depends not only on innate potentialities but also upon the quality of environment where he/she lives. He must know that both nature and nurture are potent factors in the development of the child and their relationship is just like a seed and the soil. Without heredity the individual will not come into existence at all and without environment it will not grow. All development, therefore, depends upon both heredity and environment.

The following are the more specific role of the teacher:

1. Teacher should know that children differ in their capacities and accordingly he should provide education or create congenial environment for them.

2. Teacher should see that adequate and proper environment in the educational premises are prevailing.
3. The teacher should not think that he cannot bring change in the child as heredity is inherent. He should provide various kinds of opportunities for development.
4. Teacher should be optimistic in attitude while dealing with the students.
5. Teacher should see that poor families are given all necessary help to facilitate development for the child.
6. Teacher should have the data of inborn traits like intelligence, aptitude and personality traits of the child so that he can provide necessary guidance to them.
7. Teacher should see that the home, school and social environment of the child is conducive to proper development.

Thus it can be concluded that without heredity there is no beginning and without environment there is no continuity and an individual is said to be the product of nature and nurture. In this context the role of the teacher is like this:

Teacher is like a tank, student is like a tap,
Pure water within the tank, gives pure water out of the tap.
Good teachers make good schools,
Good schools make good students,
Good students make good citizens, and
Good citizens make good nations.

Summary

Man is the unique creation of the Almighty. Whether man is the product of heredity or environment is a debatable question? To understand the development of human personality it is necessary to study the actions and reactions of heredity and environment. Heredity provides raw materials and how the materials are moulded depends upon the environment.

Heredity means all those traits and characteristics which a person possesses at the time of conception from parents. It is heredity which determines the structure, colour of the skin, the hair structure, height, facial features, nasal index, cephalic index, etc. It has two aspects—biological and psychological.

The mechanism by which heredity is passed on to a person is a debatable question. How life begins is the crucial point under the mechanism. Due to coitus, the male germ cells millions in number usually come in contact with the female germ cells. When the male germ cells (sperm) are deposited at the mouth of the uterus and try to contact with the female germ cells (ovum), only one sperm is able to contact with the one ovum and makes it fertile. This is called zygote. There are 23 pairs of chromosomes in the human sex cell. Each chromosome consists of genes. Growth and development takes place by the multiplication of the fertilized cell through continuous division. It is also found out that there is a variation in behaviour because of dominant and recessive genes. The dominant genes determines the characteristics in an individual. Therefore, brothers and sisters, even twins either fraternal or identical are different from one to another. Similarly, sex chromosome determine the sex of an individual. There are two sex chromosomes—X and Y. Male is the carrier of X and Y and female is only X and X chromosomes. Mother's role in the determination of sex of the child is neutral.

There are three laws of heredity. These are law of similarity (like begets like principle), law of inheritance or law of variation (though all the members of a family looks like equal, yet there is a great deal of variations among themselves) and last one is law of regression (bright parents may have children of average IQ and vice-versa).

Recent studies try to explore the influence of heredity on personality development. The study of biographies of great men, on family history, study of Edward's family, Kallikak family, Juke family, and study of twins, etc., have indicated the importance of heredity on human life.

On the other hand, environment is everything, other than heredity, that influences an individuals growth and development. It is the sum total of the forces and stimulations, i.e., social, moral, economic, political, physical and intellectual factors which the individual receives from the conception until death is known as environment. Environment is of three types, i.e., natural, social and cultural. In addition to that environment may be free or restricted, poor or rich, and controlled or uncontrolled.

Recent studies on environment help in understanding how it influences the behaviour of an individual. The study of Fly and Edith, James and Reece, Amala and Kamala, Donald and Gua and the Wolf boy—Ramu, etc., indicates the importance of environment on human life.

There is a long controversy regarding the influence of heredity and environment on human development. It is found out that both the forces are complementary to each other and their relationship is like a seed and soil. While heredity is the raw material, the environment gives the shape to it. Heredity explains man the animal, environment man the human being. Thus, the individual is the byproduct of both.

In this context, the role of the teacher is very important. He is to deal with the child in the real classroom situation. Therefore, he should not only know the inner potential of the child but also should provide congenial environment so that innate animalistic tendency can be changed and develop a humanistic character with him. Thus, it can be said that without heredity there is no beginning and without environment there is no continuity and development.

Questions

1. What do you mean by Heredity? What is the importance of heredity in Education?
2. What are the different approaches to prove heredity is vital in personality and intelligence development? Explain.
3. Discuss the implication of heredity-environment controversy for a teacher.
4. How is the individual a product of both heredity and environment? Explain.
5. Examine the relative importance of heredity and environment in human behaviour.
6. Discuss the importance of nature and nurture in the development of a child. What is its bearing on education?
7. What do you mean by environment? Give suggestions for the improvement of environment at home and schools.
8. Sketch with suitable illustrations the interactions of the individual and the environment.
9. To what extent is 'human nature' inborn? How much is it modified by the environment?
10. Distinguish between biological and social heredity. What is the contribution of each to the making of an individual?

References

Anastasi, A (1954): *Differential Personality*, Macmillan and Co., New York.

Bhatnagar, S. (1976): *Educational Psychology*, Loyal Book Depot, Meerut.

Chauhan, S.S. (1978): *Advanced Educational Psychology*, Vikas, New Delhi.

Eson, M.E. (1964) : *Psychological Foundations of Education*, Aolt Pub., New York.

Goddard, H.H. (1911) : *The Kalikak Family*, Macmillan, New York.

Jennings, H.S. (1930) : Biological Basis of Human Nature, Nortan and Co., New York.

Kundu, C.L. and Tutoo, D.N. (1980) : *Educational Psychology*, Sterling Publishers Ltd., New Delhi.

Newman, H.H. *et al.* (1937) : *Twins: A Study of Heredity and Environment,* University of Chicago Press.

Skinner, C.E. (1962) : *Essentials of Educational Psychology*, Asia Publishing House, Bombay.

Walia, J.S. (1977) : *Foundations of Educational Psychology*, Paul Publishers, Jullandur.

Woodworth, R.S. *et al.* (1953) : *Psychology*, Methuen and Co., London.

INDIVIDUAL DIFFERENCES

Introduction

It is a well known fact that human beings differ from one to another. Not only it is true in case of animate beings but also it is true in inanimate things. Today the principle of individual difference has so much influenced the education system that without knowing, it is difficult to provide good education in the educational institution. Similarly when a teacher has to deal with a large number of students who are different from one to another in the class it is very essential to know about individual difference which will help him/her to handle the students in a more efficient way. Although all human beings possess certain universal common characteristics, i.e. qualitative in nature (physical, mental, emotional, psychic, social, etc.), yet they differ in respect of their quantitative aspects. The individual not only differ from one another but also differ from one ability to another within his/her own self. Thus, the teacher has to pay adequate attention towards the individual differences in the class otherwise development of abilities of the child up to the maximum extent cannot take place. Therefore, it can be said that individual differences are a matter of degree, not of kind.

Meaning and Nature of Individual Differences

Individual difference means that no two persons of the world are alike each other. Even two sons of same parents or two twins are different from each other. This lack of similarity is called individual difference.

The concept of individual differences refers to quantitative differences found among individuals in respect of a specific point or various traits.

It is due to this reason that all individuals do not behave in the same manner. Dececco defines the Psychology of individual differences is largely the study of group differences. When we observe the differences within and between those groups is called individual differences. Similarly, it can be said that Individual differences are those differences which separate the human beings from one to another in all psychological characteristics and physical abilities.

When individuals in general are studied, it is found that instead of two opposed types, there is a continuous gradation from one extreme to the other, with a concentration of individuals about a central point, and the frequency of occurrence decreasing as the deviation from the mean increases. If we consider the IQ of a very large group of adolescence, we shall find that majority have an IQ between 90 and 110, a few of them will have their IQs between 110 and 120 on positive side of normal probability curve and may be an equal number will have their IQ betwen 80 and 90 on the negative side of the Normal probability curve and this situation may occur till the ± 3 degree of NPC.

Types of Individual Differences

The Individual differences may be divided in two broad types, i.e., Inter and Intra Individual differences.

i. **Inter-Individual differences**

When the difference between two or more than two individuals are studied is called Inter-Individual differences. Different individuals have different types of abilities, interest and personality. Thus when we try to find the differences from one to another in respect of physical, cognitive and psychological traits is called inter-individual differences.

ii. **Intra-Individual differences**

An interesting fact is that variations are found within the same individual when he is studied in respect of various traits or an individual also differs from one ability to another within his/her own self. These differences are called intra-individual differences. This means difference is noticed in the same individual with respect to his/her performance on a particular task at different times.

Areas of Individual Differences

Inter and intra individual differences are found out with the following areas:

1. *Physical and Psychological differences:*

Individuals vary in physique, i.e., some are tall and some are short, fat and thin, strong and weak, black and fair, and height and weight, etc. These differences are found not only in the same class but also all over the world. The nature of interests, needs and psychology of these children may be different from each other.

2. *Mental or Intellectual differences:*

People differ with reference to their cognitive (intelligence) abilities. On the basis of the IQ one can be classified as idiot or normal or Superior or Genius categories. It is generally found out that there are very few possessing low level of intelligence, most children possess average and very few children have high degree of intelligence.

3. *Age Differences:*

In the class it is found out that there is a difference in age group and because of that abilities and capacities also differ from one to another.

4. *Difference in Motor Ability :*

In Motor activities children are different from one to another. While some are interested more vigorously in mechanical task others may be in technical one or vice-versa.

5. *Race and Nationality Differences :*

People coming from one race is different from other. Similarly people living in one nation or state is different from another nation or state in custom, tradition, beliefs, habits and living patterns. It is said that Russians are tall and stout, Ceylonese are short and slim, Germans have no sense of humour, yellow races are cruel and revengeful, Americans are hearty and frank, White possess superior intellect than black and Indians are timid and peace loving.

6. *Sex Differences :*

Some of us are men and some are women and this influences the performance in various fields. While on an average man has been observed superior in reasoning, in ability to detect similarities and in skill with numbers, etc., whereas in case of women's superiority is shown in memory, aesthetic comparisons and in sentence compilation, etc.

7. *Differences in Interest :*

It is true that people differ in interests, while some are in literary others are in scientific, artistics, musical, executive, agricultural, political and religious interest, etc.

8. Differences in speed of learning and retention :

It is found out that different individuals have different ability and capacity to learn. While some learn quickly and very fast others take very long time to complete it and some do not learn at all.

9. Differences in personality :

Another aspect of individual difference is personality. Psychologists have divided the people in different categories. While some are sanguine, choleric, melancholic and phelegamatic others have classified as extroverts, introverts and amiverts, etc. Similarly some individuals are able to adapt to social situations more easily than others, emotionally stable, sober, and friendly, etc., whereas others are just opposite of it.

10. Miscelleneous :

In addition to the above people also differ with respect to their development, health, achievement, attitudes, temperament and regional situation. Hence, the teacher should have the adequate knowledge about individual differences so that he/she can meet the challenge effectively in the class.

Factors/Causes of Individual Differences

Individual difference is caused by various factors. The following factors will give sufficient indication why do individuals differ from each other.

1. *Heredity/Genetic/Nature*

The pioneer psychologist is of the opinion that heredity is the main cause of individual difference. They are of the view that during the process of fertilization the individuals inherit many qualities and trait from their parents and ancestors through specific genes which is completely different from one set up to another or child to child. Hence siblings resemble one another more than unrelated children. Thus there is every possibility that individuals will differ from each other and within themselves because of the types of genes he/she receives.

Generally it is seen in the many studies, i.e., Galton, Dugdate, Goddard, Winship, and Nunn, etc., that (see Heredity and Environment chapter for more details) heredity is responsible for individual difference. Genetic differences cause differences in intelligence, personality, physical features and psychological traits. Hence it is said that Genes are responsible for individual difference.

2. *Environment/Nurture*

In addition to genetic factors, environment also cause individual differences among children.

The environment consists of sum total of the stimulation that the individual receives from conception until death. Environment moulds one's personality up to the maximum point. Environment is of many varieties. The extent of the influence of the environment, however, depends on the individual and the strength of the environment. Studies have shown that (see heredity and environment chapter for more details) children who are shifted from poor to better environment show clear gain in I.Q scores, interests, abilities, emotional and social aspects. It is also no way exception in case of identical twins. Thus this shows the strong influence of environment.

The influence of these two factors cannot be clearly demarcated. Teacher should not overemphasize the importance of any single factor. The interaction of both the factor so subtly that it is impossible to say whether heredity or environment is the stronger factor. Hence it can be said that both the factors are complementary and not conflicting in nature.

3. *Age and Intelligence*

Age causes differences in physical, psychological and

emotional aspects of an individual. When age increases, children differ in these qualities. Interests of an individual also differ with age.

Similarly all children do not have the same intelligence. While some are exceptionally genius others may be mentally backward or normal. This causes the individual difference.

4. *Sex and maturity*

There is a difference in the boy and girl in physical and mental activities. Studies indicates that maturity process differ from person to person. While some are more matured the others are less. Because of this situation there is a great difference in boys and girls. Hence, there is individual differences.

5. The caste and race and socio-economic status, etc., also leads to individual differences

Measurement of Individual differences

The measurement of individual differences can be possible through psychological tests. The following are the tests of measurement:

1. *Intelligence tests*

In order to ascertain the intelligence of the children different type of tests, i.e., verbal, non-verbal and performance tests are applied. This may be either individual or group based. Through intelligence test we can measure the child as normal or abnormal or idiot or genius. This helps the teacher to adjust his teaching effectively.

2. *Aptitude test*

Through aptitude tests we can measure the possibilities of success of an individual in future performance. This may be either special, or mechanical or differential type in nature. What is the actual capacity of an individual can be measured which help the teacher to guide him/her properly in the class.

3. *Achievement tests*

In order to ascertain the achievements of the children in different subjects these tests are used. Here the students are asked to answer as per their subject separately. This may be either standardized or teacher-made test through which individual differences among the students in academic achievement can be measured.

4. *Personality test*

In order to know whether a child is introvert or extrovert or to know the personality structure different type of personality tests are used. With the help of the different personality tests it is possible to ascertain the individual differences.

5. *Interest inventories*

The interest inventories are used to measure differences among the individuals about their interest. What type of person he/she is and what is his/her interest is judged through this technique. The liking and disliking of an individual towards an object, person or subject are also known through these inventories.

6. *Attitude test*

The internal feelings of an individual towards certain persons and object, etc., are judged. When we talk about the acceptance or rejection of certain kind of activities we refer it as attitude.

7. Similarly the adjustment test, values test, moral judgement test, emotion test and memory test, etc., are used to measure the individual difference among the children for effective teaching.

Educational Implications or Importance or Significance of Study of Individual Differences

Today, individual difference occupies a very significant place in the field of education. Without knowing it fully the teaching-learning process becomes ineffective. Thus the following are some of the implications of individual difference:

I. ***Size of the class***

It is true that people differ from one to another. Now-a-days the size of the class is normally increasing. Therefore it is not possible to pay individual attention to all the students. If a teacher knows that there is individual difference then he/she will try to limit the size of the distribution of the class for adequate personal attention for effective teaching.

II. *Homogeneity in grouping*

With the help of the knowledge of individual difference the teacher can make homogeneous groups according to the level of ability and can plan his teaching more effectively. Ross said "we should classify our people according to which they belong". Though it is not possible to have perfect homogeneous grouping yet the teacher with the help of it can pay individual attention effectively.

III. *Attention towards the interest, aptitude and abilities*

The knowledge of individual differences will help the teacher to form proper attention towards the aptitudes, interest and abilities of children. The teacher should have the capacity to encourage the child for proper development.

IV. *Methods of teaching*

Keeping in view the individual difference various methodology like activity based, assignment, demonstration, participatory, etc., have been developed. Thus on the basis of difference in groups the teacher is to adopt different methodology depending upon the suitability for the class.

V. *Proper environment*

The teacher should know that heredity provide raw materials and environment gives the shape to the raw materials. So, the teacher should try to provide the best possible environmental conditions to the child so that he/she will become a effective person in the society in future.

VI. *Attention towards the personality and physique*

It is generally found out that all children do not have similar physique and personality. Some are good and others are weak. Thus children with poor physique and imbalanced personality should be dealt effectively in the class.

VII. *Provision of self learning at their own rate*

It is a fact that children are the future citizens of our country. But they behave and learn differently and the difference between the rate of learning speed is different from child to child. So, the teacher should take care of the above while delivering goods to them.

VIII. *Curriculum*

It is a fact that there are different sorts of students in the class and accordingly curriculum should be framed. The teacher can achieve his/her end product only when he/she is able to construct the curriculum while keeping the individual difference in mind.

IX. *Organisation of special classes for exceptional children*

There are individual exceptional children in the class. Some are gifted while others are handicapped, backward and socially disadvantaged. While dealing with gifted children emphasis should be given on enrichment programme along with segregation and ability grouping so that development of their potential can be optimum. Similarly for different types of handicapped students different educational provisions should be made. In order to help the socially disadvantaged children remedial instruction and incentives, etc., should be provided to them. For slow learner children backward positive motivation, encouragement and closer supervision be made for their development.

X. **Home assignment and Guidance**

It is a general notion that the teacher give hometask of similar type to each and every student irrespective of their calibre and interest. Due to this situation it is seen that intelligent students complete the task as comfortably as possible than the dull ones. This situation is not really conducive for teaching. Therefore the teacher should give the home task of different difficulty level as per the ability of the student. On the other hand, students should be provided with proper guidance because they are different from one another.

XI. *Role of the teacher and Individual difference*

The teacher is the pivot in teaching-learning process. The teacher must consider, individual differences of her pupils as a challenge. The study of individual differences will help the teacher to plan instruction systematically and sensitively to enable learners to learn excellently. In addition to the above it also helps the teacher to employ all his/her ingenuity to meet the needs and abilities of all his/her students, to plan different types of in and out of school activities to help children, to prepare better curriculum, to give proper attention on exceptionals and providing remedial education and better understanding of children. Thus, if the teacher is careful, alert and dedicated then he/she can meet the individual differences effectively.

Summary

The concept of individual difference refers to quantitative differences found among individuals in traits. It means there are no two individuals equal in respect of specific or general traits or characteristics. The lack of similarity is called individual difference.

Basically there are two broad types of individual differences. These are Inter-individual, i.e., comparing two or more individuals on any aspects of characteristics and Intra-individual, i.e., within the same individual when differences are found on various traits it is called inter or intra Individual differences.

Individuals also differ in various areas. These differences may be physical, mental, age, motor, race and nationality, sex, interest and aptitude, speed of learning and personality characteristics from one to another.

The differences in individual is caused mainly by two factors, i.e., heredity and environment. But the psychologists have given many more factors which also causes the difference, i.e., sex and maturity, age and intelligence, caste and race and social conditions of the society.

The measurement of Individual differences can be possible through psychological tests like intelligence test, aptitude test, achievement test, personality test, interest inventories, attitude test, value judgement test, adjustment test and memory test. The study of individual differences is essential for the teacher. For effective teaching-learning process the teacher should have the ideas about Individual difference which will help him/her to know about the class so that he/she can know what should be the size of students in the class; what methodology is needed for the class; how to develop congenial environment; what should be the curriculum, how to give proper attention to exceptionals, and what type of guidance and home tasks are needed for the students, etc., which will ultimately help him/her for effective teaching-learning process.

Questions

1. What do you mean by Individual difference? What are the factors responsible for Individual differences?
2. "Individuals differ from each other"—comment.
3. What are Individual differences ? Why should a teacher know them ?
4. What are the meaning and nature of Individual differences? What provisions you have to make to meet Individual difference in the classroom?
5. Discuss the various causes of Individual differences with suitable examples.
6. What are the educational implications of the study of Individual difference. Explain.
7. Write short notes:
   (i) Inter and Intra Individual differences.
   (ii) Causes of Individual differences.
   (iii) Role of the teacher in Individual differences.
   (iv) Nature of Individual differences.
   (v) Measurement procedure of Individual differences.

References

1. Brophy, J.E. *et al.* (1974) : *Teacher-student relationships : Causes and Consequences*, Holt, Rinehart and Winston, New York.
2. Chauhan, S.S. (1987) : *Advanced Educational Psychology*, Vikas Publication, New Delhi.
3. Dandekar, W.N. (1976) : Psychological Foundation of Education, The Macmillan Company of India, New Delhi.
4. Dececco, J.P. (1975) : *The Psychology of Learning and Instruction*, Prentice Hall, New Delhi.
5. Gates A.I. *et al.* (1948) : *Educational Psychology*, The Macmillan Company, New York.
6. Glaser, R. (1972) : Individuals and Learning : The new aptitudes. Educational Researcher, 1 (6), 5-13.
7. Lindgren, H.C. (1962) : *Educational Psychology in the Classroom*, Wiley, London.
8. Lovell, K. (1969) : *Educational Psychology and Children*, University of London Press Ltd. London.
9. Mayer, R.E. (1987) : *Educational Psychology*, Little Brown and Company, Boston.

LEARNING

Introduction

Learning occupies a very important place in our life. When the child is born, his/her mind is just like a clean slate. As soon as he/she comes in contact with his/her environment, he/she starts reacting and in this process of interaction of the individual within his/her environment, the foundation of learning are laid down. It is only with the help of the learning that the child learns many things and modifies his/her behaviour. Thus, experience, direct or indirect is found to play a dominant role in moulding and shaping the behaviour of the individual from the very beginning. The changes in behaviour brought about by experience are known as learning. The following are some of the definitions of learning.

Meaning and Definition of Learning

It is very difficult to give a universally acceptable definition of learning because various theories developed by psychologists attempt to define the term from different angles. Thus the definitions of learning as given by different psychologists are given below :

(a) Mayer (1982) defines learning is a relatively permanent change in a person's knowledge or behaviour due to experience practices. This definition has three parts :

(i) The duration of the change is long-term rather than short term.

(ii) It is a change that takes place through experience or practice, changes due to growth or maturation such as increase in height or weight, development of muscles, etc., are not to be considered as learning.

(iii) The change must be relatively permanent. This rules out changes due to motivation, fatigue, illness, brain injury, drugs or physiological intervention.

(b) According to Garrett, learning is that activity by virtue of which we organise our responses with new habits.

(c) Woodworth (1945) defines that any activity can be called learning so far as it develops the individual in any way, good or bad and makes him alter behaviour and experiences different from what they would otherwise have been.

(d) Murphy (1968) defines the term learning covers every modification in behaviour to meet environmental requirements.

(e) Kingsley and Garry defines learning is the process by which an organism in satisfying its motivations adopts and adjusts its behaviour in order to overcome obstacles or barriers.

(f) Skinner defines that the process of learning implies something more than the acquisition of facts and skills through mechanised procedures such as repetitive practices. Instead the learner organises and evaluates learning materials, endows them with many meanings and interpretations, and becomes conscious of working goals.

(g) Nunn (1955)defines learning is more or less permanent incremental modification of behaviour which results from activity, special training or observation.

(h) Gagne (1976) defines learning is a change in human disposition or capability, which persists over a period of time, and which does not simply ascribe to processes of growth.

(i) Gates and others define learning is the modification of behaviour through experience and training.

(j) Booz defines learning is the process by which the

individual acquires various habits, knowledge and attitude that are necessary for meeting the demand of life in general.

(k) Smith defines learning is the acquisition of new behaviour or the strengthening or weakening of old behaviour as the result of experience.

(l) Crow and Crow (1973) defines learning is the acquisition of habits, knowledge and attitudes. It involves new ways of doing things, and it operates in an individuals's attempts to overcome obstacles or to adjust to new situations. It represents progressive changes in behaviour and enables him to satisfy interests to attain goals.

(m) Hilgard (1958) defines learning is the process by which an activity originates or is changed through reacting to an encountered situation, provided that the characteristics of the changes in activity cannot be explained on the basis of native responses, tendencies, maturation, or temporary states of the organism, e.g., fatigue or effect of drugs, etc.

In brief, we may enumerate the following facts about the learning process :

1. Learning means acquisition of experience.
2. Learning means acquisition, retention and modification of experience.
3. Learning is a change of behaviour.
4. Learning depends on practice and experience.
5. Learning is acquisition of habit, skill and knowledge.
6. Learning is a process and not a product.
7. Learning is a continuous process and continues till death.
8. Learning is purposive and goal directed.
9. Learning is a creative experience.
10. Learning is Universal.
11. Learning is transferable.
12. Learning takes place in both formal and informal situation.
13. Learning means establishing new relationship between stimulus and response.
14. Learning is both incidental and intentional.
15. Learning involves both overt and covert processes.

16. Learning prepares an individual for any adjustment and adaptation that may be necessary.
17. Learning does not include changes in behaviour on account of maturation, fatigue, illness or drugs, etc.

Nature of Learning

The nature and general characteristics of learning are as follows :

1. *Learning is universal*

Learning is not having any boundary. It is not restricted to any particular age, sex, race or cultures. It is applicable to all the living creatures, although, the degree of learning varies from creature to creature.

2. *Learning is purposeful and goal directed*

Learning is not an aimless activity. It provides clues and hints to the learner that there is something behind in learning and children learn with that hope and aspiration.

3. *Learning is a continuous or never-ending process*

Learning starts from birth and continues till death. It is a never ending process. At each stage the learner acquires new ideas and achieves something new, which is a continuous process.

4. *Learning occurs both formal and informal situations*

The child learns many things. He/She acquires new habits, skills and gains new information. Many things the child learns in a formal situation like that of a school. But a great many of these the child learns in informal situation in a family or with his/her friends when he/she is travelling, playing in an incidental manner.

5. *Learning is the process of solving problems*

In fact, all learning is problem solving. The child learns many thing during the course of time and try to apply all these to achieve a solution for a novel situation. Learning rules and principles help him/her to produce changes in his/her behaviour and abandonment of existing behaviour.

6. *Learning is adjustment*

Learning is the process of adjustment. The individual must learn to adjust himself/herself to the changes that take place around him/her. It prepares an individual for any adjustment and adaptation that may be necessary.

7. *Learning involves various dimensions of psychological and mental activities*

For the effective learning both psychological, e.g., motivation, interest and ability and physiological bases, i.e., nervous systems, brain, spinal cord, glands, etc., are essential. Therefore in schools children must be provided opportunity to learn by doing or learn by activity for effective learning.

8. *Learning is more than academic mastery of subjects*

In schools we generally think that learning is concerned with subjects and acquisition of information of facts. But learning is beyond to that and we learn different traits or characteristics, attitudes, values, interests, etc., rather than only mastery on academic subjects.

9. *Learning is the function of practice*

There is a saying that practice makes a man perfect. In this context practice does not mean repeating a response. It is repeated efforts of an individual to react to a situation effectively. Thus, practice help to drop out awkward, unhythmic and unnecessary responses and leads to improvement in learning.

10. *Learning is a Process*

Through learning modification of behaviour takes place. It constantly enlarges the child's understanding, leads to growth of abilities, perception and intellect. Though the entire learning situation is a very complex process yet the favourable environment can bring desirable and satisfactory growth on the part of the individual which is the ultimate goal of the learning.

11. *Difference in learning is due to environment*

There is a difference in learning due to stimulating environment. It has been found children coming from depressing environment suffer in their learning as compared to the children having stimulating home and school environment. We learn if there are opportunities and facilities to learn. There are children who have great capacity to learn but due to no opportunities and backwardness they do not learn much. Thus, stimulating environment must be provided for better learning.

12. *Learning is a self-directed activity*

If there is sufficient motivation and opportunity to participate in the various kinds of experiences then learning without teacher is possible. Thus attainment of goals is possible if the child is motivated to learn.

13. *Learning may be correct or incorrect*

Learning can be right or wrong or socially desirable or undesirable depending upon the situation. Thus precaution must be taken that learning should be socially desirable and acceptable.

14. *Learning is manifold in nature*

Psychologists have classified learning into various types. These are concept learning, skill learning, verbal and non verbal learning, learning of rule, learning of attitudes and values, etc. Therefore, learning has many facets.

15. *Learning involves perceptual operation and motor processes*

Perception in the learning context refers to the acquisition of specific knowledge about objects directly stimulating the sense at any particular movement. In perception, objects are seen or interpreted in the light of pertinent experience from the past.

Similarly, learning involves motor processes, which include habits, ideational acquisitions which involve information, and affective elements which include emotions. Manual skills are relatively simple acquisitions and are dominantly motor in character. On the other side we have likes and dislikes or biases and prejudices. Ideational acquisitions are facts, meaning, precepts and concepts. Thus, learning must be the combinations of all these otherwise it leads to negative learnings.

Factors Affecting Influencing/Associated with Learning

Psychologists and teachers are concerned with the various factors which influence learning. The factors which are responsible for bringing about the betterment and improvement in learning or influence or associated with learning are given below :

While some of the author's have given emphasis on physiological, psychological and environmental factors others have given emphasis on learners, teachers, school and home factors responsible for affecting/influencing learning. Similarly there are some authors who have given emphasis on subject, task and method variables as compared to individual, internal and personal and social forces responsible for learning process. Thus whatever may be the nomenclature the following variables or factors represent some avenues and discover the better routes to learning. These are as follows :

(a) *Maturation*

Development of a child takes place because of two basic but complex processes—learning and maturation. Learning is possible only when a certain stage of maturation is reached. We may try to teach a six month old child to walk but it will be in vain because muscles have not matured enough to learn to walk or premature training may do more harm than good. Thus particular activity is possible only when the nerves and muscles have attained a particular stage of maturity and learning. Therefore, psychologists have suggested that learning is effective if the activities or subject matter is at a rate commensurate with the development of the child. In this context teachers should explain this principle to parents who are over ambitious and over-enthusiastic in the education of their 3 to 4 year old child.

(b) *Motivation*

Motivation is the very heart of the learning process. Motivation sets the activity which results in learning or it is the art of stimulating interest in the pupil and gives the direction to learning. It may be intransic or extransic. Motives energise, select and direct behaviour. Praise and blame, rewards and punishment, knowledge of progress, etc., devices are the external factors of motivation help in learning. Thus the teacher should apply various devices in the class room to motivate the children.

(c) ***The Organism and Perception***

All knowledge is based on some sense perception. The loss of or defects in any sense means that knowledge and learning are impoverished in proportion to the loss. Perception is not merely the visual, auditory or other image of an object present to the senses; it involves cognition or the consciousness of a number of facts associated with the object perceived. Thus learning is dependent on the relative perfection of the senses and the general condition of the organism. If there will be organic defects (visual, auditory, focal infections and adenoids, etc.), then learning will be affected.

(d) ***Intellectual Ability or Capacity***

It is a fact that various species of animals have different capacities to learn. Man is known to have greater capacity to learn then other living things. We know that human beings differ in their abilities to learn. On the basis of the Terman and Merril Intellectual classification we classify them as feeble-minded, normal or in the genius class in terms of their ability to learn. Thus the teacher should see that mental health/ability is properly strengthened in learning.

(e) ***Psychological Safety***

Learning is a process of interaction in which the learner actively participates in the learning situation. Thus, the learner should be provided psychological satisfaction or safe situation so that he/she can participate freely and safely in the learning process.

(f) ***Readiness***

If a person is ready to learn, the learning process will be more active. Thus the teacher should stimulate and develop the mental readiness in the children for effective learning in addition to seating arrangement, ventilation, light facilities and excessive noise.

(g) ***Drawing of a Study Schedule***

A schedule is often useful in setting up regular habits of study and thus enabling the learner to make maximum use of his/her time and energy. A schedule acts as a challenge, as well as a guide and monitor. Thus drawing of a study schedule makes the learner attentive and persistent in learning.

(h) *Attacking the Assignment Vigorously*

Learning is an active, effortful process. There is no more effective method of study than merely to read the words of a book passively, waiting for the material somehow to register itself on the "mind". If the learner attack the learning task vigorously he/she can be a successful person than the passive group.

(i) *Family Background and Socio-economic Status*

Research in the field of family background and socio-economic status proved that learning achievement, attitudes, values and ability of the students are different due to urban and rural environment and socio-economic conditions of the family. Therefore, for effective learning proper stimulation may be provided from the family irrespective of the background and socio-economic conditions of the family because it is responsible for developing adequate and correct attitude towards learning.

(j) *Knowledge of Results*

Knowing how he/she is doing offers strong incentive to the learner to put forth additional effort. It is found that the group which is provided information about improvement, is able to make satisfactory progress than the group which is deprived of this information. This suggests the importance of use of knowledge of results in a teaching programme.

(k) *Effect of Age on Learning*

Learning capacity varies with age. Age accompanies mental maturation. The teacher, while constructing curriculum should keep in mind the various stage of the development of the child and adopt various methods of instructional process according to the age and grade level of the students.

(l) *Sex and Physiological Differences*

Many studies have been conducted to find out whether there is any difference in learning of various subjects, skills, attitudes, etc., among boys and girls due to differences in sex or they are the product of culture and social roles assigned to males and females in our society has not been established so far. But this aspect must be taken into consideration while learning takes place.

(m) ***Environment***

The progress and process of learning is very much under the influence of the environment. Therefore, the teacher should see that environment of the institution is congenial and cheerful otherwise it may affect the learning process, if it is not healthy.

(n) ***Fatigue and Bad Working Conditions***

Fatigue is the state in which the organism is exhausted and requires rest. In a state of fatigue, the output is diminished or lowered efficiency or the quality is impaired. Fatigue may be muscular, sensory or mental. This may be due to bad seating arrangement, unhealthy atmosphere, poor environment, poor light, noise and over crowdedness, etc., affects the learning capacity. Similarly, learning is hampered by bad working conditions or distraction both at home and school.

(o) ***Organisational Set-up***

The organisational set up of the school also affect learning. The time-table, teacher-pupil relations, democratic organisation, inter-class competitions and guidance personnal, etc., affect the learning process if the organisational set up of the school is not conducive and strengthened.

(p) ***Difficulty, Meaningfulness and Length of Material***

It is a fact that more difficult the learning material, the poor is the learning. Therefore, experimental studies have clearly indicated that more meaningful the material, the rapid is the learning. Being meaningful means that the material conveys some sense and has some associations and previous experience with the learner. There is little learning without meaning. Therefore, the teacher should provide more meaningful material to the learner for effective learning. Not only this the teacher should see that the length of the materials is reasonable and can be completed within the time frame.

(q) ***Nervousness, Worry over Finances, Emotional Tensions with Personal and Family Problems***

It is a fact that no student can do effective intellectual work when distracted by worries, fears, and frequent emotional upsets. There are some situations which develop worries, tensions and rooted in feelings of inferiority and hamper study habit in spite of the interest and ability of the learner. Thus, the teacher should see that all these hindrances are overcome as far as possible while learning takes place.

Types of Learning

Learning has been classified by psychologists and educationists in various ways depending upon the domain specific (cognitive, affective and conative) aspects of human behaviour, i.e., verbal learning, concept learning, learning of principles, problem solving, attitudinal learning, and learning of skills or motor learning as compared to the learning according to the methods or techniques that are employed for the introduction of behavioural changes, i.e, conditioning (Classical and Operant), discrimination learning, chain learning, serial learning, associative learning and insightful learning and so on.

However, as an alternative basis Gagne has classified learning into eight types in a hierarchical order. These eight types are the following.

1. Signal or classical conditioning
2. S-R learning or instrumental or operant conditioning
3. Chain learning
4. Verbal associate learning
5. Discrimination learning
6. Concept learning
7. Learning of principles, and
8. problem solving

1 & 2. *Conditioning (Classical and operant)*

Conditioning is considered by many psychologists to be the fundamental form of learning. Conditioning always involves the substitution of one stimulus for another and the forcing of an association between them. A child sucks a nipple when hungry and withdraws from painful stimuli. Thus a child acquires new patterns of responses. Both the classical and operant conditioning are given in details subsequently.

3 & 4. *Chain learning (Verbal and motor)*

There are mainly two types of chaining, i.e., motor and verbal. Chaining means the connection of a set of individual S-R in sequence. Virtually all the learning taking place in formal education is verbal learning. The language we speak and the communication devices we use are the product of verbal learning signs, pictures, symbols, words, figures, sounds and voices are employed by the individual as essential instruments for engaging in the process of learning.

Similarly, when learning involves primarily the use of muscles, it is called motor learning. In this type, the individual acquires new muscular coordinations as a mode of response to some situation. Learning to walk, to operate a typewriter, to swim, to play hockey, to play a musical instrument, drawing a geometrical design, riding a horse, driving a car, flying a plane, etc., are examples of motor learning.

5. *Discrimination learning*

In this type of learning, the subject is presented with two or more stimuli which differ in some detail. Here the task is to distinguish between the two situations. An infant before he can talk, generally learns to distinguish between his mother and his aunt, between milk and some other drink, and a dog and doll and so on.

6. *Concept learning*

A concept is a generalized idea about things, persons or events in the form of a mental image. The concept of "tree" is a mental image that throws up the similarities or common properties of all the different trees we know. We will call a thing "tree" when it had some specific characteristics, the image of which we have already acquired in our mind on account of our previous experience, perception and exercise of imagination. All our behaviour, verbal, symbolic, motor as well as cognitive are influenced by our concepts.

7. *Learning of Principles*

It depends on learning of concept formation and other forms of learning. There is a large number of principles that every individual masters in order to function properly in the environment. Most of the classroom learning contributes to the development of principles.

8. *Problem Solving*

It comes at the highest stage in the hierarchy of learning process. This learning requires the use of the cognitive abilities like reasoning, thinking, the power of observation, discrimination, generalisation, imagination, the ability to infer, draw conclusions and try out novel ways and experimenting, etc., by the learner. Details are given separately.

Theories of Learning

In order to explain the process of learning various theories have been put forth by psychologists. How does an individual learn or what we learn is answered by the psychologists through various approaches of learning. Broadly we may categorise all these approaches or theories under two major heads. These are:

A. ***Associationist or Connectionist or Behaviourist or Stimulus response (S-R) theories of learning.*** They interpret learning in terms of connection or association between stimulus and response. Under this category the theories like Thorndike's theory of trial and error, Hull's drive reduction theory and Skinner operant conditioning theory (all these are S-R theories with reinforcement) and Pavlov's classical conditioning, Watson's learning theory and Guthrie's continuity theory of learning (all these are S-R theories without reinforcement), etc., are included.

B. ***Cognitive or Field or Gestalt or Organismic or Central theories of learning.*** These theories emphasize the role of purpose, insight, understanding, reasoning, memory and other cognitive factors in the process of learning. The important theories in this category are: Gestalt theory or insightful learning by Kohler, Lewin's field theory of learning and Tolman's sign theory.

Some of the important theories of learning are described below.

1. *Thornsdike's Theory of Trial and Error (S-R theory with Reinforcement or Reward)*

Meaning

Edward Lee Thorndike (1874-1949) was the first American psychologist who introduced the concept of reward (reinforcement) for learning and conducted a series of experiments as learning with animals. All learning, according to him, is the formation of bond or connections between stimulus response. In any act of learning, the learner is only acquiring a series of new responses and hence any description of the learning process is only a description of how a learner acquires and stabilises a new series of responses.

Thorndike conducted a number of experiments on animals to explain the process of learning. His most widely quoted experiment is with cats placed in a puzzle or problem box. He put a hungry cat in a puzzle box. There was only one door which should be opened by correctly manipulating a latch or by pulling a loop of string hanging inside the box. A fish was placed outside the box. The smell of the fish acted as a strong motive for the hungry cat to come out of the box. The cat indulged a number of random activities or movements inside the box indicating trial and error type of behaviour—clawing at the bars, biting at the bars or wires, scratching the box, walking around, pulling and jumping, etc., to come out to get food. After a number of random movements the latch was manipulated accidentally and the cat came-out and got the food (reward). Over a series of successive trials the cat took shorter and shorter time and committed less number of errors and was in a position to manipulate the latch as soon as it was put in the box and learnt the art of opening the door.

Thorndike found that it was only after many random trials that the cat was able to hit upon the solution. He said it is a trial and error learning. An analysis of the learning behaviour of the cat in the box conforms that there was motivation, goal, exploration (random movements) and reinforcement, etc., in the learning process. Thus learning is the result of connection or bond formation between the stimulus and response.

Laws of Learning

On the basis of the experiments Thorndike suggested certain laws which governed human learning. The primary laws suggested are the laws of readiness, exercise and effect.

1. The Law of Readiness

The term readiness refers to preparedness of the organism in a certain manner which immediately precede the action. If the child is ready to learn, he/she learns more quickly, effectively and with greater satisfaction than if he/she is not ready to learn. Thus the law of readiness means mental preparation for action and not to force the child to learn if he is not ready. Therefore, the teacher should make an attempt to motivate the students by stimulating their attention, interest and curiosity.

2. The Law of Effect

The law explains the importance of effect or consequence in strengthening and weakening of connection. While success brings with it satisfaction and strengthening of the relation the failure increases dis-satisfaction and the absence of the relation among the facts weakens them. Therefore, all pleasant experiences have a lasting influence and are remembered for a long time, while the unpleasant ones are soon forgotten. Thus the law emphasises the role of rewards and punishment in the process of learning.

3. The Law of Exercise

The law explains the role of practice in learning. It has two sub-laws, i.e., law of use and law of disuse. With practice the connection is strengthened (use) and when practice is discontinued, connection is weakened (disuse).

All these three laws are significant in many kinds of learning in our life and can be mentioned like "you can lead a horse to the water but you cannot make it drink". "Nothing succeeds like success", and "practice makes a man perfect". In addition to the above Thorndike mentioned five subordinate laws of learning. These are as follows :

Subordinate Laws of Learning

a. *Law of multiple response or varied reaction.* This laws implies that when an individual is confronted with a new situation he responds in a variety of ways trying first one response and then another before arriving at the correct one.
b. *Law of attitude or mental set.* Learning is guided by a total attitude or 'set' of the organism. The learner performs the task properly if he/she has developed a healthy attitude towards the work.
c. *Law of partial activity*: This suggests the capacity of the learner to deal with the relevant part of the situation which is directly related to his learning effort. The law states that the learner makes selective responses in a learning situation.
d. *Law of analogy* : This law suggests that new situations are tackled on the basis of older ones or previous experience.

e. ***Law of associative shifting*** : This law states that we may "get any response of which a learner is capable, associated with any situation to which he is sensitive.

Educational Implications of the trial and error learning

Thorndike's theory is of great significance in the field of education or teaching-learning process. He has stressed the following five things which assist in the progress of learning. These are :

(i) interest in the work,
(ii) interest in improvement,
(iii) significance,
(iv) attitude,
(v) attentiveness.

He encouraged the psychological revolution in the field of education and emphasized the study of elements according to specific situations and motivation in learning. It has also given an impetus to drill and practice and highlighted the importance of rewards and praise in the field of learning.

II. *Skinner Operant or Instrumental Conditioning Theory (S-R Theory with Reinforcement)*

B.F. Skinner's Operant Conditioning or Instrumental Conditioning Theory of Learning proved the importance of reinforcement in learning rather than the connections being formed between stimuli and responses. The theory is called the operant conditioning as it is based on certain operations or actions which a person has to carry out. In classical theory of Parlov, the dog was harnessed on a table and was passive. The dog performed no operations.

The presence of a stimulus is essential to evoke a response. The subject (e.g., child express fear only when he hears a loud noise and the dog waits for food to arrive salivation) had no control over the happening and is made to behave in response to the stimulus situations. But Skinner revolted against it and argued that in practical situation of our life we cannot wait for things to happen in the environment and it is not always essential that there must be some known stimuli or cause for evoking a response. In operant conditioning the subjects performed acts or 'carried out' operations and were active. A dog, a child or an individual does something, behaves in some manner, which, operates, on the environment which in turn responds to the activity. Based on the findings of his experiments Skinner concluded that "behaviour is shaped and maintained by its consequences. It is operated by the organism and maintained by its results. The occurrence of such behaviour was named operant behaviour and the process of learning that plays a part in learning such behaviour, was named as operant conditioning. More precisely operant conditioning refers to a kind of learning process where a response is made more probable or more frequent by reinforcement. It helps in the learning of operant behaviour, the behaviour that is not necessarily associated with a known stimulus.

The Experiments regarding Operant Conditioning

Skinner conducted a series of experiments with animals. For conducting the experiments with rats, he constructed a sound proof box which was equipped with a bar and a food tray. He put a hungry rat in the box. It is so arranged that when the rat presses the lever, the feeder mechanism is activated, a light or a special sound is produced and a small pellet of food is released into the tray. All these activities were connected to a recording system. Thus the rat learned the task of pressing the bar more frequently when the food pellet reinfored the behaviour. Here, giving out the correct response is more important and succeeded in changing the traditional S-R formula to R-S formula. He believed that there are responses without known stimuli and these responses are called "emitted" responses. Responses to known stimuli are called elicited responses. He believes response first then stimulus and recognizes two kinds of reinforcers—positive and negative.

Mechanisms of Operant Conditioning

The important thing in the mechanism of operant conditioning is the emitting of a desired response and its proper management through suitable reinforcement. Here the organism responds in a certain way so as to produce the reinforcing stimulus. The subsequent reinforcement gradually conditions the organism to emit the desired response and thus learn the desired act. The following are some of the mechanisms of operant conditioning :

(a) Shaping : It refers to the judicious use of selective reinforcement to bring certain desirable changes in the behaviour of the organism. Suppose we want to train a child for toilet training. Simply putting the child on the toilet is not successful because as soon as the child is placed on the stool, he/she begins to cry. To shape his/her behaviour, the child is given a chocolate whenever he/she is placed on the toilet. It has been observed that successful elimination follows. Similarly other techniques may also be used. In this way, shaping may be used as a successful technique for training individuals to learn difficult and complex behaviour and also for introducing desirable modification of their behaviour.

(b) *Chaining* : It is a sort of chain reaction where one object sparks the other object in its proximity and in turn causes sparking in the next object in the chain and so on. When we see someone we know, it is an effective stimulus for starting the chain responses. We greet him and he greets in response. His response to our greeting acts not only as a reward for our greeting but also as a stimulus for generating further response and in this way one generated response gives birth to another response and so on indicates chaining.

(c) *Generalisation* : It is a fact that both animals and human beings are capable of generalizing experiences and knowledge acquired in one learning situation to another. Thus due care should be taken by the parents and teachers to reinforce the behaviour of the children only after they demonstrate the ability to generalize correctly.

(d) *Discrimination* : Ability of discrimination is very important in the behaviour formation. For example, in the Skinner box the animal learns to press the lever when the light is on and not to press it when the light is off. Thus the light becomes a clue or signal for the operant behaviour, i.e., the lever press response. Here the animal develops a discriminative operant which is an operant response extended to one set of circumstances but not to another. Similarly in the learning process the teacher should see that feedback is provided to the children as and when they are able to discriminate the good from bad or to provide proper feedback in correctness of his responses.

(e) *Reinforcement* : The concept of reinforcement is central in operant conditioning theory and is identical to the presentation of a reward. A reinforcer is the stimulus the presentation of which increases the probability of a response. Skinner used reinforcement as a procedure for controlling behaviour which produces stimulus response connection and recognizes two kinds of reinforcers—positive and negative.

Positive Reinforcement

A positive reinforcer is any stimulus (such as food, money, water, social approval, praise, knowledge of results) the introduction or presentation of which increases the likelihood of a particular behaviour. In the educational context, praise, grades, medals, and other prizes awarded to students are examples of positive reinforcers.

Negative reinforcement

A negative reinforcer is any stimulus or those unpleasant stimuli the removal or withdrawal (such as loud noise, electric shock, social disapproval, condemnation) of which increases the likelihood of a particular behaviour. In the educational context, a teacher saying to the students that whoever does drill work properly in the class would be exempted from homework act as a negative reinforcer.

The schedules of Reinforcement

The term schedule of reinforcement suggests the particular pattern according to which reinforcers follow responses.

Some important schedules of reinforcement are the following:

1. *Continuous schedule of reinforcement:* It is an arrangement of providing reinforcement after every correct response. In the teaching-learning process a student may be rewarded for every correct answer in the form of warm regards or praise or praise or approval indicates continuous schedule of reinforcement.

2. *Fixed interval reinforcement Schedule :* In the fixed or periodic interval schedule the reinforcement is presented after a prescribed interval of time, i.e., every 2 minutes or 4 minutes. Here emphasis is not given on correct responses rather it is only at the expiry of the fixed interval reinforcement is given.

3. ***Fixed ratio reinforcement schedule :*** In this schedule the reinforcement is given after a fixed number of responses. It means the performance of the learner is important rather than anything else. A learner may be rewarded (receives a chocolate) after he/she answers a fixed number of questions say 2 or 3. Another example of fixed ratio schedule is a rat gets a pellet of food only after pressing the bar say 7 to 8 times.

4. ***Variable reinforcement schedule :*** When reinforcement is given at varying intervals of time or after a varying number of responses, is called a variable reinforcement schedule. In this case, reinforcement is intermittent or irregular. Here the learner does not know at which time he/she is going to be rewarded and consequently he/she remains motivated with a hope of reinforcement.

Implications of the Theory of Operant Conditioning

The following implications emerged from the theory of operant conditioning :

(i) The theory provides the basis for programmed Instruction. It is a kind of learning experience in which a programme takes the place of tutor for the students and leads him through a set of specified behaviours.

(ii) The theory has drawn attention to the inadequacy and unsuitability of reinforcement procedure adopted in our educational system. Thus the element of reinforcement can be strengthened in the teaching-learning process.

(iii) Generally, in our schools, the desirable behaviour of the learners is not immediately reinforced to raise the probability of the recurrence of the same behaviour in future. Thus it suggests delay of reinforcement destroys the effect of reinforcing stimuli, hence, reinforcement should be given at an appropriate time and at each step.

(iv) The principle of operant conditioning can be applied in behaviour modification and ultimately desired behaviour can be strengthened depending upon the manipulation of reward.

(v) Operant conditioning emphasizes the importance of schedules in the process of reinforcement of behaviour.

(vi) Operant conditioning suggested appropriate alternatives to punishment in the form of rewarding appropriate behaviour and ignoring inappropriate behaviour, for its gradual extinction.

(vii) The root of mechanical learning in the form of teaching machines and computer assisted instruction have taken a shape in place of usual classroom instruction due to operant conditioning.

B. *Pavlov's Classical or Respondent Conditioning Theory (S-R Theories without Reinforcement)*

The theory of classical conditioning was developed by a Russian physiologist named Ivan P. Pavlov in the year 1904. It is defined as a process in which a neutral stimulus, by pairing with a natural stimulus, acquires all the characteristics of natural stimulus. It is called substitution learning because we substitute a neutral stimulus in place of a natural stimulus. This is also called as respondent conditioning because the subject has noting to do himself and becomes conditioned and does the things. To understand the nature of the process of conditioning, the experiments performed by Pavlov is given below:

Experiment

Pavlov kept a dog hungry for a few days and then placed it in a sound proof room which was fitted with certain mechanically controlled devices. The observer himself remained hidden from the dog but was able to view the experiment by means of a set of mirrors. Arrangement was made to give food to the dog through an automatic mechanism. But everytime before giving food a bell was rung. When the food was given and the bell was rung it was marked that there was a automatic secretion of saliva from the mouth of the dog. This activity was repeated several times. After several trials the dog was given no food but the bell was rung. It was found that even the absence of food (the natural stimulus) the ringing of the bell (an artificial stimulus) caused the dog to secrete the saliva (natural response).

The above experiment thus, brings to light four essential elements of the conditioning process, i.e., unconditioned stimulus (US, natural stimulus) is food results in a natural response called the unconditioned response (UR). The conditioned stimulus (CS, artificial stimulus) elicit conditioned response (CR). It is given below.

1.	UCS	-	UCR
	(Food)	-	(Saliva)
2.	CS + UCS	-	UCR
	(Bell + Food)	-	(Saliva)
3.	CS	-	CR
	(Bell)	-	(Saliva)

Principles of Conditioning

1. *Reinforcement :* The salivary response to the bell was strengthened as a result of the food being repeatedly presented just after the bell rang.

2. *Extinction* : If the bell was rung too many times without the food to reinforce, the response could have disappeared.

3. *Generalisation :* The dog tended to respond to any sound roughly similar to the ringing of the bell.

4. *Discrimination :* To teach the dog to distinguish the right sound and other sounds, selective reinforcement was used, that is, the dog was given food only after the sound of the bell, but never any other sound.

Educational Implications

(i) The formation of positive attitudes, fears, love, prejudices or hatred towards an object, phenomenon or event can be developed through conditioning. Thus classical conditioning can be used to develop favourable or unfavourable attitude towards learning, teacher and the school.

(ii) We should associate faults with punishment so that whenever a child feels like committing faults, he/she anticipates the punishments. Thus rewards and punishments may be given right at the time of the act and not to be delayed.

(iii) Repetition and habit formation is to be strengthed in the process of learning.

(iv) Most of our learning is associated with the process of conditioning from the beginning. Thus the teacher is to develop the good reading habits through conditioning.

(v) The process of conditioning not only helps us in learning what is desirable but also helps in eliminating, avoiding or unlearning of undesirable habits, unhealthy attitudes, phobias through deconditioning.

COMPARISON BETWEEN CLASSICAL AND OPERANT CONDITIONING

Classical Conditioning	*Operant Conditioning*
1. It was developed by Russian Physiologist Ivan P. Pavlov.	1. It was developed by B.F. Skinner.
2. It is known as Respondent/ Types or signal conditioning.	2. It is known as Type R/Instrumental conditioning.
3. In classical conditioning the CR and UCR are the same.	3. In operant conditioning they are different, i.e., pressing the lever is different from eating food.
4. In classical conditioning reinforcement is provided by the unconditioned stimulus.	4. In operant conditioning the response causes conditioned reinforcement to appear.
5. In classical conditioning the association between (S-R) is on the basis of law of contiguity.	5. In operant conditioning association between (S-R) is on the basis of law of effect.
6. Reinforcement, i.e., food is presented first to elicit the response here.	6. Reinforcement is provided after the response is made by the organism.
7. The essence of learning is stimulus substitution.	7. The essence of learning is response modification.
8. In this type of conditioning beginning is made with the help of specific stimuli that bring certain responses.	8. Here beginning is made with the responses as they occur naturally.
9. It is stimulus oriented.	9. It is response oriented.
10. Classical conditioning is limited to autonomic response.	10. Operant conditioning is limited to skeletal behaviour.

II. Cognitive/Field/Gestalt Theories of Learning

Dissatisfied with the approach of behaviourists, the cognitive psychologists tried to see learning as a more deliberate and conscious effort of the individual rather than a product of mere habit formation or a stimulus response machine like mechanism. According to them, in a learning process, the learner does not merely receive or make responses to the stimuli, but definitely interacts with and does something about what he receives and his response is determined by that processing. Accordingly a group of German psychologists called gestalists and particularly Wolfgang Kohler originated a learning theory named insightful learning.

Learning by Insight

Wolfgang Kohler, a German psychologist, put forth this theory of learning. This theory is based on the basic concept of Gestalt school of psychology that "whole is more meaningful than sum of its parts". The word Gestalt in German language means "whole" total pattern or configuration. Similarly, it is a fact that learning also takes place as a whole. According to him learning is a process of discovering and understanding relationships and organizing and finding significance in the sensory experience aroused by the external situation. Thus learning by insight means sudden grasping of the solution or a flash of understanding.

Experiments

Kohler conducted various experiments on Chimpanzees. In one of the experiment, he put the Chimpanzee inside a cage and hung a bunch of bananas from the ceiling/roof of the cage. A box was placed inside the cage. But after several trials suddenly the Chimpanzee got an idea and used the box as a jumping platform by placing it just below the hanging bananas and succeeded.

Secondly to make the experiment more complex and to reach the bananas two/three boxes were required and accordingly boxes mere put inside the cage. But after several trials, Sultan was able to learn the placing of one box on the other and succeeded.

Similarly in a more complicated experiment, a bunch of bananas was placed outside the cage. Two sticks were placed inside the cage. Unless two sticks are joined together bananas cannot be picked up. After several trials suddenly the animal had a bright idea and joined the two sticks together and reached the bananas.

Characteristics of Insightful Learning

(i) Insight is sudden.
(ii) Insight alters perception.
(iii) Old objects appear in new patterns and organisations is by virtue of insight.
(iv) In case initial mode of response proves in-adequate, alternative mode of response is tried.

(v) Repetition and generalization of response is found out.

Educational Implications

(1) *Proceeding from whole to the part:* It is better to proceed from the whole to the part, so as to give a complete insight into the subject. It means the teacher should teach the whole concept, i.e., begin from the globe and then come to country, state, district and block, etc.

(2) *Arousal of motivation*: In the class the teacher should try to arouse motivation among the students in the teaching-learning process because all the learning does not come suddenly. Constant encouragement and motivation can solve many of the problems of learning.

(3) *Emphasis on understanding:* What is needed in the learning process is deep understanding and insight rather than mechanical repetition or learning by rote.

(4) Development of reasoning power and capacity of discovery of new facts are essential in learning process to meet the challenges of life. Thus the task of the teacher is not in spoon feeding and transmitting knowledge but in helping the child to acquire knowledge himself.

(5) Here the role of the teacher is much broader than merely establishing connection between a stimulus and a response. Thus the teacher should organise the learning situation in such a way so as to bring out certain relations.

(6) The field theories lay emphasis on the classroom and child-centred approach in teaching learning. Thus freedom should be given to the child to think in terms of his own interests and come out with the ideas more relevant to the situation.

(7) This theory emphasises on the psychological organisation of the subject matter because of the individual difference. Thus the child is allowed to enter into the total situation rather than part method.

(8) The whole-part-whole method is emphasised because it provides the general outline or broad features of the topic before analysing part by part. Thus it develops the analysis, generalisation and integration of the learning situation in front of the students.

II. *Lewin's Field Theory*

Kurt Lewin as a Gestalt Psychologist profounded his theory on the basis of gestaltonian elements with a little change or modification. According to him, learning is a process of perceptual organization or reorganization of one's life space involving insight and emphasizes on behaviour and motivation in learning. He further stressed upon that learning and insight can always be viewed as a change in the cognitive structure of the situation. He shares the theory of insightful learning as a process of structuring or restructuring the perceived area. So, perception is the main issue in Lewin's theory of learning and further suggested that learning is a change in cognitive structure, is a change in motivation, is acquisition of skills and is a change in group belonging. Let us now try to explain some basic concepts utilised by Lewin in propounding his theory.

(a) *Concept of LIfe-Space*

The concept of life space may be defined as "the totality of facts which determine the behaviour of a given individual at a given time" or how an individual interprets a particular stimulus at a particular time and how that interpretation influence the behaviour. If an object does not exist but of which the person thinks to be there and reacts to it, becomes a part of the his life space. If a child thinks there is a snake on the wall, even if it may be purely an imaginary idea, the snake is a part of child's life space. Even life space of two persons in an identical situation may be entirely different. Thus, one's life space is the space in which one lives psychologically involving one's own perception and depicting one's own view point. It includes each and every object, person or idea with which one is concerned at a given time.

(b) *Foreign Hull*

It consists of those aspects of a person's environment which are perceived not by the person himself, but by one who is studying the person. It lies outside the life space.

(c) *Valence*

Lewin describes two types of valences (positive and negative) operating in one's life space. It may be liking (positive) or disliking (negative) valence depending upon the object. Thus a person tends to move towards a region in life that has positive valence and restrict or move away that has negative valence. The valence may be strong, medium or weak depending upon the psychological status of the individual, his needs and other factors. Hence valence motivate the individual to learn.

(d) *Vector*

A vector is a psychological force which is influencing movements towards or away from a goal. It indicates the relative strengths of tendencies to approach or to avoid different points in the life space. If only one vector (force) then movement is as per the direction but if more than one vector acting simultaneously then depending upon the magnitive of force movement will be decided.

(e) *Concept of Conflict*

In a complicated situation a person is not able to make compatible responses. Each incident, object or person in the life space attracts or repels in some degree. The conflicts are three types. These are:

(i) Approach-approach conflict (two equally strong force) indicates when a student wants to score high marks in the class and also in final examination or choose between watching a movie of his choice or going to picnic with his class-mates.
(ii) Avoidance-avoidance conflict indicates two almost equally strong and negative valences work, i.e., the student wants to avoid home work as well as punishment from the teacher.
(iii) Approach-avoidance conflict revealed when a student wants to eat lot of ice-cream but fears getting soar throat or bad teeth.

(f) *Barrier*

The individual has to cross the number of difficulties, barriers and problems to reach his desired goal. These may be physical or psychological. Thus psychological changes in the life space of an individual is taken place to over-come the barrier.

(g) *Motivation*

Lewin's gives an important place to motivation in his theory. According to him motivation is the process in which motives are related to specific goals and the satisfaction of motive is determined by achieving it. It may be intransic or extransic and both are essential for better learning.

(h) *Rewards and Punishment*

Lewin's highlighted the role of both rewards and punishment in the process of teaching-learning and so also warned against their excessive and improper use.

(i) *Levels of Aspiration*

According to him aspiration is also an important fact in the learning process. It depends upon the potentialities of the individual and on the influence of the group to which he belongs. Thus proper development of the level of aspiration is essential in the learning process.

Educational Implications

(i) Lewin's field theory emphasises on motivation and perception. Therefore for effective learning the teacher should provide suitable psychological environment and have an insight and understanding into the relationship between individual, environment and his behaviour.
(ii) The teacher should keep in setting the goals for different individuals to attain according to their capacities and abilities and try to guide the learners effectively to overcome difficulties, threats and barriers of learning.
(iii) Total situation of the problem should be made very clear and understandable to the learner so that they will be motivated to learn.
(iv) Teacher should use reward and punishment according to the needs of the situation, as Lewin's accepted the value of reward and punishment for learning.

Modern Methods of Learning

1. *Transfer of Training or Learning*

While the term transfer of learning is transfer of knowledge the term transfer of training is transfer of skills, which is being used interchangeably. As education is said to be preparation for life, whatever we learn in educational institution, should be useful only when we can apply the same in day-to-day life. Hence, the need for transfer of learning emphasises on application of knowledge in various fields or is a process in which responses are used in one situation which it is acquired.

Meaning and Definitions

The process of carrying over habits of thinking, knowledge, skills and attitude from one learning situation to another is called the transfer of learning. For example, a child will carry over the arithmetical abilities he/she learns in a class room to the solution of problems that he/she may actually face in later life, in business or in the management of personal finances is called transfer of learning.

The following are the definitions of Transfer of Learning:

1. Bigge defines " Transfer of learning occurs when a person's learning in one situation influences his learning and performance in other situations."
2. Walter defines "Transfer is the application or carry over of knowledge, skills, habits, attitudes or other responses from one situation in which they were initially acquired to some other situation".
3. Eills defines "Transfer of learning means that experience or performance on one task influences performance on some subsequent task".
4. Crow and Crow defines "The carry-over habits of thinking, feeling or working of knowledge or of skills, from one learning area to another usually is referred to as the transfer of training".
5. Sorenson defines "transfer as recognition, use and application to a given situation of knowledge, skills and habits that were learned in another situation".

Types of Transfer of Learning

The following are the different types of transfer of learning.

(a) *Positive Transfer* : When learning in all situation facilitates the learning in another situation is called positive transfer.

(b) *Negative Transfer* : When the learning of one task makes the learning of second task harder is called negative transfer or the previous learning interferes or hinders the learning of new task is called negative transfer.

(c) *Zero Transfer* : When the learning of one subject or previous learning neither facilitates nor hinders the new learning is called zero transfer.

(d) *Vertical Transfer*: When one lesson facilitates understanding for another lesson in a subject, e.g., habits and values of the family influences the child to adopt them in their day to day life is called vertical transfer.

(e) *Horizontal Transfer:* When the knowledge of one subject helps in understanding the other subjects, e.g., the knowledge of the history of vedic period helps in understanding the literature of that period is called horizontal transfer.

(f) *Bilateral Transfer:* When the training given to one part of the body is transfered to other part, e.g., writing with right hand may be transfered to the left one is called bilateral transfer.

(g) *Unilateral Transfer*: When the training given to one sided parts of the body is used for future is called unilateral transfer.

Factors responsible for transfer of training

Transfer is dependent on a multitude of factors which are given below :

(i) Transfer depends very much upon the intelligence and innate efficiency of the learner. It depends upon one's ability to generalise and the ability to perceive relationships between two situations. But a dull student learns by rote and hence cannot apply it to a new situation.

(ii) Formation of attitudes and ideals helps one to transfer the knowledge and the skill from one situation to another.

(iii) Transfer relies heavily on meaningfulness of material. So, proper teaching and encouragement to pupils are essential for transfer of training.

(iv) Transfer depends upon the use of facts learnt. Transfer is not possible unless the subject learnt is put into practical use. The transfer of the knowledge of Ethics gained in school to social education is possible only in the event of the students use of the former daily life.

(v) Discovery leads to transfer. When a child discovers the solution to a problem himself, he is likely to transfer this knowledge to the solution of other problems.

(vi) Techniques of learning, congenial environment and motivation to the subject help in transfer of training.

Educational Implications of Transfer of Learning

(a) Subject matter should be taught and learnt in close contact with its applications. When a child knows that what he/she learns has a bearing beyond the classroom, he/she is strongly motivated to learn it well.

(b) Whatever is taught to the student should have a practical applications in actual life. Thus, good teacher should keep in mind that for greatest transfer the generalizations should be thoroughly mastered and completely understood.

(c) Students should be encouraged to see beyond specific details to the underlying relationships or principles and provided opportunity for applications of generalization.

(d) It is now well established fact that greater transfer from subject matter can be achieved by changing the methods of teaching. if the subject matter is taught in isolation from the problems of daily life the utility of the knowledge gained is extremely limited.

(e) Emphasis should be given on developing ideals and attitudes so that proper transfer of learning can take place.

(f) Teacher should know that transfer is not accomplished with equal facility. It depends upon one's ability to generalise his experiences and the ability to perceive relationships between two situations. Thus emphasis should be given on intelligence and the teacher should teach the student according to the mental ability.

(g) Teacher should given the meaningful matter in the class and try to develop the attitude for the application of theoretical content into practical life. Students should be made alert to new situations.

(h) The teacher should give several examples when teaching concepts and skills. Through examples student understanding of new concepts can be strengthened and its applicability to life situations can be judged.

(i) Teacher should see that the ideas which are presented to students are not creating confusion and developing negative transfer habit among them. Thus the teacher should encourage critical thinking on the part of the students while teaching.

II. **Mastery Learning**

Meaning of Mastery Learning

'Mastery learning' is a new term in educational vocabulary, developed by B.S. Bloom in 1968. He is considered as the father of mastery learning strategy for his systematic investigation into the problem of helping each child to achieve mastery of a subject and thereby to remove individual differences among children.

When Bloom was doing research in the field of learning the prevailing construct was : There are good learners and there are poor learners. It is believed that good learners can learn the more complex and abstract ideas, whereas poor learners can learn only the simplest and most concrete ideas. From the research Bloom concluded that most students become very similar with regard to learning ability, rate of learning and motivation for further learning, when provided with favourable learning conditions. However, this research also demonstrated that when students are provided with unfavourable learning conditions, they become even more dissimilar with regard to learning ability, rate of learning and motivation for further learning. It is this idea which underlies Bloom's theory of school learning. In this theory Bloom advocated for mastery learning strategy with an aim to promoting learning under favourable learning conditions.

Mastery learning is an optimistic theory about teaching and learning. It asserts that a teacher can help most student to learn excellently, that is dumb like smart, slow like fast, and retarded like gifted student. Thus it is an effective set of individualised instructional practices that consistently help most student to learn excellently. Thus chief objective of mastery learning is to promote excellence in learning. This objective is achieved through systematic planning, proper motivation, better methods and materials for learning, self guided instruction and objective based evaluation.

Procedure for Mastery Learning

There are two approaches for mastery learning:

1. Group based or teacher paced approach

In this approach, the teacher is considered as the most important person in teaching learning situation. Here the student learn co-operatively with their classmates and the teacher controls the delivery and flow of instruction (Bloom).

2. Individual based or student paced approach

In this approach students learn independently and controls the delivery and flow of instruction. Thus this approach puts emphasis on independent study by the individual (Keller plan).

Steps in Mastery learning

Bloom has suggested the following steps for effective mastery learning.

1. Defining the Mastery

The teacher should first define what materials students will be expected to learn or what is meant by mastery of the subject. They are also explained the concepts involved, the processes to be followed and adopted, the skills to be employed and the amount of time to be taken for the mastery of a particular content area. The teacher also prepares a summative test by covering all objectives and decides the standard. Suppose a teacher decides that scoring at least 80% to 90% in the examination would indicate mastery of the subject. Students who perform better than this predetermined standard would be regarded as 'masters' and those who do not would be regarded as 'non-masters'.

2. Planning for mastery

Planning must be consistant with the way in which mastery has been defined. Specially, the plan must include activities, materials, related to the unit objectives, and also include additional supplementary activities and materials for those students who fail to attain the performance standard on the unit formative test.

Planning for mastery involves following tasks

1. The teacher divides the course to be taught for mastery into a series of smaller sequence learning units, each of which cover in two weeks time.
2. For each unit, teacher constructs a formative test or a brief diagnostic progress test. These tests are designed to provide specific information of feed-back to both the teacher and the student about how the student is changing as a result of group-based instruction.
3. Then the teacher specifies a score or performance standard on each formative test, which will be indicative of unit mastery. Generally a score of 80-90 % indicated mastery.
4. If the instruction material is not followed, the teacher develops a set of alternative instructional material or correctives for each unit (individual tutoring, learning aids such as, text book, audio-visual materials, etc.), to master the content, and to overcome the learning problems before proceeding to the next step or subsequent learning.

Orienting for Mastery

After planning for mastery, the teacher is now ready to teach. But students are not accustomed to mastery learning. So before the teacher starts teaching for mastery, it is essential that he/she should explain to the students, what they are going to learn, how they are going to learn, what should be the outcome of learning and what standard of attainment is expected of them. This will provide the necessary orientation and motivation to the students for learning.

Teaching for Mastery

After proper orientation and motivation the teacher teaches the 1st learning unit using the group based teaching methods. After teaching one unit of the lesson, the teacher administers the unit's formative test to the entire class. On the basis of the test score the teacher identifies those who have achieved the unit mastery standard and those who have not. For non-master the teacher follows the alternative instructional material and corrective formative test till the achievement of mastery. The masters are engaged either in enrichment activities or serve as tutor for non-masters. This procedure continues till the completion of all the units.

Grading for Mastery

The final step and major task is grading for mastery. After teaching all the units the teacher administers the summative evaluation test and awards grades. The teacher awards A grade, whose scores are at or above the predetermined mastery performance standard and scores below this level are awarded grades appropriate to the level they have achieved.

Evaluation of MLS

An effective MLS requires two types of evaluation.

(1) ***Formative Evaluation :***

Formative evaluation is used to provide information useful for directing students study and teacher practice. Formative tests have two purposes.

(a) To find out how much the pupils have learned in a restricted area of content at the end of a unit of instruction.
(b) To diagnose pupils difficulties.

(2) ***Summative evaluation :***

Achievement test at the end of periods of instructions are summative test and its attempt to sum-up total achievement in a course. In mastery learning, the primary purpose of summative evaluation is to grade students according to their achievement of the aims of the course or the criteria.

Essential Conditions for Mastery Learning

According to Bloom there are seven essential conditions for successful mastery learning.

(1) *A learner's aptitude* plays an important role in mastery learner. A learning will show more progress in the fields of learning for which he has the aptitudes, as aptitude is the innate ability of the learner in a particular area of learning. According to Carrol, aptitude is the amount of time required by the learner to attain mastery of a learning task. According to Bloom the aptitude for particular learning task is not stable. It may be modified by appropriate environmental conditions or home and school

learning experiences. So Bloom viewed that the central task of educational programme should be to produce positive changes in the student's basic aptitude.

(2) *High quality of instruction* is very essential for mastery. Bloom observed that if every student had a well trained tutor, then most of them would be able to master a particular subject. The main point to be stressed is that quality of instruction must be developed with respect to the needs and characteristics of individual learners, rather than group learners.

(3) *The ability of the learner* is also important for mastery learning. The curiosity to learn and the ability to learn are important factors in achieving mastery learning. This can be defined as the ability of the learner to understand the nature of the task to be learnt and the procedures he/she is to follow in its learning.

(4) *Perseverance* : This is another important condition for mastery learning. This implies that the learner must have the necessary will-power to learn. In other words, long and continuous practice is essential for mastery learning.

(5) *Time allowed for learning*: The time allotted must be appropriate for acquiring mastery over the subject matter. A lot of time is required for practice resulting in the mastery learning. According to Bloom, it is not sheer amount of time spent in learning that accounts for the level of students learning. He believes that the students should be allowed the time they need to learn a particular subject.

(6) *Mastery learning*: necessitates the use of learning materials like text books, library, audio-visual aids like charts, models, pictures, etc. These are the essential requirements of mastery learning.

(7) Another very important requirement is thorough preparation by the teacher. A full previous preparation of instructional units by the teacher is necessary. A teacher must be fully conversant in the content unit to be set for the learning of the students.

Advantages of Mastery

1. It systematises instruction. The learning content is

divided into units and the instruction proceeds from unit to unit.

2. It employs varieties of techniques of teaching and learning and instructional materials for achieving mastery learning.
3. It makes a teacher life-long learner, as the teacher has to keep up his learning because he has to employ new stratagies of instruction for mastery learning.
4. Every student is expected to attain mastery. So there is least of wastage and stagnation.
5. It reduces differences in individual paces of learning, for majority of learner.
6. It helps for motivation, as they provide sense of success in steps.
7. It helps for transfer of learning.
8. It helps immediate readers in providing adequate time to them to do sufficient practice and thus help to develop power of retention.

Limitation of Mastery Learning

1. Vast amount of time, money, and labour may be required to organise mastery learning strategies in school.
2. It requires special training to be given to teachers.
3. It requires special preparation on the part of the teacher for which they are reluctant generally.
4. Mastery is not object of all courses and many courses are meant for providing experience. In such situations mastery learning approaches cannot be employed.
5. The curricula and the syllabus, the text books and other reading materials in all cases are not developed properly to emphasise mastery learning.

III. Problem Solving

Society is not static. It is changing day by day. Not only the individual is facing numerous problems in the society but also the life of the individual has become complicated in the process of change. To overcome from this situation it is important to develop scientific attitudes in students so that they may solve their problems and maintain balanced adjustment in the society. Problem solving is the highest level of learning in the hierarchy proposed by Gagne. It is one of the method which involves the use of the process of reflective thinking or reasoning to solve the problem. The following definitions can provide the meaning and nature of problem solving :

Definition

1. Gates and others defined "problem solving is a form of learning in which the appropriate response must be discovered".
2. Skinner defines "problem solving is a process of overcoming difficulties that appear to interfere with the attainment of a goal. It is a procedure of making adjustment in spite of interferences".
3. Woodworth defines "problem solving behaviour occurs when there is an obstruction of some sort to the attainment of an objective". If the path of the goal is straight and open, is no problem.

Features

On the basis of the above definition the main features of the problem solving are.

(a) Removing obstacles that appear to interfere with the attainment of goals
(b) Development of perception and establishment of relationship
(c) Emphasis on relevant experiences are recalled and selected
(d) Insightful, reflective, creative and critical thinking attitude should be formed to test the tentative hypothesis
(e) Deliberate, conscious and serious efforts on the part of the problem solver should be developed.

Steps in Problem Solving

Psychologists have studied the behaviour of animals as well as of the human beings to understand the process of problem solving. The following are the steps involved in the process of problems solving

1. *Confrontation or the emergence of a problem :*

Sometimes it is found out that the individual himself has experienced a problematic situation or someone else has created a problem for the individual. This is the first step of problematic situation.

2. *Identifying and Defining the problem in a definite term:*

After confrontation with the problem the investigator starts analysing the situation, identifies the problem and defines it in definite terms. It means understanding the problem is very important in the problem solving process.

3. *Search for Solution or Exploring possible strategies:*

Here the investigator formulates certain hypothesis/ possible hunch that guide him/her to reach the goal. He/She collects relevant data information about the problem by all possible means. Appropriate tools are gathered, books and magazines are collected. He may consult experienced persons and read the available literature to collect comprehensive data and knowledge about the problem. Even it has been experienced that final solution occurs in a flash of inspiration although it is not fool-proof but paved the way for solution.

4. *Selection of the Correct solution or acting on the strategies:*

The possible solutions are analysed and evaluated thoroughly. Before finalisation of the correct solution it has been suggested by Gates *et al.,* that solution should be consistent with well established or accepted fact.

5. *Verification of the concluded solution or hypothesis:*

The conclusions which are drawn must be verified by applying it in the similar situation. If it works in the process of problem solution then become a useful product of one's problem solving behaviour and be utilized in solving other future problems.

6. *Making generalization and application :*

Once the problem is solved it is better to dissiminate the ideas and making it public so that it will help the individual in future. Making a generalisation will help the student in solving other problems in future.

Factors of Problem Solving

The following are some of the factors which influence problem solving behaviour.

1. Intelligence
2. Initiation on the part of the subject
3. Experience related to success and failure
4. Flexibility in approach
5. Divergent thinking ability
6. Cooperative work culture
7. Systematic manipulation of facts and materials
8. Motivation

Teachers role in Problem Solving

No universal law can be formulated for solving each and every type of problem. It is an individualized process which requires various strategies to tackle. The following are the tentative problem solving role of the teacher:

1. Atmosphere of freedom in the class by the teacher should be initiated. He has to create the problematic situation and assist the student in defining and stating the problem. He has to help the student to develop an attitude of open mindedness and critical enquiry, an attitude of respect for the other person's view points and indicate the techniques of problem solving to the student.
2. Motivation is another aspect of problem solving. So both intransic and extransic motivation may be raised among the students, which may help in problem solving.
3. Reorienting school work. Both curricular and co-curricular activities of the institution should be recasted so that students will gather useful experiences in their life which will help in problem solving of their future life.
4. Through teaching-learning process (method of instruction) problem solving mechanism can be strengthened. Thus the teacher should present the problems in the class as a whole so that the student may have the perception of the total situation for the solution which will help in strengthening problem solving behaviour.
5. The teacher should discuss problems of great variety among students to develop proper mental readiness to solve similar types of problems in future.
6. The teacher should encourage the divergent thinking among the students. he should see that more

flexibility and original approach to problems are used by the student.

Advantages of Problem Solving

1. In problem solving situations try to develop good habits of planning, thinking and reasoning among the pupils and help in developing the habits of solving the problem independently.
2. Through problem solving situations students are encouraged to search materials in order to arrive at a satisfactory solution.
3. Problem solving creates a condition of strong mental perplexity and acts as a motivating force for activities.

Limitation of Problem Solving

The limitations of the method are not inherent in it. They are the result of poor selection of problems or of the ineffective use of the techniques of problem solving. If the teacher is not able to think reflectively and does not have an attitude of critical enquiry, or when the classroom situation is dominated by him/her and the atmosphere is not conducive and full of ready-made answers, the problem solving method fails miserably. This will also happen when the problems are not chosen correctly and are unreal and artificial and have no relationship with the needs of children.

Summary

Learning is the key topic of Educational Psychology. Not only it is defined as a process which brings relatively permanent change in the behaviour of a learner through experience or practice but also it prepares an individual for adjustment and acquisition of habit, skill and knowledge.

The nature of learning are universal, purposive and goal directed, continuous, process of solving problems, involvement of mental activities, adjustment and function of practice and involves perceptual and motor processes of an individual. In addition to the above the following factors like maturation, motivation, psychological saftey, readiness, intelligence, study schedule, socio-economic conditions, age, environment, working conditions, length and meaningfulness of materials, emotional involvements and organizational set up, etc., are influencing the learning process.

The theories of learning can be classified as connectionist theories and cognitive theories. The first type emphasises on stimulus-response connection and the second type emphasises the role of cognition in learning. The theories like Thorndike theory of trial and error, Hull drive reduction theory, and Skinner operant conditioning comes under the learning theories with reinforcement and the theories of Pavlov's classical conditioning, Watson's learning theory and Guthries contiguity theory of learning are S-R theories without reinforcement. Similarly important field theories are Kohler insightful learning theory, Lewin's field theory and Tolman's sign theory.

The theory of trial and error learning propagated by Thorndike emphasizes that we learn through a trial and error mechanism. On the basis of his experiments he has suggested certain laws of learning like law of readiness (one can learn if one is ready to learn), law of exercise (practice makes a man perfect or learning needs repetition) and law of effect (the effect or consequence decides the fate of one's learning). Further he has suggested five subordinate laws, i.e., law of multiple response, law of mental set, law of partial activity, law of analogy and law of associative shifting.

In 'operant conditioning' Skinner proved that reinforcement is the key factor in learning and behaviour which are reinforced and are likely to be repeated. Thus the success of operant conditioning is dependent on the right choice of a reinforcement schedule and found to be quite useful in the field of behaviour modification, programmed learning and computer-assisted instruction. The shaping, chaining, generalization, discrimination and reinforcement are the basic element of operant conditioning.

Similarly classical conditioning was developed by Pavlov. Through his experiment he found out that a dog is conditioned to salivate when he hears a bell. It means the artificial stimulus (bell) becomes so strong that it can produce saliva in the mouth of the dog even though natural stimulus (food) was not accompanied or supplied. Thus the basic characteristics of the classical conditioning is a process in which a neutral stimulus acquires all the characteristics of natural stimulus and produce the response.

Insightful learning was propagated by Kohler. He emphasised that human learning is purposeful and goal directed and is essentially based on ones cognitive powers. Thus whole situation should be presented in front of the learner to arrive at an insightful solution. Lewin's field theory considers learning to be a process of perceptual organisation of one's life space

or field in which he moves psychologically or is the result of change in cognitive structure. One is supposed to structure one's life space into an appropriate pattern for achieving the desired goal. Thus ones future behaviour depends upon the way one manages to bring about desirable changes in one's cognitive structure on the basis of previous learning and insight.

In addition to the above three modern methods of learning are presented. These are transfer of training (the process of carrying over habits of thinking, knowledge, skills and attitudes from one learning situation to another); mastery learning and problem solving. Transfer of learning may be of various types. These are positive, negative, zero, vertical, horizontal, bilateral and unilateral. Thus the school should provide life-like situations so that good transfer of learning can take place.

Mastery learning was developed by B.S. Bloom. This theory asserts that a teacher can keep most students to learn excellently if individualised instruction and proper time is provided to them. The chief objective of mastery learning is to promote excellence in learning and this can be achieved through systematic planning, proper motivation, better method and materials for learning, self guided instruction and objective based evaluation.

Similarly problem solving is a form of learning in which the appropriate response must be discovered or is a process of overcoming difficulties that appear to interfere with the attainment of a goal. There are different steps of problem solving, i.e., selection of a problem, identifying and defining the problem, search for solution of strategies, selection of the correct solution or acting on the strategies, verification are drawing conclusions. Role of the teacher, advantages and limitations of problem solving are also mentioned.

Questions

1. Define Learning. Describe in brief Gagne's classification of learning.
2. What is learning? How is it different from maturation? Explain in brief the role of teacher in learning.
3. Describe Thorndike"s learning by trial and error and state its laws and educational implications for the teacher.
4. Explain the difference between classical and operant conditioning and suggest the role of reinforcement in learning.

5. What is the contribution of Pavlov to psychology? State the educational importance of the theory.
6. What do you mean by learning by insight? What are the characteristics of insight learning? State its implications for the teacher.
7. Discuss the essential features of learning by classical conditioning and state their educational implications.
8. What do you mean by reinforcement? State its relationship to learning and motivation or what are the various schedules of reinforcement? Explain with examples.
9. What do you mean by learning? State its nature. Discuss the factors influencing/affecting learning.
10. Explain the main principles of Skinner's theory of learning? State its educational implication.
11. Discuss that Lewin has not presented any theory of learning? Point out its implications for learning.
12. What do you mean by transfer of learning? what are the important factors that influence transfer of learning.
13. How can a teacher promote or maximize the percentage of transfer ability in his students? State the importance of transfer in education.
14. What is mastery learning? Discuss the steps and essential conditions of mastery learning.
15. Is mastery learning needed in our educational system? If so, why and at what stage of education? Explain.
16. What do you mean by problem solving? How can the teacher develop problem solving behaviour among children?
17. When does problem solving method fail? Give specific examples to illustrate your answer.
18. Define problem solving? Describe the various steps of teaching through problem-solving.
19. How does the problem solving method contribute to the development of mental skills, concepts and attitudes? In what way does it affect the 'personality development' of students and teachers.
20. Write short notes :
    (i) Main-tenets of Lewin's theory
    (ii) Laws of learning
    (iii) Conditioning

(iv) Learning Curve
(v) Schedules of reinforcement
(vi) Learning and Maturation

References

Ausubel, D. (1963) : *The psychology of meaningful verbal learning,* Grune and Stratton, New York.

Bandura, A. (1977) : *Social Learning Theory*, Englewood Cliffs, Prentice-Hall, N.J.

Biggie, M.L. (1967): *Learning Theories for Teachers*, Universal Book Delhi.

Biggie, M.L. and Hunt, M.P. (1968) : *Psychological Foundations of Education*, Harper and Row, New York,

Bower, G.H. and Hilgard, E.R. (1986) : *Theories of Learning*, Prentice-Hall of India, New Delhi.

Block, J.H. (1971) : *Mastery Learning,* Holt, Rinehart and Winston, New York.

Crow, L.D. and Crow, A. (1973) : *Educational Psychology*, Eurasic Publishing House, New Delhi.

Ellis, H. (1965) : *Transfer of Learning,* Macmillan, New York

Ferester, C.B. and Skinner, B.F. (1957) : *Schedules of Reinforcement*, Appleton Century, New York.

Gagne, R.M. (1973): *The Conditions of Learning,* Rinehart and Winston, New York.

Guthrie, E.R. (1952) : *The Psychology of Learning*, Harper and Row, New York.

Hilgard, E.O. (1976) : *Theories of Learning*, Appleton-Century Crofts, New York.

Kingsley, H.L. and Carry, R. (1957) : *The Nature and Conditions of Learning*, Prentice Hall, New Jersey.

Klausmeier, H.J. (1961) : *Learning and Human Abilities*, Harper and Row, New York.

Logan, F.A. (1970) : *Fundamentals of Learning and Motivation*, Duluque Brown, Iowa

Mayer, R.E. (1987) : *Educational Psychology*, Little and Brown Company Canada.

Murphy, G. (1968) : An Introduction to Psychology, in *Education*, University Book Stall, Delhi.

Pavlov, I.P. (1957) : *Experimental Psychology*, International Pub. New York.

Skinner, B.F. (1974) : *About Behaviourism,* Knopf, New York.

Smith, H.P. (1962) : *Psychology in Teaching*, Prentice Hall, New Jersey.

Sorenson, H. (1948) : *Psychology of Education*, McGraw Hill, New York.

Spence, K.W. (1956) : *Behaviour theory* and conditioning, Yale University Press, New Haven.

Thorndike, E.L (1931) : *Human Learning*, MIT Press, New York

Watson, J.B (1924) : *Behaviourism*, Norton, New York

INTELLIGENCE

Introduction

To define the word intelligence is a very difficult task. But the psychologists have defined it according to their own ways and there is great difference among them regarding the meaning of intelligence. It is thus clear that there is no agreement about the definition of intelligence. It is also a common fact that teacher has to meet variety of students in the classroom and has to adjust his/her teaching accordingly. Unless he/she is aware of the term intelligence the teaching-learning process would be baseless. Therefore, it is necessary for him/her to know about the word intelligence and its measurement for better, efficient and effective classroom transaction. Let us now discuss some of the definitions of intelligence.

Definition/Meaning of Intelligence

The term intelligence means 'intellect' and 'understanding'. Generally speaking, 'alertness' with regards to the actual situation of life is an index of intelligence. From the layman point of view intelligence means common sense or application part of knowledge. Intelligence is generally guessed from the way a person appears to understand a fact or a group of facts, and the manner in which he/she responds to those facts. But in ancient India our great rishis called it viveka or 'Vivekatmaka Budhi'.

As far as possible the definitions of intelligence is grouped under the following categories. These are as follows:

1. *Intelligence Means Ability to Adjust*

The following psychologists are strong supporters of this category of definition.

(a) Stern: Intelligence is the general capacity of an individual consciously to adjust his thinking to new requirements. It is the general mental adaptability to new problems and conditions of life or the ability to adjust oneself to a new situation.
(b) Ebinghous: Intelligence is the capacity to integrate the things.
(c) Ross: Intelligence means conscious adaptation to new situation.
(d) Wells : Intelligence is the property of recombining our behaviour pattern so as to act better in a novel situation.
(e) Burt: Intelligence is the capacity of flexible adjustment.
(f) Colvin: Intelligence as ability to adjust to environment.

In addition to the above the other psychologists like Spencer, William James and McDougall, etc., are also the supporters, belonging to this group.

II. *Intelligence Means Ability to Learn*

The second group of psychologists emphasise on ability to learn. The following are the psychologists who support the above definitions.

(a) Woodworth has defined intelligence 'as intellect put to use'. It is the use of intellectual abilities for handling a situation or accomplishing any task. It is the capacity to acquire capacity or it is an indicator of the ability to cope successfully with novel situations.
(b) Thorndike has defined Intelligence as the power of making good responses from the point of view of truth and fact or it may be defined as the ability to make profitable use of past experiences or intelligence is the ability of learning.
(c) Buckingham defined intelligence is the ability to

learn.

III. *Intelligence Means Ability to Carry on Abstract Thinking*

The following are the psychologists who strongly advocated the meaning of intelligence as follows:

(a) Terman: He defined intelligence as the ability to carry on abstract thinking or the ability to think abstractly.
(b) Spearman: Intelligence is the analytic and synthetic ability of mind.
(c) Binet: Intelligence is a capacity to think well, to judge well and to be self-critical.
(d) Burt: Intelligence is ability to judge well, to comprehend well and to reason well.

In addition to the above large number of psychologists have also defined intelligence according to their own way. These are the following:

I. Wagnon: Intelligence means the capacity to learn and adjust to relatively new and changing conditions.
II. Piaget: Intelligence is the ability to adapt to one's surroundings.
III. Peterson: Intelligence is a mechanical means for adjustment and control.
IV. Pintner: Intelligence is the capacity of the individual to adapt himself adequately to relatively new situations of life.
V. Galton: Intelligence is the power of recognition and hearing.
VI. Stout: Intelligence is the power of attention.
VII. Ausubel and Robinson: Intelligence refers to a general level of cognitive functioning as reflective in the ability to understand ideas and to utilise abstract symbols in the solution of intellectual problems.
VIII. Heim: Intelligent activity consists of grasping the essentials in a given situation and responding appropriately to them.
IX. Hollingworth: An intelligent person learns how to do and how to get what is wanted.
X. Rex: Intelligence is the ability to discover relevant qualities and relation of the objects and ideas that are before us and provide other ideas.

All the above mentioned definitions convey the meaning of intelligence only in one aspect or the other rather than in global manner. Hence we are in need of comprehensive and modern definition of intelligence.

IV. *Comprehensive and Modern Definition of Intelligence*

In view of the lacunae in the various definitions, the following psychologists have suggested the comprehensive and global ideas on intelligence.

(a) David Wechsler defined Intelligence as the aggregate or global capacity of an individual to act purposefully, to think rationally and to deal effectively with his environment. In his definition he has given emphasis on three aspects, i.e., purposeful activities, rational thinking and effective dealings of an individual to consider intelligence.

(b) Stoddard defined Intelligence is the ability to undertake activities that are characterized by difficulty, complexity, abstractness, economy, adaptiveness to a goal, social value, emergence of originals and to maintain such activities under the condition that demand a concentration of energy, and a resistance to emotional forces. If we analyse the attributes of intelligence given by Stoddard the nature of intelligence will be very clear. The attributes are the following:

1. *Degree of difficulty:*

This refers to the degree of difficulty of a task to be performed by a person. A person performing tasks at a higher level is said to be more intelligent or an intelligent person is able to solve problems of greater difficulty level in comparison to one who is less intelligent.

2. *Complexity:*

This refers to the varieties of tasks at a given level of difficulty, which can be successfully completed by a person. A person performing several different kinds of tasks in a given difficulty level is more intelligent than a person performing fewer tasks.

3. *Abstractness:*

This refers to performing task particularly during analysis and interpretation with the use of symbols, number, diagrams, formulas and words, etc. An intelligent person can more intelligently use symbols and all the above in analysing situations and interpreting facts.

4. *Economy:*

This refers to economy of time or works with accuracy and speed. An individual performing mental tasks more rapidly than another individual is more intelligent.

5. *Adaptivess to goal:*

This refers to directing action towards a well defined goal. An intelligent individual has clear cut goal or behaviour is goal directed. It is purposive and quite distinct from trial and error action.

6. *Social Value:*

This indicates that an intelligent act is that act which is socially acceptable in nature and it should be group acceptability rather than profitability. It has some bearing, meaning and value to the society.

7. *Emergence of Originals:*

The emergence of originals as an attribute of intelligence suggests that intelligent persons have the ability to create something new; i.e., they are creative and divergent thinking. They are the authors of new ideas.

8. Resistance to emotional forces:

The intelligent person is emotionally controlled and balanced. This non intellectual aspect of behaviour must be found out in a superlative degree in intelligent person than the ordinary being. Thus it can be summarised that intelligence is the ability to deal with abstractions, ability to deal with problems, ability to learn, ability to withstand stress and distraction, ability a person has to respond effectively to the environment, the cummulative set of competencies an individual has acquired through interaction with an environment over a period of time, an ability of a person who chooses to measure on an intelligent test, the mental capacity or energy available with an individual at a particular time in a particular situation, capacity helps him in the task of theoretical as well as practical manipulation of things, objects or events present in his environment in order to adapt to or face new challenges and problems of life as successfully as possible and leading a happy and well contented life.

Nature of Intelligence

It is not an easy task to depict the nature of intelligence. But modern psychologists, in order to determine the nature of intelligence, have put forward various definitions to understand its meaning, discussing various theories explaining its structure in terms of the several constituents and factors, and identifying the numerous other aspects and characteristics related to intelligence and its functioning. The meaning and theories have already been covered which indicates the nature of intelligence. Let us now discuss the other view points regarding the nature of intelligence.

(1) The distribution of intelligence is not equal among all human beings. It is distributed according to the law of normal probability curve or by a definite principle which states that the majority of people are at the average, a very few individuals possess a high degree or bright and a very few possess dull.

(2) Wide individual differences exist among individuals with regard to intelligence. The assessment of intelligence by various tests has given enough ideas that not only intelligence vary from individual to individual but also it varies in the same individual from age to age and situation to situation.

(3) The growth of intelligence is orderly and cummulative and is not a specific trait of the individual. It is a composite of many abilities.

(4) Intelligence is an inborn personal quality of an individual. Although it is transmitted genetically yet environment has tremendous influence on it. It has now been established that the bright and the dull can be found in any race, caste or culture group.

(5) The study of intelligence and the sexes have proved that there is no significant difference between male and female. So it can be stated that difference in sex does not contribute towards difference in intelligence.

(6) The idea that intelligence continues to grow throughout life is not strictly true. Studies have proved that intellectual development is very rapid during infancy and the pre-school years and then gradually slow down but the growth of a person's intelligence reaches its maximum sometime between the age of 16 and 20 years after which the vertical growth of intelligence almost ceases. However, horizontal growth, i,e., achievement, accumulation of knowledge and acquisition of skills, etc., may continue throughout an individual's life.

(7) Intelligence helps a man to solve even complicated and comprehensive problems and situations. The study of the development of the intelligence has proved that if a child is brought up in a healthy and proper environment, then his I.Q. shall be more than a child brought up in a different environment.

Types of Intelligence

Basically the term intelligence has been classified into three groups. They are as follows:

(a) *The Abstract Intelligence*

Abstract intelligence refers to the ability to understand and deal with symbols—words, numbers, formulas and diagrams. It means the capacity to solve problems presented in the above form. This type of intelligence can be predicted by testing level of aspiration, capacity to do various types of work and his special interest and speed of work. Generally the lawyers, physicians, literary men, students, statesmen, businessmen and professionals possess abstract intelligence on high degree.

(b) *The Concrete/Mechanical/Motor Intelligence*

This intelligence refers to the ability to deal readily and effectively with Machines and Mechanical contrivances or the ability of an individual to concrete situations and to react to them adequately. The motor intelligence is more related to physical education, i.e., the activities of games and sports. Thus the person who is engaged in the work of engineering, highly trained persons of mechanic and industry belong to this group of intellectuals.

(c) The Social Intelligence

The person who is able to deal effectively with the people and maintain good social situations possess more social intelligence. These people make friendship easily and understand human relations. The people like salesman, diplomat and politician, etc., belong to this category.

Though there is no specific demarcation of distributing intelligence yet it can be said that some may be more in abstract and others may be mechanical and social intelligence. If a person is very good in abstract intelligence may not be equally fruitful in mechanical work but may be better than average and vice versa.

Characteristics and Distribution of Intelligence

(a) Characteristics of the Intelligence

The following are the signs of an intelligent person:

1. An intelligent person is capable of facing difficult circumstances, problems and complicated situations very effectively.
2. Intelligence helps a man in learning new things, solve problems and adjust effectively in the environment.
3. Due to intellect an individual keeps himself neat and clean and able to maintain it throughout his/her life.
4. The study of development of intelligence has proved that both heredity and environment play a vital role for the formation of intelligence.
5. Intelligence is orderly and cummulative but the development ceases at the end of adolescence.
6. An intelligent person attends to the tasks assigned to him very positively.
7. It is true that an intelligent person is a very clever person and tries to manage the affairs very effectively.
8. An intelligent person knows how to behave in a particular situation whereas it is difficult for others.
9. An intelligent person has sense of discrimination and capacity to proceed in the right direction.
10. An intelligent person possesses the capacity of rational, original, creative and constructive thinking which are essential ingredients/components of a civilized person.

(b) *Distribution of Intelligence*

Various attempts have been made to classify intelligence according to the IQ. Table 7.1 illustrates the relationship between I.Q. and degree of brightness on the basis of the experiments of Terman and Merril.

When analysis is done it is found out that Idiot mental age is not exceeding 5 and their I.Q. is up to 25. The mental age of the Imbecile again is about 8 and their I.Q varies from 25 to 50. Thirdly, the Moran is only 11 in mental age and from 50 to 70 in I.Q. Further it can be said that idiot is not capable of carrying on even the elementary functions of self preservation like feeding, dressing, bathing himself and avoiding the common danger of life. The Imbecile can be taught the above function but not capable of the higher process of thinking. The moran can be trained and receive education if efforts are made. The dull can rise up to the level of a graduate by dint of hard-work and perseverance whereas the normal can carry on all intelligence functions. Similarly the bright, normal and superior can do intelligence work with greater case and facilities. At the end the near genius very superior and the genius show originality and creativity in every intelligent work that they do.

TABLE 7.I

Sl. No.	*I.Q.*	*Classification of Intelligence*	*Percentage in approximately*
1.	140 and above	Genius	2.5 %
2.	130 - 139	Very Superior	4.0 %
3.	120 - 129	Superior	6.0 %
4.	110 - 119	Above Average (bright)	15.0 %
5.	90 - 109	Normal or Average	45.0 %
6.	80 - 89	Below Average	15.0 %
7.	70 - 79	Dull or Borderline	6.0 %
8.	50 - 69	Feeble minded, moran (Educable)	4.0 %
9.	25 - 49	Imbecile (Trainable)	
10.	24 and below	Idiot (Untrainable)	2.5 %

Theories of Intelligence

The theories of intelligence propagated by psychologists from time to time have explained the meaning and nature of intelligence. Some of the important theories are present below.

(I) *The Monarchic Theory or Unitary Theory*

According to this theory intelligence is one power or energy which affects all the activities of the individual. The propounder like Johnson, Binet, Terman and Stern, etc., emphasized that intelligence consists of one factor which is universal to all activities of the individual or it is general ability of the individual that enables him to succeed in every sphere of life. The propounder are also of the view that a person who can perform one intellectual task very well, can also perform another task equally well.

In spite of all its advantages this theory fails to explain that all the mental abilities of a person cannot be explained as element of a single factor and, therefore, is not acceptable or to believe that the intelligence affects all the activities of the individuals equally is not true.

(II) *The Eclectic Theory or Two Factor Theory*

This theory was developed by Spearman. He was of the opinion that intelligence consists of two factors, i.e., General Intelligence 'g' and Specific Intelligence known as 's'. The first factor 'g' general mental ability is always the same for the same individual or present in all the intellectual exercises and common for all activities and the second factor 's' varies from task to task according to its nature. It is also noticed that different individuals differ both in their 'g' as well as 's' factors. He/She believed that 'g' is innate, omnipresent and varies with the individuals ability whereas 's' factor is acquired and differ from different actions. For example, an individuals performance in literature is partly due to his/her general intelligence and partly due to some specific aptitude for language, i.e., g+s, in mathematics his/her performance may be the result of g+s2, in drawing, may be due to g+s3 and in social sciences, i.e., g + s4, and so on. Thus the factor 'g' is present in all specific activities and the amount of 'g' and 's' factors required in an activity will depend upon its nature.

It is also further noticed that a person having more of 'g' and less of 's' fares well in life. Therefore, the amount of 'g' is required everywhere in life and depends on the amount of deposit in cerebral cortex.

Limitations

In spite of many advantages there are serious limitations of the two factor theory of intelligence. These are as follows:

1. Pears asserts that adequate experimental data in its favour is not available and consequently even Spearman's theory cannot be said to be universally acceptable.
2. Spearman theory was based on two factors but it was noticed that there are not only two but several factors like S_1, S_2, S_3, S_4 and so on.
3. Thomson has criticised Spearman for his statistical technique and inferences drawn from his results.

III. *Anarchic Theory or Multi-Factor Theory*

After discarding/criticising Spearman's two factor theory E.L. Thorndike, the famous psychologist propounded this multi factor theory of intelligence. This theory holds that intelligence is the means of undermined independent rudimentary elements or intelligence is the combination of numerous separate elements or the factors of intelligence are independent to each other. These are numerical reasoning, vocabulary, classification and sentence completion, etc. This theory believes that every task needs different abilities or a host of highly independent factors and there is nothing like general ability. Thorndike believes that if a person gets 60 marks in Mathematics and English it means there may be 2 or 3 factors are present and correlating to each other. He concluded that in every task a group of abilities are manifested and out of which few of them correlates because of their resemblances. Thus these common abilities may belong to certain faculty and clear that the intelligence is composed of highly particularised and independent faculties.

Lastly, Thorndike distinguished four attributes of intelligence. These are Level, Range, Area and Speed.

(a) *Level*: It refers to the difficulty of a task that can be solved. It means if a task arranged in a sequential order and the person attain the task up to a certain level indicates his/her degree of intelligence.

(b) *Range*: It means the total number of situations at each level to which the individual is able to respond indicates his/her intelligence.

(c) *Area*: It means the total number of situations at each level to which the individual is able to respond indicates his/her intelligence.

(d) *Speed*: It means the rapidity with which the individual can solve or respond to the test items.

Thus, to say about the theory of intelligence it can be interpreted that when we test a person we give him/her a certain number of task (area). these tasks vary in difficulty (level), there are certain number of items at each level of difficulty (range) and they respond in a given time frame (speed). This is all about the ideas of Thorndike on intelligence.

IV. *Group Factor Theory*

This theory was propounded/advocated by L.L. Thurstone and his associates after criticising the theories of Spearman and Thorndike. According to this theory intelligence is composed of a group of primary mental abilities. Each of these abilities is relatively independent of the other. But there are factors which are common to certain activities comprising a group and different from others. Thus this theory is known as the Primary Mental Abilities or the Group Factor Theory of Intelligence.

Thurstone conducted number of experiments and came to the conclusion after factor analysis that intelligence is made up of the following seven primary mental abilities. These are as follows:

1. *Verbal comprehension*: It means the ability to use words and ideas in planning, thinking and communication.
2. *Numerical factor*: It is concerned with the ability to do numerical calculations rapidly and accurately.
3. *Visual or Spatial factor*: It indicates the ability to visualize and manipulate an object imaginatively in space.
4. *Perceptual Ability*: It reveals the ability to perceive objects accurately and speedily.
5. *Reasoning* : It means the ability to draw inferences or conclusions and to make use of generalized results described in symbols and discover rule or principle.
6. *Word fluency*: It is the capacity to express himself/herself in words about an object or things at a rapid rate.
7. *Memory*: It means the ability to recall and associate previously learned items effectively or memorise quickly.

Later on another dimension, i.e., problem solving ability factor was incorporated. It means the ability to solve problems with independent efforts.

But this theory was also criticised in the sense that it fails to give weightage to the common factor which is vital in the formation of mental abilities.

V. *Sampling or Oligarchic Theory*

This theory was developed by Thomson, a British Psychologist. According to this theory the mind is made up of several independent bond/components or intellectual abilities belonging to certain groups and independent from each other but there is close relationship between the abilities belonging to the same group and there is little correlation between the abilities belonging to the other groups. From this it can be said that cognitive abilities are manifestations not of a single faculty but of a few main intellectual powers or group of abilities. This means that a student of class VII may secure and does fairly well in one group of knowledge, e.g., in mathematics but may not be equally intelligent in the other group of knowledge, e.g., English or vice-versa. It means in related subjects he/she does well but fails in unrelated subjects.

Thus the individual has got number of mental abilities. When he/she has to perform certain type of work he/she makes sampling of abilities and samples out certain important abilities out of the whole world of abilities. Because of the selection of abilities through sampling this theory is called sampling theory of intelligence.

VI. *Hierarchical Theory of Intelligence*

P.E. Vernon, a British Psychologist, has suggested a hierarchical structure of intelligence. Vernon compares the mind to a genealogical tree, where the 'g' factor is the most prominent component, i.e., an overall factor measured through intelligence tests or it accounts for the greatest proportion of differences in abilities. Under 'g' we have two major group factors, termed as Ved, i.e. (verbal numerical-education factor) and KM, i.e. (spatial-mechanical-perceptual-practical and physical factor). These two major factors can be divided into minor group factors and ultimately these minor factors may be further sub-divided into various specific factors related with minute specific mental abilities.

The following figure will give the hierarchical structure of human intelligence.

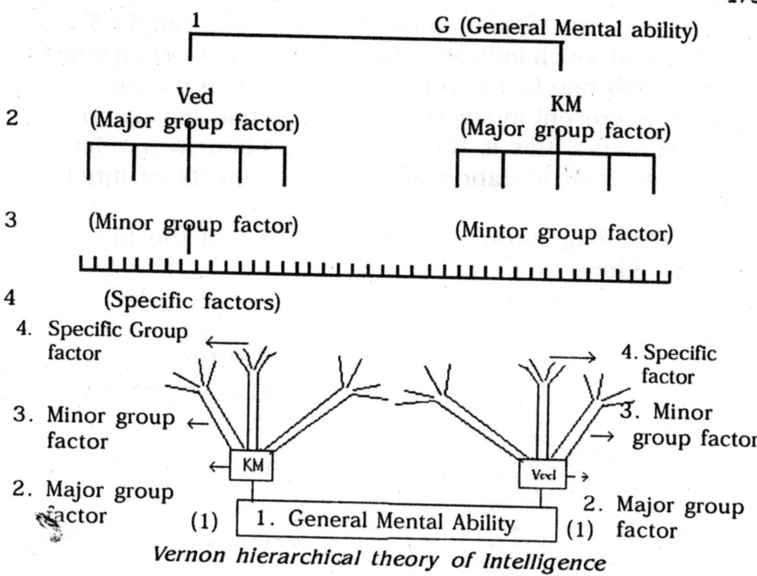

Vernon hierarchical theory of Intelligence

VII. *Guilford Theory of Intelligence*

This theory of intelligence is known as three dimensional theory or the Structure of Intellect Model. The propounder of this theory was J.P. Guilford and his associates while working in the psychological laboratory at the University of Southern California in U.S.A. This theory is the result of factor analytical research studies conducted by them which involved a number of intelligence tests.

Guilford and his associates concluded that every intellectual activity is based on three basic parameters and these are operation, content and products. Operationally operation means the act of thinking; content means the subject matter or areas in which we think and products means the ideas in which we arrived at conclusions or come up with.

The following are the details of intellectual activity.

I. *Operation*: Under this dimension there are five kinds of operation, namely, cognition, memory, divergent thinking, convergent thinking and evaluation.

II. *Content*: Similarly there are five kinds of content, i.e., visual or figural, audiotory, symbolic, semantic and behavioural.

III. *Products*: Lastly there are six types of products, viz., units, classes, relations, systems, transformations and implications.

Thus, the maximum number of factors can be 5 × 6 × 5 = 150 in all which indicates the mental process of an individual and at least one factor from each category of the three factors has to be present in any specific intellectual activity on mental task. However, this is the most comprehensive model which takes into consideration all possible aspects of intellectual activity.

The diagrammatical representation of the SI model is shown below:

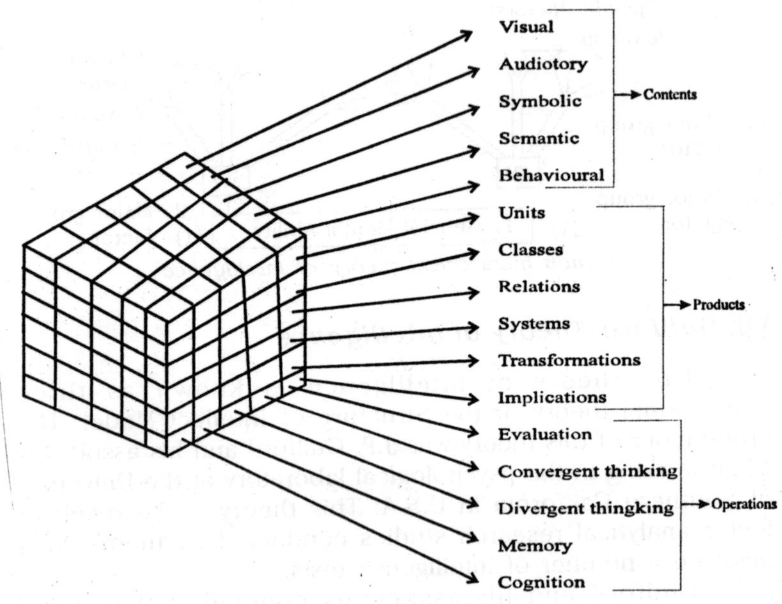

Structure of Intellect Model

Educational significance

1. It is comprehensive
2. It is the only theory which considers creativity (divergent thinking) along with convergent thinking (intelligence) in the same model.
3. It applies factor analysis technique identification of factors or common abilities which constitute one's intelligence.
4. When some students with adequate knowledge fail to learn this SI model can provide an academically acceptable method by dealing with the problem.
5. This theory can look into three different angles i.e., developmental, genetic and clinical point of view

GUILFORD 16 CATEGORIES OF INTELLIGENCE

Category	*Nature of the category*	*Examples of Possible test items*
I. Content		
1. Visual	Information in visual form	Colour, shape, texture, size, continuity, dimensionality
2. Auditory	Information in auditory form	Music tones, phone calls, discrimination of spoken words, melodies
3. Symbolic	Information in the form of signs, the elements have no significance by themselves	Letters, numbers, codes, etc.
4. Semantic	information in the form of meaning	Words commonly attached to verbal thinking and communication
5. Behavioural	Non verbal information involved in human interactions, awareness of other people and self.	Interpret moods, states, and traits of oneself and others.
II. Operation		
6. Cognition	Awareness, immediate discovery, recognition of information in various forms, comprehension	Recognition of stimuli that are incomplete (e.g., mutilated words or pictures), vocabulary words
7. Memory	Recognition and/or recall of previous stimuli in various forms and relations.	Free recall, memory span, test for numbers.
8. Divergent production	Generation of information from given information emphasis on variety and quantity	Generate ideas, brain storm, flexibility and fluncy
9. Convergent production	Generation of information from given information—emphasis on one solution	Relate diverse objects where a specific answer is required (In what way are a cat and dog alike)

Category	*Nature of the category*	*Examples of Possible test items*
10. Evaluation	A process of comparing a product of information with known information	Must answer a "which", "is" or "does" question.
III. Product		
11. Units	Things, segregated wholes, figures on grounds or "Chunks"	The student produces a product such as filling in multicated words, filling in incomplete words, defining vocabulary words, or identifying a characteristic of a person.
12. Classes	Set of objects with one or more common properties	Student identifies the common attribute between two or more stimuli
13. Relations	Some kind of connection between two things	Student identifies the relational nature of two or more stimuli, e.g., greater than analogies, serial order, etc.
14. Systems	Patterns or organizations of interdependent or interacting parts	Student identifies the rule to find the solution to problem, e.g., which letter comes next A, C, E—What is the rule
15. Transformations	Changes, revisions, modifications from one state to another	How would something look if it were changed ? what would something be like if ? How can the purpose of an object be changed to get a new result
16. Implications	Something expected, anticipated or predicted from given information	The ability to plan ahead or predict what will most likely come next.

where SI factorial abilities play an important role in human life.

Thus Guilford suggests that Intelligence consists of 150 discrete abilities. These abilities result from an interaction among the types of stimuli in the environment (content), the types of mental processes used to respond to the stimuli (operations) and the resulting response (product).

VII. *Piaget's Stages of Cognitive Intellectual Development and Its Educational Implications:*

Jean Piaget, a Swiss Psychologist/Biologist was one of the most remarkable figures in contemporary behavioural science and had produced the world's most comprehensive theory of cognitive development. According to Piaget, there are four recognizable stages of cognitive development or pattern of intellectual development. These are as follows:

Sl. No.	*Stage*	*Period*	*Characteristics*
1.	Sensori-Motor Stage	(0-2 years)	Basic perceptual—motor development, infant begins motoric interaction with the environment, begins to manipulate the environment.
2.	Pre-operational (a) Preconceptual (b) Intuitive phase	(2-7 years) (2-4 years) (4-7) years)	Begins to use language in an egocentric manner, very self-centred intellectually, in latter part of this stage child can reach intellectual conclusions, but the conclusions are based on feeling perceptual judgements: not based on a conceptual system of thought.
3.	Concrete operations	(7-11 yrs)	Uses language system in a reliable although in concrete fashion; understands concrete concepts such as A>B>C :A> (or A+B = B + A); begins to approach problems systematically, acquires conservational skills (knowledge that the amount of something does not change just because the outside appearance, shape, or length changes)
4.	Formal Operations	(11+ years)	Can think abstractly, uses hypothetical-deductive reasoning,

{cont.}.....

generalizes, can solve problems systematically, understands implications of past and future.

Thus in the sensori motor stage (0-2 years) much of the basic practical knowledge needed for the foundation of complex thought is formed. During the pre-operational stage (2-7 years) the beginning of language and the reconstruction of the sensory motor experiences takes place. Images also develop during this stage. It is during the concrete operational stage of development (7-11 years) that the child begins to solve concrete problems, dealing with objects by using concrete mental operations. In this stage the child develops the ability to solve most of the famous conservation tasks (the principle that the number, volume, amount, weight and mass of objects are not changed regardless of the shape or appearance of an object). The child in the concrete stage of development, however, cannot solve abstract problems requiring hypothetical-deducting mental operations. The child is also not very systematic in solving problems. As the child moves into the fourth stage of development (formal operations—about 11 years of age), the child begins to use hypothetical-deductive reasoning in a systematic fashion, loses the egocentric perspective of viewing the world, and comes to understand fully the implications of the past and the future.

Let us now discuss the stages of development in detail:

I. *Sensory-Motor Period*

Piagets description of cognitive growth begins with the sensori-motor period, lasting roughly from age zero to two. According to him, the new born infant does not perceive or represent the world in the same way that adults do. During this period, the child tends to represent the world in terms of motor behaviour or deals directly with objects because he lacks language. This stage is limited to direct sensory and motor interactions with the environment.

This sensory motor period is sub-divided into six stages through which progressively complex pattern of intellectual behaviour appears. The stages are reflex (0-1 month), the primary circular reaction (1-4 months), secondary circular reaction (4-8 months), co-ordination of secondary circular reaction (8-12 months), tertiary trial and error circular reaction

(12-18 months), and mental combinations (18-24 months). This stage help the child to experience or see the object in his/her mind by making its mental image. After that the stage of pre-operation begins with the child.

II. *Pre-Operational Period*

This stage is a period of about 2 to 7 years. Here, the child begins to replace direct action in the form of sensory or motor exploration with symbols. The learning of the language provides him with a good tool for thinking and able to talk and form simple concepts.

This stage is of two parts, i.e., the pre-conceptual stage (2-4 years) and the intuitive phase (4-7 years). During the first phase the child does not understand the nature of classes and class memberships. He does not have the ability to understand the dimensionality of an object. For example—he/she takes a 'red pen' as 'red pen' and does not know that 'red' is one of the columns and 'pen' is one type of article used for writing. This period is extremely concrete and strikingly egocentric.

But during second phase, i.e., the intuitive stage theme is decrease of gross absurdity in thinking and reasoning. The child conceptualises more and groups objects by similarity. If two rows have equal number of coins then he/she can illustrate but if line is different but coins are same then the child says these are different.

The speech of the child is ego-centric from ages 2 to 4 years but it is found socialised between ages 4 to 7 years. Logical thought takes place. But as a whole it can be said that the child at this stage fails to realize that the amount or quantity of a material (example, water), etc., does not change with the change in the shape or appearance of its container. Thus the concept of the conservation of numbers, etc., is not yet developed in the child and his/her thinking at this stage is characterized as illogical and full of contradictions.

III. *Concrete Operational Stage (7 to 11 years)*

This stage covers the period from 7 to 11 years. Reasoning process becomes logical in relation to objects or persons and understand transformation. It is not the final stage in thought development because the child is still restricted to concrete thinking.

Piaget believes that the child after age seven is able to classify objects on the basis of similarities and classify ideas into a logical system. He develops ideas and thinks of a set of red objects even in the absence of any object in front of him. This is called internalization of a concept. Even two kinds of classes can simultaneously be thought of and comparison can be made. Sensation is another process which is observed during this phase. Piaget believes that in the concrete operational stage the child has the ability to generalise and reaches a satisfactory level in terms of intellectual development because of his thinking becoming quite systematic and logical. Thus, it can be said that it is a pre-preparation for the final stage of formal operations mainly concerned with abstractions.

IV. *Formal Operation Stage (12+ and above)*

This is a period of final form and the child's cognitive structure reaches at maturity. He applies formal logic to solve his problems and approaches them more systematically. He/She comes to acquire ideas of social justice and proper modes of social interaction. He is liberated from the bonds of the concrete, i.e, the child takes a rational outlook towards problems. In fact Piaget was of the opinion that the thought processes and the intellectual functioning of a child at the formal operational period reflect the beginning of the most advanced stage in the functioning of his cognitive system. It provides a ladder to reach the limits of a person's intellectual development and actualize his potentiality to the maximum in the available circumstances. Thus after the expiry of the formal operation stage (say up to 15+ or so) the child may reach full intellectual potential or attain mental maturity with respect to the development of his cognitive abilities.

Educational Implications of Piaget's theory :

1. Children should be active. They learn best when actively exploring their environment.
2. Children should not be pushed or accelerated into learning material beyond their level of development. The child will be incapable of accommodating to the experience.
3. Activities selected by the children act as a aid in their cognitive growth. Thus in primary classes it should be strengthed.
4. Teachers should arrange their classroom environments in such a manner that it facilitates cognitive development and to encourage active exploring.

5. While interacting with a child, the teacher should attempt to understand the child's cognitive level of development by applying the 'clinical interview' technique to determine what the child believes is true.
6. Piaget's general theory would suggest that the open education or free-school format might be essentially fruitful (Weber, 1971).
7. Children should be provided a great deal of direct first hand experience before they can be expected to cope with abstract ideas and concepts. This theory also stress the importance of readiness.
8. Children should be provided facilities to participate in group discussion for enhancement of creative thinking.

The Concept of CA, MA, BA and IQ

It is a matter of fact that the function of psychological tests is to measure individual differences. But the ideas of intelligence test was first mooted by the French Psychologist, Alfred Binet to measure intelligence and before that attempts were made to measure intelligence through unscientific or crude manner. Now intelligence test is used in a variety of situations and provides a single score such as I.Q. indicating individuals general intellectual level.

Before we make an attempt to assess the intelligence of an individual the following basic concepts must be understood. These are as follows.

(1) *Chronological Age:*

It refers to the actual age of an individual or his/her date of birth. It is symbolically called as CA.

(2) *Mental Age*

The concept of Mental age was introduced by Alfred Binet in the year 1908. MA merely indicates the level of development which a child has reached at a given age. It shows the mental level but it does not tell us how bright the child is. It gives us an idea whether the child is advanced or retarded or average when compared to normal children of his/her age.

The concept of MA has made the interpretation of intelligence easier. If the MA of a child is equal to his chronological age then he is normal. When he is greater than the CA, he is advanced and less than the CA is retarded. It is otherwise called the mental maturity achieved by the child at some particular age or MA is a kind of score which gives an idea of about the intellectual development of the child. Maximum mental age of a person is 19 or 20. The procedure of calculation of mental age is as follows. A child's mental age is calculated by adding the basal age and the credits (in terms of months) obtained by him in subsequent levels.

Suppose a child takes a test of intelligence and there are six sub-tests in the test. Success in passing one sub-test means a credit of 2 months and passes all the six sub-tests means a credit of 12 months. Take for example a five year child and his success and credits earned at various levels are given below.

1. Passed all tasks at 5 years level - 5 years (Basal age)
2. Passed 4 out of 6 tasks at 6 years - 8 months credit level (4 x 2)
3. Passed 4 out of 6 tasks at 7 year - 4 months credit level (2 x 2)
4. Failed all tasks at 8 years level - 0 months credit

MA Total: 5 years 12 months = 6 years

Thus, the child MA would be 6 years though he is chronologically 5 years old. Thus mental age = basal age + partial credit or fractional credit for the items up to the terminal age.

3. *Basal Age*

Basal age is that age of the child where he or she can solve all questions in a given test. It is the basal age which helps in the calculation of mental age. Suppose a child is 5 year age (CA). He solves all questions in a given test meant for a child of 6 and 7 years and solves only one question out of 6 questions in a test of 8 years and unable to solve any of the questions of 9 years. Thus his basal age is 7 years 2 months though his CA is 5 years.

4. *The Concept of I.Q.*

Intelligence Quotient is the ratio between mental age and chronological age multiplied by 100. Symbolically it is called I.Q. I.Q. is calculated with the formula, i.e.,

$I.Q. = \frac{MA}{CA} \times 100$. In the year 1916 Stern gave us this concept to know the degree of brightness or dullness. It is a method of defining relative intelligence because IQ is independent of the scores which he happens to make at a particular age.

It has been observed by Terman in 1916 revision test that individual mental age increases along with his chronological age up to 16 years. Though the CA goes on increasing yet for the purpose of calculation of IQ, chronological age may be taken as 16 years. Again in the 1937 scale, Terman assumed that for computing IQ, the CA for all adults was taken as 16. Since mental growth continues beyond the age 16, the highest chronological age included in the IQ tables is 18, in the 1960 scales. Accordingly the CA of any adult taking the test is taken as 18 for computing the IQ. Thus Intelligence Quotient in fact a ratio of the physical and the mental age of the child or ratio of mental growth or the rate of mental growth of a child.

Limitations of I.Q.

1. IQ s on one test are not comparable to those obtained on another test.
2. IQ in case of adults are only hypothetical and are open to doubt.
3. IQ. tells the rate of maturity but two children having an I.Q. of 120, may not be equally mature.
4. The difference between an I.Q. of 70 and 80 is not the same as the difference between an I.Q. of 110 and 120.

Measurement of Intelligence

Intelligence being only a concept or an abstraction rather than a substance, it cannot be measured in physical units like a length of cloth or temperature of the body. When we measure an individuals intelligence by means of an intelligence test, we try to interpret his score in terms of the norms set (group of performance) by the author of the test. A piece of cloth may be measured in absolute terms whereas relative measurement or assessment has to be resorted to in the case of intelligence.

Intelligence test may be individual or group test. If one individual is tested at a time is called individual and a group of individuals tested is called group tests. On the basis of their form—intelligence test may be verbal or language test and non-verbal or non-language tests. Let us now discuss about the different types of test to assess the intelligence.

A. Verbal or Language Test

A verbal test of intelligence is that test where reading and writing are involved. Here the subjects make use of language in which the instructions are given in words, written, oral or both, or the ability to read, write or understand words. The test content is loaded with verbal material of varieties of the items which are as follows.

(a) *Vocabulary*: Here the subject is to give the meanings of words or phrases like what is the difference between shop and soap?

(b) *Memory* : Here the subject's immediate and long term memory is judged by asking recall and recognition type of items. For example, the subject is asked to tell the full name of teachers who had taught him in different subjects and different classes.

(c) *Comprehension* : By means of these, the subject's practical judgement and common sense is judged. Example—Why are shoes made of leather ?

(d) *Information test*: Here the subjects knowledge about the things around him is judged, i.e., where is the Taj Mahal situated?

(e) *Reasoning test*: Here the subject knowledge regarding arithmetic reasoning, analogies, analysis—synthesis, inductive-deductive and common sense questions, etc., are asked. For example, How may apples can you buy for 10 rupees if one apple cost 50 paise. Secondly, complete the series like 1, 2, 4, 7, 11,16, 22, 29, ..., etc.

(f) *Digit forward and backward* : Here the subject is asked to repeat 3 to 9 digits presented to him. He may be asked to repeat them backward.

(g) *Similarities and dissimilarities*: Here the subject is asked to point out his ability of similarities and dissimilarities between two or more concepts or objects or in what ways the two things are alike, e.g., air and water, and orange and banana.

Thus it can be said that in verbal test—language is used adequately and examine the reasoning power, power of comparing and contrasting, sense of direction, ability in numerals and language. In case of verbal individual intelligence test the following test like Binet and Simon test, Terman and Merrill scale and in case of verbal group intelligence tests the test like Army Alpha (for literate) and Beta test (for illiterates), S.S. Jalota's test of general mental ability, etc., are used.

Limitations of Verbal Intelligence Test

The difficulties of the verbal group intelligence tests are fundamentally as follows.

1. It is difficult to judge whether the examinee is extending his full cooperation or not.
2. It is difficult to determine whether the physical and emotional balance of the examinee is perfect or disturbed.
3. It is difficult to ascertain whether examinee is feeling comfortable and free to respond or restrain.
4. It is difficult to check cheating and testify whether the person has written the answer himself or copied it from his neighbour.

B. Non-Verbal Intelligence Tests

Verbal nature of intelligence tests, though of great advantage in general, turns out to be great handicap in certain cases. A child who has a serious speech defect or whose language development is retarded will be handicapped on such tests. In this case non-verbal test is used.

In non-verbal test of intelligence, paper and pencil are used rather than language. This test otherwise known as non-language test or paper pencil test or visual test or culture free test. Items of non-verbal tests are in the form of pictures and diagrams. One example of the non-verbal tests is the performance intelligence tests. The main features of these test are the following:

(a) The contents of the tests are in the form of material objects.
(b) What is required of the subject is conveyed by the tester through oral instructions or by pantomime and signs.
(c) The subject responses are assessed in terms of how he reacts or what he does rather than what he says or writes.
(d) This test is basically individual in nature.

The difference between performance tests (used for an individual) and non-verbal tests (used for a group) is one of degree as far as their non-verbal nature is concerned. The individual performance test require the manipulation by the subject of concrete objects or materials, supplied in the test. The responses are purely motor in character and seldom require the use of paper and pencil by the testee whereas the test material in the non-verbal tests, used for group testing, is provided in booklets and requires the use of a pencil by the testee.

The types of items included in such test are: figure analogies, figure classification, following directions and reverse drawings, etc. What the subject is required to do is explained clearly by the examiner usually through demonstrations so as to make the least possible use of language. Some examples of such tests are: Army beta test, the Cattell culture-fair intelligence test, Raven's progressive matrices test, and Jenkin's non-verbal group test of intelligence, etc.

Advantages of Non-verbal group intelligence tests

1. The comparison between different human groups of various languages and culture can be possible.
2. The abilities of illiterate persons are assessed and possibilities of their learning are known.
3. Intelligence testing in children can be possible because the linguistic ability is very low in them.

C. *Performance Test of Intelligence*

In a performance test, the items are usually presented in a concrete form and the response is manual or based on Motor activity. Here the subject is to do something rather than to make a verbal response. Performance tests have been found useful particularly in testing intelligence of persons with language handicaps, feeble minded (blind, deaf and mutes), illiterates, foreigners and slightly retarded children.

Performance tests are different from non-verbal tests in the sense that in the latter writing is involved and there is very little motor activity. Performance test/scale includes the following 5 sub-tests. These are picture completion (subject is to point out the missing part of the picture), picture arrangement (the subject is asked to rearrange sets of cards containing picture in a way that the arrangement suggests a meaningful story), object assembly (the subject is asked to put together the cut-out objects), block-design (the subject is asked to produce a complex design by fitting together various cubes painted in different colours), and digit symbol (where the subject is asked to mention the digit symbol). Some of the widely used performance tests are Koh's Block Design test, Bhatia's performance test of Intelligence, Drever-Collins performance scale, Maze test, the Pinter-Patterson scale, Alexander's battery of performance tests, and Draw-a-man test, etc., are used.

Advantages of Performance Tests

1. When an individual has limited command of the language, he is handicapped and it is useful in such cases.
2. For the study of pre-school children, who have not begun reading and writing these are suitable tests.
3. These tests are useful for clinical purposes for testing feeble minded persons.

Uses of Intelligence Tests

The following are the important uses of intelligence test:

1. *Understand the Capability of a Child*

Intelligence tests are of valuable aid to the educationist as a means of diagnosis of the capacity or efficiency of pupils. The scores of intelligence test reveal the mental age of a child and indicates the readiness of a child for learning.

2. *Homogeneous Grouping*

A class consisting of students with widely different abilities, is difficult to handle. Thus homogeneous grouping of pupils can be done on the basis of intelligence test results.

3. *Purpose of Admission/Selection to Various Courses*

It has been known that success in school is to a great extent, correlated with intelligence. While admitting pupils it is desirable to consider their M.A. rather than C.A. Thus, it is an asset (intelligence test) and help the professionals and students to choose the right institutions and right courses.

4. *Identifying Gifted and Backward Children*

Intelligence tests help in classifying individuals according to their mental make up. On the basis of results the students can be named as gifted, backward and average, and accordingly educational opportunities can be provided.

5. *Educational and Vocational Guidance*

The results of intelligence tests help in providing educational, vocational and personal guidance to students by teachers and guidance personnel. It gives clue in guiding the students into those courses where they have some likelihood of being successful and suggesting a few other courses and careers. This test is also used as a screening device for selecting suitable candidates from among a large number of applicants and possibility of entering into an occupation in future.

6. *Use in Assessment for Promotion, Reporting to Parents and Degree of Responsibility*

The results of intelligence tests along with the achievement tests can be successfully used for promotion of students to the next higher grades and help in promotion of people in next higher post. Similarly intelligence test help the teacher to sent progress report to the parents about the mental ability and the achievement level of the students. Sometimes the teacher assigns responsibility, etc., on students on the basis of intelligence test, which is really a praiseworthy activity.

7. *Raising the Quality of Teaching*

Intelligence test help the teacher to plan his/her teaching-learning activities according to the needs of the child or what the child can learn and how quickly he/she can learn.

8. *Use in Research Work*

Intelligence tests are very much needed for research in the field of education. Mental measurement is a very important aspect in any study whether it aims at survey or comparison. Intelligence test help us to know the general level of intelligence of a particular country or race.

Limitations of Intelligence Test

1. Results of intelligence tests should not be considered final because sometimes it may not give accurate results. In such cases interpretation of intelligence of the individual becomes wrong.

2. Intelligence tests are constructed and standardised on a definite population. In such cases accurate results may not be predicted in another population.
3. Intelligence test becomes unreliable if accurate chronological age is not real.
4. Intelligence tests especially individual tests are too costly and teachers cannot make use of it.
5. Sometimes intelligence test by itself or in combination with others cannot measure the true psyche potential or mental functioning of an individual or the real cognitive ability of an individual.
6. Sometimes it is quite surprising and rather confusing when a child scores very high on one test and very low on another. This may be quite misleading.
7. The I.Q. scores of the testees are highly influenced by the conditions prevailing at the time the intelligence tests are administered.
8. There is every possibility of language difficulty, poor test questions and vague instructions, etc., in the intelligence test, which may not give accurate ideas of the students.

Summary

Intelligence is the general capacity of an individual or a mental energy or altertness of an individual which enables him to adjust effectively in the environment and deal with novel situations of life. The most important definitions of intelligence was given by Stoddard which are characterized by difficulty, complexity, abstractness, economy, adaptiveness, goal, social value, emergence of originals and resistance to emotional forces. On the basis of the modern definitions of intelligence the following nature emerged. These are as follows: Intelligence is inborn natural power; with the help of intelligence we are capable of overcoming difficulties and problems of life; it helps man in learning things; no difference in intelligence due to difference in sex; I.Q will be more if a child is brought up in healthy environment, and intelligence is orderly and cummulative.

There are basically three types of intelligence, i.e., abstract, concrete and the social intelligence with the following characteristics. An intelligent person is capable, adjusts effectively, learns new things, clever, knows how to behave in a situation and constructive thinking. The distribution of intelligence is based on the I.Q. In the society there are genius, very superior, superior, bright, normal, below average, dull, educable, trainable and untrainable persons available.

The theories of intelligence are of many types. These are the monarchic theory or unitary theory, the eclectic theory or two factor theory, the anarchic theory or multifactor theory, group factor theory, oligarchic theory or sampling theory and Guilford theory of intelligence. Similarly, Piaget's stages of intellectual development are as follows. These are sensori-motor stage (0-2 years), pre-operational (2-7 years) which are divided as pre-conceptual (2-4 years) and Intituitive phase (4-7 years), concrete operations (7-11 years) and formal operations (11+ years) onwards.

The measurement of intelligence cannot be done like a piece of cloth or temperature of our body. It can only be assessed through intelligence test. These are either verbal individual test, verbal group intelligence test, non-verbal individual test and non-verbal group intelligence test. Excluding that the shy, illiterate, language handicapped, foreigners and the deaf and dumb can be tested through performance tests.

The concept of mental age, chronological age, basal age help the individual to find out the I.Q. of an individual. The intelligence tests are the following uses such as to make homogeneous grouping, understand the capability of child, help in taking admission, to provide guidance, identity gifted and backward children, improve in quality of teaching and use in research work.

Questions

1. What is intelligence ? How do you assess intelligence of an individual ?
2. Define modern definitions of intelligence? Describe any one theory of intelligence with educational implications.
3. Describe the salient feature of an individual and a group test of intelligence.
4. Define the nature of intelligence? Describe the characteristics and limitations of a culture-fair test.
5. Critically examine the merits and demerits of an intelligence test.
6. What are the various uses of intelligence tests in the field of education?
7. Briefly discuss the various theories of intelligence with their educational implications.
8. What is Intelligence Quotient? How to calculate it?

9. Intelligence tests do not test true intelligence but they test the product or result of schooling. Comment.
10. Write short notes on the following :
    (a) Types of intelligence
    (b) I.Q.
    (c) Assessment of intelligence
    (d) Uses of intelligence test in real classroom
    (e) Piaget's views on intellectual development
11. Describe the Guilford SOI model theory of intelligence with educational implications.
12. Define the concept of intelligence. How is intelligence measured ?

References

1. Binet, A and Simon, T. (1916) : *The Development of Intelligence in Children*, Baltimore, Williams and Wilkins, New York.
2. Brody, E.B. and Brody, N., (1976) *Intelligence: Nature, Determinants and Consequences,* Academic Press, New York
3. Butcher, H.J. (1968) : *Human Intelligence : Its Nature and Assessment,* Methuen, London
4. Chauhan S.S. (1987) : *Advanced Educational Psychology*, Vikas Pub, New Delhi.
5. Crow, L.D. and Crow, A. (1973) : *Educational Psychology*, Eurasia Pub. House, New Delhi.
6. Dutta, N.K. (1971) : *Psychological Foundations of Education*, Doaba House, Delhi
7. Garrett, H.E (1996) : *General Psychology,* S. Chand and Company, Ltd. New Delhi.
8. Gulliksen, H. (1958) : *Theory of mental test,* Wiley, New York.
9. Guilford, J.P. (1967) : *The nature of human intelligence*, McGraw - Hill, New York.
10. Kundu, C.L. and Tutoo, D.N. (1980) : *Educational Psychology*, Sterling Publishers Ltd. New Delhi.
11. Kuppuswamy, B. (1988): *Advanced Educational Psychology*, Sterling Publishers Ltd., New Delhi.
12. Kamath V.V. (1940) : *Measuring intelligence of Indian children*, Oxford University Press, London.
13. Mayer, R.E. (1987) : *Educational Psychology: A cognitive approach,* Little, Brown and Company Ltd. Canada.
14. Piaget, J. (1952) : *The origins of intelligence in children*, International Uni. Press, New York.
15. Rastogi, K.G. (1983) : *Educational Psychology,* Rastogi Publications, Meerut, India.
16. Sawray, J.H. and Telford, C. (1964) : *Educational Psychology*, Prentice Hall of India, New Delhi.

17. Sherman, M. (1945) : *Intelligence and its Deviation*, The Ronald Press Company, New York.
18. Skinner, C.E. (1962) : *Essentials of Educational Psychology*, Asia Pub. House, Bombay.
19. Stoddard, G.D. (1943) : *The Meaning of Intelligence,* The Macmillan Company, New York.
20. Terman, L.M. (1937): *Measurement of Intelligence*, Houghton Mifflin Company, (Boston).
21. Thorndike, E.C. (1948) : *The measurement of intelligence*, Bureau of Publications, Teachers College, Columbia Univ.
22. Thurston, L.L. (1938) : *Primary Mental Abilities*, Univ. of Chicago Press, Chicago.
23. Vernon, P.E. (1950): *The Structure of Human Abilities*, Methuen and Co., New York.
24. Walia, J.S. (1977) : *Foundations of Educational Psychology and Guidance*, Paul Publications, Jullandur.
25. Wechsler, D. (1958) : The Measurement and Appraisal of Adult Intelligence, The Williams and Wilking Co., New York.

CREATIVITY

Introduction

We encounter with increasingly complex problems in today's world. Success in the complex world depend on our ability to solve these problems. New discovery and development is possible only due to creative thinking. Thus, whatever good and beautiful that has survived through the passage of time in human civilization and culture, is designed and determined by the creative thinkers. Creativity, thus, the highest order of human potentiality of a country that contributes optimum growth and development, progress and prosperity, and nurtures the greatness and glory of a nation's destiny. The creative persons are really the assets of the nation and the greater the creative potential that a nation holds, the better it is exploited for the cause of the nation. Therefore, in the educational process we should develop the creative abilities among children.

Meaning/Defining Creativity

Creativity has many meanings, probably because it arouses interest among a wide variety of scholars—including philosophers, historians, educators, psychiatrists and psychologists who view it from their separate perspectives. Some think of creativity as personal idiosyncrasy while others associate it with special competency. Thus, creativity is that which appears new to every moment or it is the responses that are novel to the society as well as to the individual.

Drevdahl (1956) defined creativity as "the capacity of a person to produce compositions, products or ideas of any sort which are essentially new or novel and previously unknown to the producer".

Skinner defined the creative thinker is one who explores new ideas and makes new observation, new predictions and new inferences. Thus, creativity is the capacity or ability of an individual to create, discover or produce a new idea or object including the re-arrangement or reshaping of what is already known to him.

Kobie (1958) defined as "creativity implies invention, the uncovering of new facts or new relationships among new or old data.

Guilford (1960) said that "creativity refers to abilities that are most characteristics of creative people. Thus creativity refers to the abilities of individuals to create or produce results of creative nature.

Torrance (1962) defined creativity is the process of becoming sensitive to problems, deficiencies, gaps in knowledge, missing elements, disharmonies, and so forth".

McKinnon (1963) defined "creativity is a process extended in time and characterized by originality, adaptiveness and realization".

Ausubel (1963) defined "creativity is a generalized constellation of intellectual abilities, personality variables and problem-solving traits".

Thurstone defined creativity is an act of the thinker which comes suddenly to him and implies some novelty to him.

Tylor (1964) defined a process is creative when it results in a novel work that is accepted as tenable, useful or satisfying by a group at a point in time.

Stein (1974) defined creativity is a process which results in novel work that is accepted as tenable or useful or satisfying to a group of people at some point in time.

Willach and Kogan (1965) defined creativity lies in producing more associations and in producing more that are unique.

Thus for creativity there is no correct response. It is new or original and unique. It is the capacity or ability of an individual to create, discover or produce a new idea or object including the rearrangement or reshaping of what is already known to him.

Baker (1962) defined creativity as bringing about notable

changes in things, thoughts and social structure through action thinking which results in a situation not previously known to us.

Vernon (1967) considers creativity mainly as "an ability" and, 'a form of cognitive activity'. According to him, creativity means the abilities and personality characterstics that underline the production of artistic or scientific work which is generally recognised as creative and original.

The creative person is a divergent thinker. He discovers or offers uncommon thoughts or ideas, unexpected suggestions and unconventional views. Andrews (1961) defines a creative person has a positive self-integrating force, a process of self-actualization and expression of being. Creativity in terms of product refers to the capacity of individual by which something new is produced, i.e., an idea or an object including a new form or arrangement of old elements. Creativity in terms of process refers to the act of mind, that calls into play, motivation, perception, learning and thinking. According to Rogers "the creative process is the emergence in action of a novel relational product growing out of the uniqueness of the individual on the one-hand and materials, events, people or circumstances of his life on the other". A creative environment is that which motivates a person to produce new ideas, patterns or relationships. Rogers also mentioned four environmental conditions that may foster creativity, i.e., accepting the individual as of unconditional worth, providing climate free from external evaluation, understanding the child empathically and providing psychological freedom.

Nature of Creativity

The following are the nature of creativity:

(a) *Creativity is universal* : Creativity is not confined to any individual, groups of individuals, caste, colour, sex or creed. It has no boundary of age, location or culture. It is applicable to all stages of education and universal in nature.

(b) *Creativity abilities are natural* : It is not surrounded and developed with artificial and forceful situation. It can be nourished and nurtured by training and proper education. It is both innate and acquired.

(c) *Creative expressions are new or novel* : All individuals are creative in diverse ways and in different degrees. It is not restricted to a chosen few.

It brings newness or novelty in the system or something new into being. The emphasis is on the newness and lack of previous existence of the idea or product.

(d) *Creative expressions are wider in scope* : It has no limit or boundaries. It is a kind of adventurous and open thinking. It covers multifarious human accomplishments and all fields of human life.

(e) *Creative expressions carries ego involvement* : No one other than the creator can experience the warmth, happiness and satisfaction which he receives through his creation. The creator takes pride in his creation and hence makes ego involved statements like 'it is my idea' and I have solved this problem, etc.

(f) Creative abilities are not completely spontaneous rather it requires constant understanding, discipline, hardwork and patience to produce something new and unique. It is a kind of adventurous thinking and a departure from the closed thinking.

(g) Creativity is the ability to go beyond the immediate solution, redefine the problem or some part of it and unusual ideas and new approach to the problem. It involves many abilities like fluency, flexibility, originality and elaboration.

Characteristics of a Creative Person

According to Tylor, the characteristics of a Creative Person are the following:

(a) Strong momory powers and full of new ideas about things;
(b) Tendency to evaluate the ideas and actions of self and others;
(c) Flexible and open minded;
(d) All the four qualities like originality, fluency, flexibility and power of elaboration;
(e) Sensitivity to problems, openness to new ideas and experiences;
(f) Curiosity and having intellectual persistence;
(g) Tendency to seek challenges and manipulative ideas;
(h) Prefering complex ideas and tolerance for ambiguity;
(i) Commitment to work and inclination to take risk;
(j) Resourceful, adventurous and extrovert; and
(k) More perseverance and less traditional-bound.

Torrance indicated that a creative person is a (i) divergent thinker; (ii) forming ideas or hypothesis—concerning problem; (iii) testing these hypothesis and communicating the results; (iv) capable of modifying and retesting the hypothesis; (v) original, useful and socially accepted abilities and (vi) development of novel approach to solve problems.

The researchers in their findings concluded the following behavioural characteristics of a creative person:

1. Flexible and open minded
2. Suggest better ways of doing a job
3. Originality of ideas and expression
4. Ability to use material, words or ideas in new ways
5. Bold and emotionally sensitive, resourceful, radical or a sense of adventure and curious nature
6. A high degree of awareness, enthusiasm and concentration
7. Self-discipline and capacity to integrate things
8. Respect for the opinions of others
9. Humorous, playful, dominant and self-assertive
10. Lack of rigidity, high values, intolerant for injustice, enjoy strange ideas, rich imagination and expressive
11. Need for autonomy and have high aspirations
12. Sense of self-confidence and reserve and
13. Venturesome and pursuit of self-chosen interests

Steps or Stages of Creative Thinking Process

Unlike many psychometrists and educators, those who theorize about the thoughts and emotions involved in creativity are generally not bound by the creativity—equals—divergent—thinking assumption. Instead, they look at broader aspects of human functioning. Wallas (1926) described the process as consisting of four stages, i.e., preparation, incubation, inspiration or illumination and verification or revision.

(a) *Preparation*

It is the first step in which a problem is investigated in every possible way. It means the conscious work on the problem is initiated and continued till the problem solver familiar with the various features of the problem. Here the problem is analysed and the stage or plan of action is set for its solution. The facts and materials relevant to the problems are collected or gathered for solving the problem in hand. But sometime it so happens that without solving the problem the thinkers keep aside the problem for the time being and do some other activities.

(b) ***Incubation***

In the second stage no conscious thought is given to the problem but the ideas and materials collected in the period of preparation are somehow stored below the conscious level of the psyche. This is the stage of no work or rest period. But somehow the mind continues to search or experience clue to the solution of the problem.

(c) ***Illumination***

During this stage the "Aha" feeling is suddenly experienced, often unexpectedly. This means a sudden appearance of the solution of his problem comes to the mind.

(d) ***Verification***

The final stage is verification. When the new idea is evaluated on the basis of its creator's own standards which may be sharply different from the public and criticism starts. Here the idea which appeared through insight may be considered as the correct answer. In case it does not work out, fresh attempts are made to solve the problem.

Dimensions of Creativity

According to Guilford there are four creative thinking abilities: fluency, flexibility, originality and elaboration. The intellectual operation for these abilities is divergent, and it can apply to all content areas. Generally creativity test (verbal or non-verbal) measure all the above dimensions of creativity. Let us now try to illustrate the above dimensions one by one:

(i) ***Fluency***

Researches in the field of creativity have revealed that highly creative persons are thought to be more fluent in their thinking and able to generate alternative ideas in great variety and large quantity. Examples of this competency include writing large number of acceptable plot titles for untitled literary works and imagining many consequences of a change in the environment or in the conditions of life (e.g., suppose the world's supply of oil would dry up; list as many consequences as you can imagine). This is called ideational fluency because it denotes skills in generating quantities of ideas in a language context. But associational fluency is the ability to produce many relationship or meaningful associations with a given idea. It is evident by the quantity of synonyms a person can attach to any familiar word that has many meanings or it characterises thinking by analogy. Similarly, expressional fluency refers to skills in juxtaposing words to meet sentence structure requirements. It is the production of alternative organised thoughts. A sequence of words in a sentence represents a thought system.

(ii) Flexibility

The skill of being to able discontinue an existing pattern of thought and shift to new patterns or shifts from one set of assumption or approach to another is called flexibility. Spontaneous flexibility deals with changes in direction of thinking when a person is not instructed to do so. For example, in listing the various uses of a brick, the flexible individual tends to produce ideas relating not only to the weight of the object but also to its size, colour, shape, texture and so on. Adaptive flexibility deals with changes in direction of thinking to solve problems. In this case content is figural, such as geometric forms which the persons use to make as many objects as possible.

(c) *Originality*

The process of originality is on products that are unexpected and sometimes amusing. It is found out that divergent production is the generation of logical alternatives to fit the needs of given information and that logical alternatives depend upon the original ideas of the person concerned. Thus, creativity is the process of originality, uniqueness and even sometimes idiosyncratic ways of doing things or showing problems.

(d) *Elaboration*

Elaboration is seen in facility in giving details to round out a complex innovation, such as an organised plan or how much skilled in planning and organization. For example, a person demonstrates the ability to fill in all of the various details necessary to make a briefly outlined project depends upon the elaboration.

Identification of Creative Individuals

Creativity of an individual can be seen in the interaction of his intellect, personality, motivation and the biography although its distribution is neither equal or universal. Researches in this regard have proved that creative potential are unique and divergent in nature rather than associating with intelligence. The identification of creative potential depends upon the following measures:

(i) By observation of behaviour,
(ii) Through rating scale and attitude scales,
(iii) By the help of interview/asking questions informally,
(iv) By the help of situational tests, interest inventories, aptitude test, projective techniques and personality test, etc.
(v) By studying the cummulative record, if maintained about the individual, and
(vi) By the help of standardized tests along with creativity tests.

Factors Affecting/Hindering/Obstructing or Impediments to the Promotion of Creativity

There are different factors which obstruct or block creativity development. These are the following:

(a) *Partiality or Negative Treatment of Parents*

It is found out that there is a difference in treatment from the parents with regard to facilities to boys and girls at home. The boys are provided with more opportunities, encouragement and positive attitude rather than girls, hence, creative development is suppressed and not nurtured from the very beginning.

(b) *Unfavourable Home Conditions and Unfavourable Attitudes Towards Children*

It is a fact that home is the child's first environment and it can help the child to do and undo everything when he/she is capable of doing the things. But broken home, discouragement, authoritarian discipline and not providing proper play equipments at the time of childhood and obstructive social attitudes and lack of rewards discourage creativity among children.

(c) Lack of Stimulation and Unfavourable Environment

Even though the foundations for creativity are made from the very beginning of the early childhood stage yet its development must be stimulated in the later stage. But it is noticed that due to lack of stimulation and congenial environment, the development of mental flexibility or divergent thinking is stopped. Thus, unfavourable environmental conditions have been found to influence the work of the creative person and offers less stimulation to foster creativity than the congenial atmosphere either at home or school.

(d) *Socio-economic Status and Family Size*

Socio-economic condition of the family is responsible for affecting creativity among the children. The children of lower income group experience authoritarian and lack of opportunities to express their individuality and to foster creativity. Similarly in large families it is found out that children's needs are not properly gratified due to less favourable conditions at home which hamper the development of creativity.

(e) *Inability to Detect Creativity in Time*

Generally there are different procedures to identify creativity. But sometimes it is not noticed early and too late for stimulation for full development of these potentials. Hence, creative potential is affected and not nurtured properly.

(f) *Unfavourable School Conditions*

Next to home the child spends at least eight hours a day in school. If the school conditions are unfavourable, the stimulation to promote creativity provided by a favourable home environment is a waste. Sometimes it is marked that authoritarian teaching-learning, too much memorisation, too much dependence on text-book and curricula, defective system of examination, overcrowded class, lack of co-curricular activities, lack of initiative of the teacher in the school, strict discipline and discouragement of anything that does not face within the prescribed pattern are responsible for hindering the path of creativity.

(g) *Unwilling to Take Risk and Lack of Foresightedness*

It is revealed that most of the children in schools are

not ready to take risk and to do new work either due to fear or not having the foresightedness. This situation might have occurred either due to family background or because of school conditions although every student has some form of creativity or the other. Thus unsatisfactory conditions at home and school obstruct the promotion of creativity among our pupils.

Stimulating/Developing/Promoting/Fostering Creativity in Children

Alex F. Osborn (1963) developed a five-step process of creative problem solving. These are (a) *problem finding* or the search for the nature of the real challenge from different perspectives; (b) *fact finding*, i.e., to understand the situation better and to imagine what the solution might be; (c) *idea finding,* i.e., calling up ideas from the pre and sub-conscious and to defer judgement of their quality until they have all been flushed out; (d) *solution finding,* i.e., some point of time the ideas are evaluated for their relevance and applicability, and the best one is chosen for implementation; and (e) *acceptance finding* or gaining an audience that is willing to support the idea and put it to practical use.

Parnes and his colleagues (1977) suggested the following strategies for creative problem solving:

(a) *Remove the Internal Blocks to Creativity*

In order to prepare children for creative productivity they must be helped to feel secure in their relationship with others without worrying about the acceptability of their ideas, even if they are extremely off beat.

(b) Create an Awareness of the Role of the Subconscious

Even when a problem is removed from direct attention, the subconscious somehow keeps on working at it. Since ideas and fantasies about possible solutions surface only fleetingly, it is important to jot down these thoughts so that they may eventually be clarified and organized.

(c) Defer Judgement

By doing so, the children can spend more time on a variety of perceptions about a problem and thereby increase the flow of ideas that lead to alternative solutions.

(d) *Create an Awareness of the Power of Metaphor and Analogy in Tiggering New Connections and Associations*

With the help of checklists and other devices, dealing with analogy and metaphor can be made easy if enough time is spent in practice.

(e) *Provide Experiences with Mind-stretching Exercises*

Forcing the mind to produce many alternative solutions to problems is uncomfortable at the beginning, but ideas flow more and more easily as children grow more comfortable with the task.

(f) *Keep fantasy alive*

Fantasy is not only essential in helping children's mental growth and adjustment but also a vital ingredient of creativity. Every effort, therefore, has to be made to discourage in the school and in the home from communicating the belief to children that such flights of the imagination are signs of immature thinking.

(g) *Remove Mental Breaks and Encourage Free Wheeling*

Children have to feel assured that their ideas will not be ridiculed and that any far-out thought is worth expressing and sharing with others.

(h) *Discipline the Imagination*

Although children should be encouraged to free-wheel and fantasize, they need to realize that after the incubation period ideas will be reviewed critically. Some will be rejected and those that are retained need to be implemented for humane and useful purposes.

(i) *Increase Sensitivity*

Formal awareness training, art exercises, and in-depth discussions of literature can help to increase children's sensitivity to others and to their physical environment. It will also enable them to recognize incongruities as well as new relationships and connections that can prove to be meaningful.

(j) *Increase Knowledge*

Creativity depends on the previously absorbed knowledge. Therefore, maximum information and ideas should pass on to the children to form the basis of new ideas. Learning to think, to solve problems, and to use knowledge should become an essential part of the school experience.

(k) *Help Children to Understand Why they Engage in Various Exercises Related to Creative Thinking*

Children, parents and educators have to understand the importance of creative thinking and the exercises that facilitate it in order to maximize the effects of enrichment. Otherwise, such techniques may mistakenly be seen as "fun and games" that only embellish the curriculum rather than breathe life into it.

(Source: International Encyclopedia of Education, 1985)

In addition to that parents and teachers can do a number of things to foster creativity among children. These are as follows:

1. Creative reading should be encouraged. Students should be given direction and encouragement to use unusual ideas and solutions with confidence.
2. Self-initiative learning should be initiated. Emphasis should be on more individual assignments and bring the students into contact with the best talent and knowledge available within the existing setup.
3. Both home and school must stimulate creativity by providing guidance and encouragement to use the materials that will encourage creativity. It means democratic and permissive child training in the home and school should be employed.
4. The teacher should not give everything readymade to the pupils. Dynamic methods with scientific temper and participatory approach should be adopted so that the child can take active part in discussion. In this way thought processes and imagination of the students can be enhanced which in turn can foster creative talents.
5. Students should be made self-reliant and self confident and the instinct of the child should be effectively dealt with. They should be made to feel

that whatever they create is unique and expresses what they desire to express.

6. The teacher should see that students develop positive attitude towards every work. They should be well aware that no work is big or small, prestigious or insulting or white colared. Equality in treating the students will develop confidence and foster creativity.
7. Encouraging originality and flexibility as far as possible. Children should be given enough opportunities and chance to apply their thinking and ideas into their day to day life so that they can develop creative potential.
8. As far as possible the teacher should show examples of critical and creative behaviour before the students. In addition to that the school should be well equipped with books, materials, and facilities like co-curricular activities so that creative children can exhibit their special talents.
9. Sense of humour, constant persuasion/motivation, encouragement of independent thinking, enriched experiences and removal of hesitation and fear help in promoting creativity among the children. So the teachers in the school and parents at home should try to develop the above habits for the promotion of creativity.
10. Developing healthy habits, avoidance of blocks to creative thinking like unsympathetic treatment and authoritarian outlook, frequent brain storming to explore ideas and word game in early stages, etc., enhance the scope of knowledge of children and kindle the spark of creativity in them.

Torrance (1965) has enumerated the following principles for teachers for encouraging creativity. These are:

(a) Be respectful of unusual questions,
(b) Be respectful of imaginative and unusual ideas,
(c) Show your pupils that their ideas have values,
(d) Encourage the pupils to do something for practice and ask extending questions,
(e) Tie in evaluation with causes and consequences,
(f) Be cautious not to reject nonconformity,
(g) Be willing to accept that which is new, different and even imperfect, and

(h) Use praise liberally and modify assignments to fit the students.

Measurement of Creativity

To measure creativity there are many standardized tests available in India and abroad. These are:

1. Minnesota tests of creative thinking
2. Guilford divergent thinking instruments
3. Wallach and Kogan creativity instruments
4. Torrance tests of creative thinking, and in India
5. Baquer Medhi's test of creative thinking
6. Passi's test of creativity
7. Sharma's divergent production abilities test, and
8. Acharyulu's think creativity.

On the basis of these tests the creative abilities of several dimensions of one's behaviour can be measured. The Torrance test of creative thinking is one such test which can be used in primary and secondary schools. This test consists of verbal and figural activities and measures fluency, flexibility, originality and elaboration. Some of the tasks in this test are given below. The figural forms as a non-verbal testing device make use of tasks that require drawing and picturization. The activities required in the non-verbal subtests are the following:

1. *Figural or Picture Completion Tests or Incomplete Figures*

In this subtest there are some incomplete figures. The subject is asked to complete these figures by adding new dimensions or lines for providing new ideas. Further he/she is asked to give suitable titles for the completed figures or pictures.

2. *Picture Construction Test*

In this subtest the subject is provided with a piece of coloured paper cut in curved shape and asked to think of a figure or picture of which this piece of paper may be a part. He/She is asked to provide a suitable title for this picture.

3. *Parallel Lines Test or Repeated Figures*

In this subtest there are several parts of straight lines and circles. The subject is required to draw as many objects or pictures by using each pair and circle. He/She is asked to provide a title for each of his/her drawings.

Similarly, the verbal forms incorporate tasks which require the use of language. The subject is required to provide written responses to the questions put to him/her. The tasks in this form are the following.

4. ***Ask and Guess Type***

In the asking type of activities, the subject is encouraged to show his ability in such a way so that normal human being cannot perceive it. Here the subject is asked questions needed to know exactly what is happening in the drawing. Similarly in the guessing aspect he/she is asked to guess as many causes as possible in the picture and its consequences of what is taking place in the picture.

5. ***Product Improvement Type***

Here the subject is asked to suggest ways and means of improving a toy, a machine or some other such product to make it interesting and useful as far as possible.

6. ***Unusual Uses Type***

Here the subject is asked to think about the number of ways in which a product may be used. He/She is to enumerate as many interesting and unusual uses he/she can think of a object like card board box, knife or brick be used.

7. ***Unusual Question Type***

Here the subject is asked as many unusual questions as he/she can put about a picture, scene or verbal description of a phenomena.

8. Just Suppose Type

Here the respondent is asked to guess what would happen if a certain situation occurred? It means he/she is to predict the outcomes of unusual situations like what would have happened if you had been selected as Prime Minister of India? or 24 hours would had been a day, etc.?

Thus, combining both verbal and figural forms Torrance test of creativity evaluate the creative abilities of an individual.

Summary

For the development of society, creativity stands out as an activity to be studied, cherished and cultivated. It is the capacity of an individual to create or produce a novel idea or object. It is both innate as well as acquired and a process as well as a product. The creative person possess the qualities like universality, adventures, open mindness, sensitivity, divergent thinking and novelty in thought. Thus creativity is a means and a product of ones emotional prerogative.

The creativity stages are preparation, incubation, illumination and verification. The most important characteristics of creative persons are ability to take independent decisions, ability to elaborate, ability to accept tentativeness, originality of ideas, and an investigative and curious in nature.

On the basis of standardized creativity tests, observation, interview and cummulative records, etc., it is possible to identify creativity. The tests of creativity usually incorporate the items of various components like fluency, flexibility, originality and elaboration, etc. The Torrance test of creativity, Wallach-Kogan test of creativity, Baquer Medhi's test of creative thinking, etc., are the examples of such test.

There are different hindrances which occur in the way of promoting creativity. These are SES, environment, school and home conditions, etc. In spite of these hindrances, fostering creativity among children can be possible. Thus it requires whole hearted support from parents, teachers and society for survival and growth of a nation in an effective manner. Therefore, it should be ensured that children are provided with such facilities which will ultimately nurture creativity.

Questions

1. Define creativity and describe its importance.
2. What is creativity? How can the teacher promote creative thinking in the class room?
3. Discuss the meaning and nature of creativity. State the characteristics of creative individuals.
4. Discuss the hindrances and identification of creative adolescents.
5. What is the role of parents in fostering creativity?
6. How to measure creativity? Explain a suitable strategy/ test of creativity.
7. What are the steps of creative thinking? How can the teacher measure creativity of a child?
8. Do you agree that creative process as a magic synthesis? Justify the statement with an example.
9. What do you mean by creative process? Explain in detail.
10. What are the factors affecting creativity? What role

the teacher should play to overcome in the classroom?

References

Barron, F.C. (1968) : *Creativity and Personal Freedom*, Princeton, J.N.

Cronbach, L. (1968) : *Creative Person and Creative Process*, Holt, Rinehart and Winston Inc., New York.

Deshmukh, M.N. (1984) : *Creativity in classroom*, S. Chand and Company Ltd., New Delhi.

Drevdhal, J.E. (1956) : "Factors of Importance of Creativity", *Journal of Clinical Psychology*, 12, 21-26.

Getzels, J.W. and Jackson, P.W. (1962) : *Creativity and Intelligence*, John Wiley, New York.

Getzels, J.W. (eds.) 1975 : *Perspectives in creativity*, Aldine, Chicago, Illinois.

Golan, S.E. (1963) : "Psychological Study of Creativity", *Psychological Bulletin*, 60, 548-65.

Guilford, J.P. (1950) : "Creativity", *American Psychologist*, 5, 44.

Khire, U. (1977) : "Education for Creativity", *Journal of Indian Edn.*, 3, 26-30.

Lytton, H. (1971) : *Creativity and Education*, Rutledge and Kegan Paul, London.

Mackinnon, D.W. (1962) : "The Nature and Nurture of Creative Talent" *American Psychologist*, 17, 2, 484-95.

Mansfield, R.S. (1981) : *The Psychology of Creativity and Discovery*, Chicago, Nalson Hall.

Osborn, A.F. (1963) : *Applied Imagination : Principles and Procedures of Creative Problem Solving*, 3rd edn., Scribner, New York.

Paramesh, C.R. (1972) : *Creativity and Personality*, Janatha Pub. House, Madras.

Parnes, S.J. (1963) : "Education and Creativity", Teachers College Record, 64, 1, 331-39.

Radhakrishnan, S. (1975): *The Creative Life*, Orient Pub, New Delhi.

Raina, M.K. (Ed.) 1980: *Creativity Research*, NCERT, New Delhi.

Torrance, E.P. (1962) : *Guiding Creative Talent*, Englewood Cliffs, New Jersey.

Torrance, E.P. (1966) : *Torrance Tests of Creative Thinking*, Personnel Press, Princeton, New Jersey.

Torrance, E.P. and Mysers, R.E. (1970) : *Creative Learning and Teaching*, Dodd and Mead Pub., New Delhi.

Tripathi. S.N. (1975) : "The Concept of Creativity in Education, *Journal of Indian Edn.*

Tylor, C.W. (1964) : *Creativity, Progress and Potential*, McGraw Hill Book Co., New York.

Wallach, M.A. and Kogan, N. (1965) : *Models of Thinking Young Children: A Study of the Creativity-Intelligence Thinking*, Holt, Rinehant and Winston, New York.

PERSONALITY

Introduction

Psychology of personality is of recent growth. Personality is the completed jigsaw puzzle as the whole individual is to be studied as a whole. As we come to know a person, either younger or older than ourselves, we begin to recognize and expect certain characteristic ways of behaving that distinguish this unique individual from all other people. As we observe a particular person over a period of time, we notice how his temperament, interests, and attitudes are developing, and how his behaviour tends to make a more or less consistent direction.

Sometimes we like or admire the individual who possesses "balanced personality", means dynamic, forceful, friendly or pleasant and we dislike or are indifferent to the man of 'no personality', means irritating or disagreeable. Thus in common usage personality means the impact that an individual produces on the persons interacting with him or it refers to the extent to which a person impresses other people. It also refers to special characteristics, abilities, emotional and social traits, interests and attitudes of a person or can be described in terms of behaviour of an individual, his words, thoughts and gestures. Let us now discuss the meaning of personality and its theories and dimensions to have a clear idea about it.

Personality: Its Concept, Meaning and Nature

The word personality has been described by many psychologists in different ways and each definition suggests a different approach towards personality.

Etymologically the word 'personality' has been derived from the Latin word 'Persona' which means mask or make up or cover through which an actor plays his role on the stage. Persona was meant a mask which the Greek actors commonly used to wear before their faces when they worked on the stage. For example, actors in Ramlila and Krishnalila use mask when they enact the role of a particular character from the epics.

This idea of mask using has been criticised in many ways because one plays many roles in this world. Thus the emphasis on outward appearance and observable behaviour gives us a very limited understanding of the individual to whom we are observing. In order to understand personality and its proper connotation, we have to take help from Biology, Sociology, Psychology and other allied Sciences. The following are the different view-points to define personality.

I. *Layman View Point*

From this point of view, personality means those qualities which cast their influence on others. How an individual affects other persons with whom he comes in contact or the effect or impact which an individual leaves on other people is called personality. It is also understood that personality is the stimulus value which one individual has for others or the total picture of an individuals organized behaviour.

II. *Philosophical View Point*

Philosophers are of the view that the personality is ideal of perfection or self-realisation or the internal self.

III. *Sociological View Point*

This view point thinks that the individual is nothing but a reflection of the society. Personality is the integration of all traits which determine the role of the status of the person in society, i.e., "social effectiveness". In the Warren's dictionary it is defined that "Personality is the integrative organization of all the cognitive, affective, conative and physical characteristics of an individual as it manifests itself in focal distinction from others".

IV. *Psycho-analytic View Point*

According to Freud, personality is the combination of three components, i.e., Id, Ego and Super-Ego which are manifested through behaviour.

V. *Psychological View Point*

Psychologists are of the view that personality is the sum total of all the biological innate disposition, impulses, tendencies, aptitudes, attitudes and instincts of the individual and the acquired dispositions and tendencies acquired by experience. This approach was criticized and other Psychologists emphasise on integration and organisation in defining personality. They define personality is the entire organisation of a human being at any state of his development. The way in which an individual adjusts with the external environment is personality. Thus psychologically, Personality is the integrated and dynamic Organisation of the physical, mental, moral and social qualities of the individual as that manifests itself to others in social life.

We have described the various approaches to define the term personality. Let us now discuss some of the definions of personality.

1. Watson defines "Personality is the sum of activities that can be discovered by actual observations over a long enough period of time to give reliable information".
2. Biesanj and Biesanj defines "Personality is the organisation of person's habits, attitudes and traits and arises from the inter-play of biological, social and cultural factors".
3. Freeman defines "Personality as the individuality that emerges from interaction between a psycho-biological organism and the world in which he has developed and lived".
4. Kadz and Sehank defines "Personality is the concept under which we subscribe the individual's characteristic, ideational, emotional and motor reactions and the characteristic organisation of these responses."
5. Vernon defines "Personality is an organized system of traits, sentiments, complexes and habits that distinguishes the individual, as we see him, from other individuals".

6. Guilford defines "Personality is the unique pattern of traits which distinguishes one individual from another".
7. Munn defines "Personality is the most characteristic integration of an individuals structures, mode of behaviour, interests, attitudes, capacities, abilities and aptitudes".
8. Linton defines "Personality is the organised aggregate of Psychological processes and states pertaining to the individual".
9. Cruze defines "Personality as an organised and integrated unity consisting of many elements that work together as a functioning whole".
10. Kempf defines "Personality as the habitual mode of adjustment which the organism effects between its own egocentric drives and the exigencies of the environment".
11. Eysenck defines "Personality is the sum-total of actual behaviour patterns of the Organism". Personality is the more or less stable and enduring organisation of a person's character, temperament, intellect and physique, which determine his unique adjustment to the environment.
12. Cattell defines "Personality is that which permits a prediction of what a person will do in a given situation".
13. Gestalt school defines "Personality as a pattern or configuration produced by the integrated functioning of all the traits and characteristics of an individual".
14. Young defines "Personality refers to the more or less organised body of ideas, attitudes, traits, values and habits which an individual has built into roles and status for dealing with others and with himself".
15. Woodworth defines "Personality means the total quality of an individual's behaviour".
16. Allport has attempted to give us a comprehensive definition of personality which recognises the value of wholeness, adjustment and distinctiveness of human personality. He defines "Personality is the dynamic organisation within the individual of those Psycho-Physical systems that determine his unique adjustments to his environment".

This definition of Allport underlines the following characteristics of Personality.

(a) Dynamic means that Personality is undergoing a constant change and not something static, fixed and permanent.
(b) Organisation means integration or interaction between inherited potentialities (heredity) and environmental influences, i.e., habits, dispositions, tendencies, attitudes, etc., of an individual.
(c) Psycho-Physical means two types of systems, i.e., psychological (mental) and physical elements that interact with internal and external environment.
(d) Determine lays emphasis that it is the Psycho-Physical system that activates the organism for action or regulate various behaviours.
(e) Unique adjustment of the individual to his environment means that each individual employs different methods of adjustment resulting in unique adjustment.

Thus it can be concluded that personality is unique and different from one to another.

Characteristics/Features of Personality

Personality is a sum total of various human qualities. Following are the chief characteristics of a balanced personality.

1. Personality is something unique and specific. Every one of us is a unique person and different from one to another in adjustment.
2. Personality is a dynamic and moving force. It is never fixed and rigid. It changes from day to day.
3. Personality includes all the behaviour patterns, i.e., cognitive, conative and affective and covers not only the conscious activities but goes deeper to the semi-conscious and unconscious also.
4. Personality has a structure. it consists of certain dimensions. It is the combination of inner as well as outer qualities of an individual.
5. Personality cannot be judged by only looking at his physical appearance rather it is the study of totality. It is the study of both physical and psychological and has organised and integrated system.

6. Personality is the product of heredity and environment. The development of personality is the result of continuous interaction of both.
7. Personality is the combination of id, ego and super-ego.

Jackson indicates the following characteristics of a balanced person.

(a) The Individual should have the capacity to appreciate and understand the actions and emotions of others, and he should not try to hurt their ego or self.
(b) He should be capable of adjusting himself with the changing environment.
(c) Courtesy and discipline and normal emotionality should be found out with the person.
(d) Capacity to be able to lead the group or the society.
(e) He should be capable of maintaining equality and similarity with other members of the society.
(f) He should have some goal or purpose. The behaviour of an individual is active as well as purposeful.
(g) He should have strong will power and self control.
(h) He should possess good physique and sound mental health.

In addition to the above the term personality indicates the various qualities of a person. These are the following.

P indicates Perception, *E* indicates Emotional Maturity, *R* indicates Responsiveness to situations, *S* indicates Self expression or Sociability, *O* indicates Organized, *N* indicates Noble and flexible (Not permanent), *A* indicates Appearance, *L* indicates Leadership feeling, *I* indicates Integrated, *T* indicates Tendencies, impulses, dispositions, innate and acquired, and *Y* indicates young, vital and unique.

Thus it may be said that Personality is a complex blend of a constantly evolving and changing pattern of one's unique behaviour, emerged as a result of one's interaction with one's environment and directed towards some specific ends.

Determinants of Personality/Development of Personality/ Factors Influencing or Affecting Personality

Personality is a dynamic, growing thing, different in each person in physical appearance, temperament and motivation. These differences become more pronounced and complex with increasing age and maturity due to continuous interaction with the environment and accordingly each one of us develop a personality different from the others. Now the question arises how does personality develop? What causes these variations? Why do we develop different personalities in spite of basic or fundamental similarities? All these questions can be answered if we study the various factors which influence the structure and functions of personality. Thus the development of personality or determinant of personality of an individual depends upon the following factors.

(i) The Physiological and Physical factors (Genetic or Biological Determinants).
(ii) The Environmental or Social factors (Social Determinants).
(iii) The Psychological or Mental factors.
(iv) The Cultural Determinants or Cultural factors.

1. The Physiological and Physical Factors (*Genetic or Biological Determinants*)

The biological factors affecting the development of personality are the three. These are (a) Physique, (b) Chemique (Ductless Gland) and (c) Nervous system.

(a) *Physique*

A Physical factor of personality is the individual's physique. An individual's personalty differ according to his physique. These aspects are height, weight, body-built, colour appearance and proportion, etc., which determine to a large extent the way in which he behaves towards others and how others react towards him. It is seen that in daily life the fat men are easy going and social while thin persons are self controlled, irritated and un-social. Even tall and fair persons enjoy an advantage over their short and ugly associates. Thus the physical structure has some relation with environment and makes a change in their personality.

(b) *Chemique*

Another important biological factor affecting personality is body chemistry. By chemique is meant the possible effects of the ductless glands on the personality development. Glands are small organs which change chemical substances from one form to another in the body. These glands are of two types (a) duct glands, (b) ductless glands. Ductless glands called endocrines releases chemical substances (called hormones) into the blood stream which carries them to all parts of the body. The endocrine glands (ductless glands) bring about changes in physical appearance, motor functioning, intelligence and emotional stability. Some of the important ductless glands like the Pituitary Gland, the Thyroid Gland, the Adrenal Gland and Sex Glands are interdependent. The individuals with profound imbalance of ductless glands are rarely happy or well-adjusted and play an important part in bodily, mental and emotional development and if defective, imbalanced development of personality.

(c) *Nervous System*

Similarly the nervous system is mainly classified as Central Nervous System which is under the control of our will and is connected with our sense organs and voluntary muscles; and Autonomous Nervous System which is entirely involuntary and autonomic and controls the involuntary muscles, heart, internal organs, etc., causes Personality development. The Physiological conditions of the body brought about by drugs, disease, diet, toxins and bacterial infections may also influence our behaviour and personality.

Hence heredity lies at the root of all the possibilities of personality development.

II. ***The Environmental or Social Factors** (Social Determinants)*

Environmental influences begin since the time of the conception of the child in the womb of the mother. Mother's mental, physical and emotional conditions influence the development of fetus in the womb. Physical and geographical conditions of the environment play an important role in shaping the personality of human beings at every stage of the development. The type of home atmosphere, parent-child relationship, financial conditions, types of school and the community or society, etc., are some of the factors of environment which affect the personality. The following are the description of social factor as personality.

(a) ***Influence of Home and the Family on Personality***

The environment of the home has a wide influence on the development of personality. A congenial home atmosphere, parent-child relationships, behaviour and attitudes of the parents towards their children, parental ambitions, family morale, patterns of child care, family education and economic conditions either affect the personality positively or negatively. Thus the role of the father and mother is very important in the family to determine and mould the personality patterns of the child.

Besides the role of the parents, the atmosphere in the family is greatly influencing. A peaceful and loving atmosphere results in children being orderly, peace-loving and very affectionate and develop mature and pleasant personalities. Whereas in a family where there is tension, constant quarrelling, incompatibility among parents, the child is likely to develop insecurity, inferiority and becomes emotionally confused and unstable. Rigid atmosphere, deprivation, autocratic styles of living, absence of affection and sympathy, affect adversely and the child often turns criminal. Thus, the child's personality is a creation of family and its development is fully dependent upon the child's parents and the child himself at home.

(b) ***Influence of School on Personality***

School plays an important role in moulding the personality of children because a significant part of a child's life is spent in school. In school the personality and behaviour of the teacher, class fellows and playmates, the richness of the curriculum, co-curricular activities, method of teaching, nature of school organisation, and discipline that prevails, etc., are affecting the child's personality. The child tends to identify himself with the teachers and tries to imitate his ways, manners and personality traits. Thus a good teacher and the congenial atmosphere in the institution develop the child educationally and mentally and helps in formulating balanced personality development otherwise undesirable and unethical behaviour could have been found out with the children.

(c) ***Influence of Society on Personality***

Society is a web of social relationship. These social relationship connect men and women with one another. These inter personal relations influence and mould the personality of the individual. In the society each individual has some peculiar status and roles corresponding to him. It is found out that social control is exercised by mores, traditions, myth, legends, customs, etc., and determine the style of life of an individual. The individual cannot behave in the society as he likes because there are rules, regulations, norms and law to govern the individual. Therefore, social norms influence even the ways and attitudes of the individual. This ultimately influences his personality.

III. **The Psychological or Mental Factors**

The Psychological factors like motives, interests, attitudes, character, thinking, intelligence, reasoning, imagination, creativity, habits and mental health, etc., developed by the individuals also affect their personality to a great extent.

IV. **The Cultural Determinants**

Every society is characterized by its cultural heritage which is transmitted from generation to generation in the form of social heredity. Thus personality of an individual is gradually shaped by the culture where he is born in. Tyler defines culture is "that complex whole which includes knowledge, beliefs, morals, law, custom and many other capabilities and habits acquired by man as a member of society". In simple sense culture is a way of life. It is also a fact that we are able to distinguish one person from the other on the basis of the effect of his culture over their personality characteristics. Thus, the attributes and values practised in a culture have a great effect on the personality development of its members.

Judging/Evaluation/Assessment or Measurement of Personality

Personality is a complex phenomena. It is a growing and dynamic thing. It cannot be measured quantitatively as we measure height and weight. Personality variables or traits that we try to measure are mostly vague and ambiguous in meaning. Even there is a difference in the same individual in different situations of life. As it is not possible to measure personality objectively it is desirable to use the term assessment. Before the emergence of scientific method the oldest method of assessing the personality was Astrology, Palmistry, Physiognomy and phrenology, etc. It is believed that Personality of an individual and the cause of every event in his life are determined by the configuration of the stars at the time of his birth, by reading the lines of the palm, facial counters and structure of the skull of the individual. This is otherwise known as Pseudo-Scientific method to measure personality. But in modern scientific age there are five methods of investigating or assessing personality.

These are the following methods of personality assessment.

i. Subjective Methods
ii. Objective Methods
iii. Projective Methods
iv. Psycho-analytic method (free association and Dream analysis)
v. Phenomenological approach or Battery approach. (Combination of subjective, objective and projective methods)

I. The Subjective Methods

The subjective methods are those in which the individual is permitted to disclose what he knows about himself as an object of observation. They are based on what the subject himself has to say about his traits, attitudes, personal experiences, aims, needs and interests. The following are the important subjective methods to investigate the personality.

(a) *Anecdotal Record*

An anecdotal record is a description of an actual episode that takes place inside or outside the classroom. It is a kind of diary of incidents jotted down by the teacher soon after the happenings of the incidents along with personal quality of the children. Thus a series of observations on one child may present a pattern of his behaviour. On the basis of the anecdotal record the personality of an individual can be assessed.

(b) *Autobiography*

Autobiography is a technique which permits the individual to narrate about his own self or own story feelings in his own way. It may be structured or unstructured. In structured or controlled method the examiner/teacher or investigator suggests certain headings to explain about the aspect or experiences throughout life or interests and attitudes, etc., and proceeds accordingly. In unstructured autobiography no guidelines or set plan is given to students. He is just instructed to write according to his will and wishes and accordingly freedom is given to the subject. This mechanism helps the examiner to assess the personality.

(c) *Case History or Case Study Method*

The method is more useful in understanding the personality patterns of an individual who is a problem or is maladjusted. In this method the facts concerning the life of the subject are collected. The case history supplies all the large and small facts related to his environment and heredity and in reality the personality is found out. For successful case study the following information is collected.

(i) A description of the preliminary information about the subject, i.e., name, address, age, sex, education and occupation and income of parents and social, status, etc.

(ii) Past history related to family, child's development after birth, i.e., physical, mental, emotional, social, achievement and educational career, his friendships, and medical history, etc.

(iii) Present condition related to physical, mental, social, emotional, interest and school achievement, etc.

(iv) The interpretation of the raw data collected provides the clear picture of the personality or behaviour of the individual.

(d) *Questionnaires and the Inventory Method*

Good defines questionnaire refers to a device for securing answer to questions by using a form which the respondent fills himself. It is a series of printed or written questions which the individual is supposed to answer or a list of selected questions the answers to which throw some light upon the peculiarities of personality. The subject responds to these questions in the spaces provided in columns of yes, no or cannot say, etc. These answers are then evaluated and used for personality assessment. Items like the following are included in the questionnaires.

1. Do you like to talk to people in a group? Yes No?
2. Do you laugh at a joke on yourself ? Yes No ?

The questions or statements provided describe certain traits like self confidence, sociability, emotions, attitudes or behaviours in situations revealing personality.

But it is a fact that the subject may conceal the truth and furnish such answers that does not give correct knowledge about the personality. In spite of the limitations this is most popular method and is quite useful in collecting both quantitative as well as qualitative information.

Personality inventory though it appears and resembles with the questionnaire in many respects such as administration, scoring, interpretation, etc., yet it is different in two ways. First, the questionnaire is a general device and can be used for collecting all kinds of information not connected specifically with personality traits or the behaviour of an individual whereas personality inventory is specifically designed to seek answers about the person and his personality. Secondly, the questions set in the questionnaire, are generally worded in the second person such as—Do you often feel lonely ? Yes or no—while in the personality inventory, they may be worded in the first person such as—I often feel lonely—Yes or No.

Some of the well known personality inventories to assess the personality are M.M.P.I. (Minnesota Multiphasic Personality Inventory) by McKinley and Hathaway; The California Personality Inventory, The Eysenck personality inventory and The sixteen personality factor inventory by Cattell. Thus on the basis of the personality inventory we can measure the personality of an individual in spite of the delimitations.

(e) *The Interview Method*

Interview is a technique of eliciting information directly from the subject about his personality in face to face contacts. In this, the subject and the examiner sit facing each other while the former answers questions asked by the latter and accordingly his expressions, methods and various other qualities are judged.

The face to face interaction in the interviews is of two types, viz., structured or unstructured and free directive or non-directive interview. An unstructured interview is an open or free interrogation and no limit on the area or field of subject matter to be asked from the interviewer. On the other hand the structured interview adopts a systematic and predetermined approach instead of riding on the tides of the situation. In fact interview is a relatively flexible tool. It permits explanation, adjustment and variation according to the situation and thus has proved to be one of the essential and more important tools for personality assessment.

II. Objectives Methods

In this method of assessment the observers do not depend on the subject's own statements about himself rather the examiners observe or study his overt behaviour which is shown to others in order to know the behavioural characteristics or traits.

The following are the objective procedures to study the personality.

(a) *Observation Method*

Observation is a popular method to study the behaviour pattern of an individual in an actual life situation. In this method the observer decides what personality traits or characteristics he needs to know and accordingly he observes the relevant activities of the subject in real life situations. This can be done either directly (participatory) or indirectly to observe every detail of the individual behaviour. For reliability of the observed results he may either repeat the situation or use a tape recorder or may be observed by a number of observers to know the traits of the individual. Thus what is observed and what is interpreted is very important to assess personality.

(b) *Rating Scales*

Another method of measuring personality is the rating method. In rating scale we rate an individual of the possession or absence of certain traits on a certain scale. It is used to quantify an observation or it indicates the amount of a particular Psychological trait of characteristics possessed by an individual.

This scale assesses the position of an individual in terms of other people's opinion about some of his personality traits. For example, if we want to rate students sociability, we may ask three or four supervisors or teachers to point out the place of each student on the scale. The scale may be three or five or seven points scale. To measure sociability we may use the scale like, avoids others, tolerates others, likes others, likes others well and seeks others.

The rating scales may be various types, i.e., the rank order scale, the percentage of population scale, the graphic scale and may be any specific category scale. Whatever may be the scale it suffers from some drawbacks like lacking of adequate well trained raters, personal or subjective bias, prejudices, partiality and under the halo effect (tendency to rate a person high on all traits because he makes a very good impression on one or two traits or conversely to rate him low throughout because of a poor impression on one trait).

To bring some reliability into rating scale technique, it has been suggested that instead of having rating by one judge it will be better to have more judges.

(c) *Situational or Behavioural Test*

Situational tests are of that type where certain situations are created before the students and on the basis of the reactions of the subjects in those situations their personality is measured. For example, if we want to assess the quality of leadership then candidates are assigned a group task but no body is named as a leader. Thus the candidate who has the quality of a leader assumes that role for himself. Thus the potential personality characteristics of individual related to certain qualities or traits are ascertained.

(d) *Psychodrama*

It is a technique in which the individual has to play a role spontaneously in a specified situation and his behaviour is observed by trained observers. The Psychodrama is generally played between two or more personalities depending upon the nature of their problems. Thus it is presumed that individuals project their inner feelings and conflicts in the role they play and accordingly the behaviour is judged.

(e) *Sociometric Method*

This method of assessing personality was developed by J.L. Moreno in 1946. It is a technique through which relationship among the members of a group (intra group relationship and the frequency of acceptance-rejection) are judged. This method gives clear idea of choosers, mutual choices and rejections. It will also help in locating the star, isolated, neglected and rejected type of students and may plan effectively for their better development. For example, students may be asked to give their preference in response to questions like whom would you like to sit with in the class?, with whom would you like to share your book?, and whom would you like to go with on a picnic, etc.? Thus it helps to locate and identify colleagues within group.

It gives us the knowledge of social pattern in a group and this information can be used to form of sub-groups for a specific purpose as well as to gain insight into group-structure.

(f) *Physiological Measures*

With the help of the physical examination, i.e., the movement and the speed of the pulse, blood pressure, respiratory system, etc., the personality of the individual is judged.

III. *Projective Methods*

The most famous and popular of all the methods for the investigation of personality is the projective method. Freud in his concept of personality suggested that the covert or unconscious behaviour which is 9/10th of our total behaviour can be studied in this technique. The inner urges, wishes, emotions, etc., are not visible to an outsider and to the individual himself. Through this method both inner and outer activities can be judged. Thus the evaluation of personality through projective techniques will give the whole circumference of personality or try to assess the total personality of an individual.

Projective tests are so named because they induce the individual to project himself into the test situation and thus reveal his motives, attitudes, apprehensions and aspirations. He projects his own personality through the responses just as a film projector projects the image on the screen. Hence the name projective tests. Here, unstructured test material is presented and the whole situation is vague and undefined. The subject is asked to project his wishes to the vague test situations. The way in which this projection takes place in an individual, gives an understanding of the personality of that individual.

Some of the important projective techniques are the Rorschach Inkblot test, the Thematic Apperception test, the sentence completion test, the word association test or the picture association test, and children's Apperception test. Let us see what these techniques are.

(a) ***Rorschach Ink Blot Test***

This technique was developed by a Swiss psychiatrist, Hermann Rorschach in the year 1921. The material used in this test consists of 10 cards on which there are ink-blots. Five of them are black and white and five are multicoloured. These ink-blots are completely unstructured and do not have any specific meaning.

To investigate personality, the cards are exhibited before the subject one after the other and he is asked to describe everything he sees in the blot. The tester records the subject's responses, comments and reactions; the time the subject takes to give his first response; the total time for the test; the position of the card when the responses are given; spontaneous remarks made by the subject; his emotional reactions; qualities perceived (colour, form, movement); kinds of things reported (like anatomical parts, animals, plants and people song); and other incidental behaviour during the test session.

From the various responses the clinician or the tester infers certain personality traits. For the purpose of scoring, the responses are marked as location, contents, originality and determinants.

Location: It refers to the part of the inkblot with which the subject has associated with each response. The responses of the subject may be symbolised as (W) whole blot, (D) large details, (w) part of the inkblot, (d) minor details, and (s) responses related to white spaces.

Content: It refers to the actual meaning of the word seen by the subject in the inkblot. The common symbols used for scoring the contents of the responses are : H = Human being; A= Animal forms; Hd= Human details; Ad= Animal details; N = Natural objects like rivers and O = Inanimate objects or man made objects like pot, etc.

Originality: For originality certain responses are scored as popular (p) because of their common occurrences while others are extremely infrequent or new symbolised (O) or Originality of the responses.

Determinants : It takes the note of the manner of perception which directs the perceptual activity. The common determinants are: M= movements, F= form, C= colour and K = its shading.

The scoring of each card consists of attaching the appropriate symbols to each of the subjects answers in such a way that it represents as faithfully as possible an abstract of the subject's reactions to all the inkblots which indicates subjects personality. The subject who utilizes the whole card has the ability to solve his problems in a comprehensive manner. Thus whole responses indicate high mental ability. Responses indicating large details suggest a practical approach towards problems of life and these indicating observation of minute details express emotional conflicts. Too many colour responses are related to an individuals impulsiveness. A predominance of motion of human figures indicates vivid imagination and if a subject frequently refers to animal figures in the inkblots then he expresses his stereotyped thinking and is low in intelligence. If his responses are based on the shading effects in the inkblots, then it denotes his anxiety. Thus with the help of this projective techniques we can diagnose and understand the normal and abnormal personalities. The test demands a lot of training and skill in scoring and interpretation on the part of the examiner and, therefore, the work must be taken seriously and done only by an experienced and trained psychologists.

(b) *Thematic Apperception Test (TAT)*

Morgan and Murray in 1935 developed the TAT to know the peculiarities of personality with the help of some pictures. The test consists of a set of 31 cards out of which 30 depict various scenes and one blank card.

The test consists of perception of certain picture in a thematic manner, i.e., revealing imaginative themes. Observing these pictures, the subject by projection, identifies himself with the characters in the picture. The pictures are presented one by one to the subject who has to compose a story on them in some fixed time period, say five miniutes. Unknowingly, the subject expresses many of the peculiarities of the personality in this story by projection which expresses his natural desires, emotions and sentiments, etc. On the basis of these stories, the Psychologists analyse the personality of the subject and uncovers its specialities. But there are many problems as regards to scoring, reliability and validity of TAT in spite of its suitability for adolescents and adults.

(c) *Children Apperception Test (CAT)*

The CAT was developed by Leopold Bellak to measure the personality of children between 3 (three) to 10/11 (ten/ eleven) years of age. This test consists of 10 cards depicting situations or pictures of animals. These animals are shown in various real life situations like family relationships, toilet training and feeding habits, etc. When the cards are presented one by one the subject is asked to make up stories out of them. As per the quality of the information like the theme attitude towards parental figures, nature of anxieties, confidence, language used and the time taken for completion indicates the child's personality.

(d) *Word Association Test (WAT)*

The WAT is one of the oldest projective techniques originally employed by Carl Jung. This test consists of a number of selected words which are presented before the subject and asking him to answer as quickly as possible with the first word that comes to him/her mind. The response given by the subject and the time taken by him is recorded by the tester. It is noticed that some responses come out promptly and others with delay. The contents of the responses gives clues for evaluating the individuals personality. On the basis of the responses C.G. Jung divided personality into introvert, extrovert and ambivert, among other types.

(e) *Sentence Completion Test (SCT)*

A semi-projective technique used for assessment of personality is the sentence completion method. These tests consist of a list of incomplete sentences, generally open ended which require completion by the subject in one or more words. The subject is asked to go through the list and answer as quickly as possible in any way that he likes. The incomplete sentences are like the following.

(i) I feel happy when ....

(ii) I am worried over ....

(iii) I failed due to ....

(iv) I feel proud when ....

There are many completion tasks. These are Rotter Incomplete Sentence Blank, Rozenweig Picture—Frustration Test, Good Enough's Draw-A—Man Test, Tomkins-Horn Picture

Arrangement Test and Play Technique by Lewen Field's, etc.

On the basis of the completion tasks the examiner tries to see the total pattern of attitudes and feelings revealed in the series of responses and uses it as part of the total study of the individual.

(f) *Psychodrama or Role Playing*

It is believed that role play can be a good technique to understand the personality of children. Here, in this technique the experimenter ask children to do something and he observes the child while he is doing the thing or playing his roles. On the basis of his activities the experimenter can diagnose the child's social relationship with others and his manner of dealing with others which indicates has personality pattern.

Theories of Personality

Psychologists have developed several theories of personality to study the meaning and comprehensive nature of personality. These theories in one way or another, try to describe the basic structure and underlying constructs of the personality.

The following are the theories of personality.

(a) The Type Theory
(b) The Trait Theory
(c) Psychoanalytic Theory of Freud
(d) The Phenomenological Theories or Humanistic Approach :

   (i) Carl Roger's Theory
   (ii) A. Maslow Theory of Self- actualization.

(e) The Learning Theory of Personality

   (i) Dollard and Miller's Learning Theory.
   (ii) The Social Behaviour Theory by Bandura and Walter's.

A : *The Type Theories/Type Approach*

The type theories indicate that we can predict about the personality of the individual on the basis of their physique or physical characteristics which they exhibit. The view point of

Hippocrates, Kretschmer, Sheldon and Jung belong to this category.

According to Hippocrates the human body consists of four types of fluids, i.e., blood, yellow bile, phlegm (mucus) and black bile. The predominance of one of these four types of fluids in one's body gives him unique characteristics leading to a particular type of Personality.

Dominance of fluid type in the body.	Personality type.	Characteristics.
Blood	Sanguine	Active, hopeful
Yellow bile	Choleric	Irritable, angry
Phlegm (mucus)	Phelegmatic	Cold, Calm
Black bile	Melancholic	Depressed, dejected and pessimistic

E. Kretschmer, a German psychiatrist, classified human beings on the basis of physical structure and attempted to establish relationship between personality characteristics and body build.

Personality types	*Characteristics*
Pyknic (fat bodies)	Sociable, easygoing and popular.
Asthenic (lean and thin)	Unsociable, reserved, sensitive, shy
Athletic (balanced body)	Energetic, optimistic and adjustable
Dysplastic (mixed type)	Good natured

Similarly W.H. Sheldon classified all human beings on the basis of temperament besides the physical structure.

These are the following :

Physical characteristics	*Temperament*
Endomorphic (soft, round)	(Viscerotonic) love comfort and food, sociable, affectionate.
Mesomorphic (Muscular and strong)	(somatotonic) energetic, clear and competitive nature, risk takers.
Ectomorphic (thin and tall)	(Cerebrotonic) fearful, withdrawing, sensible, stay within their limits, reserved.

Carl Jung, a Swiss Psychiatrist, attempted to classify human beings on the basis of behavioural dimensions, i.e., introverts and extroverts. An introvert is more interested in the inner world of thoughts and feelings than in the outer world of affairs and actions. They are lovers of solitude and does not easily mix with others, shy, avoid people and enjoys to be alone. The extrovert on the other hand, take more interest in others and like to mix with people of similar temperaments, out going, social and friendly in social situations. But it is a fact that an individual may show both introvert or an extrovert tendencies in different situations. Thus these intermediate people are called 'ambiverts' or those persons who could be the mixture of both the qualities.

Morgan and Gilliland have mentioned four types of personality on the basis of temperament. These are the following.

(a) Elated—They are optimistic, elated and happy.
(b) Depressed—These people are pessimistic, depressed and emotional.
(c) Irritable—They are the interfering, irritable and hot tempered type.
(d) Unstable—Their mood is unbalanced, unstable and emotional.

Berman has given a number of glandular personality types.

They are as follows :

(a) Adrenal Personality is determined by excesses or shortage of adrenal secretion. If the secretion is excess then the individual is vigorous, energetic and persistent and if inadequate the individual is indecisive, irritable and unbalanced.
(b) Pituitary type personalities are determined by an excess or shortage of pituitary secretion. Excess secretion indicates high brain power, physical development and muscular vigour whereas other one indicates dull, sluggish and unbalanced.
(c) Thyroid personalities are those who have excessive or inadequate secretion of thyroid glands. Excessive secretion indicates lack of emotional balance and inadequate leads to inadequate sexual impulse.

E. Stranger, German philosopher divided human beings on the basis of interests in the following categories.

(a) *Theoretical* : The persons who are interested in discovery of truth and systematic in knowledge.

(b) *Economic* : Persons who are interested in practice rather than in theory and interested in hoarding money.

(c) *Aesthetic* : Persons who are lovers of beauty and are busy in harmony.

(d) *Social* : Persons of humane outlook and interested in social activities.

(e) *Political* : Persons interested to gain influence desirous of power.

(f) *Religious* : Persons who devote themselves to religious activities and interest in comprehending the unity of the universe.

Terman classified human beings on the basis of intelligence quotient. This classification includes the following types.

(a) Genius, (b) Very superior, (c) Normal, (d) Backward, (e) Feeble-minded, (f) Dull and (g) Idiot.

Freud, on the basis of his theory of Psycho-sexual development, identified three types of personailty. These are:

(a) Oral-erotic type of personality shows excessive degree of pleasures associated with oral activity. Sucking, biting or putting anything in the mouth gratifies the sex in infancy.

(b) Anal type is that when the child obtains gratifications through anal activities. Here the child is at first active later on passive.

(c) Phallic type of person shows self-love. But in the later stage it is called Genital phase in which the genital organ becomes the centre of sexual pleasure. The child is creative, adaptive, dependable and co-operative.

Criticism of Type Theories

The above theories of classifying personalities are not accepted in modern psychology because of the following reasons.

(i) Experience and observation make it obvious that most people cannot be fitted into any one type.

(ii) The 'type' raises doubts on the subject of cause and effect in the sense that it would be incorrect to assert that a certain person is solitude loving because he is an introvert.

(iii) Types cannot be established by measurement. It is not essential that these qualities will remain the same in a person.

B: The Trait Theory

There are some psychologists who try to explain the 'Personality' as the basis of the theory of traits. Trait is a quality or characteristics mode of behaviour which is consistently seen in an individual's behaviour over a long period of time. Cheerfulness is a trait; a cheerful man is consistently cheerful over a long period of time in varied situations. A trait may therefore be defined as a particular quality of behaviour which characterises the individual in a wide range of his activities and is fairly consistent over a period of time. A trait of personality means such a distinctive character of a person's thoughts, feelings and actions as marked him off from other persons. The cluster of characteristics is a trait. The following are the properties of Traits.

(a) *Scalability* : Traits are scalable and can be measured quantitatively.

(b) *Inference from Behaviour* : Traits are not directly observable, they are inferred and manifested in a number of activities and verbal expression.

(c) *Flexibility* : Traits are not static. They become stable with the maturity of the person in age but some variability is always there.

(d) *Universality* : There are certain traits which are universal in nature as height and weight.

(e) *Functional Unity* : The traits must have functional utility. It means that there must be different indications which may vary or are manifested consistently in behaviour of the individual.

(f) *Traits are Higher Order Habits and Mental Sets* : It means it is a readiness to respond to any variety of situations in a consistent way.

(g) Traits are learned and a frame of reference where personality of an individual is judged.

R.B. Cattell's Classification of Trait Theory of Personality

He defined that a trait is structure of the personality inferred from behaviour in different situations. He classified traits into four categories :

(i) *Common Traits* : These traits are found in almost everybody. It may be honesty, cooperation and aggression.

(ii) *Unique traits* : It is rarely seen with the individual and uncommon, unique in nature.

(iii) *Surface Traits* : It is found out easily on the basis of the manifestation of outward/overt behaviour, such as, curiosity and integrity, etc.

(iv) *Source Traits*: It is those traits which determine the behaviour of the individual. We only infer about it from behaviour, i.e., dominance and emotionality are source traits.

H.J. Eysenck's Classification

According to Eysenck there are three fundamental dimensions of personality. These are :

(i) Introversion Vs. Extroversion
(ii) Normality Vs. Neuroticism
(iii) Psychoticism

He tried to prove that personality is genetically caused. He traced neuroticism to the autonomic nervous system and introversion-extroversion to central nervous system. He emphasized importance of heredity in the development of traits of personality.

G.W. Allports Trait Theory

He emphasized that traits are not linked with a small number of stimuli but they are general and enduring in nature. The traits may be either unique to the individual or sufficiently common so that comparisons could be made between people. For example, two persons may both be aggressive but each will be aggressive in his way, depending upon individual experiences and capabilities. He classified all human traits into three categories.

(i) *Cardinal Trait*: It is one which appears in most of the behaviour of the organism and dominates on individual's every action. Some individuals are dominated by a single trait and become reference personalities by which we describe others.

(ii) *Central Trait* : It is those traits that are uniquely characteristic of the individual and manifest in a wide range of situations.

(iii) *Secondary Dispositions* : It is a specific narrow trait and called attitudes. Thus, traits differ in intensity and magnitude from individual to individual and each individual is unique in his adjustment.

Criticism of Trait Theory

(1) There is a view that a trait is a behavioural disposition which is consistent and does not vary from situation to situation. But trait is not a permanent or static of the individual because personality is undergoing perceptual change.

(2) It is difficult to quantify the human traits.

(3) Halo effect operates when a person rates an individual. He may rate high or low the same individual.

C: **Psychoanalytic Theory of Personality**

The psychoanalytic theory was advocated by Sigmund Freud. He propagated analysis of the psyche or mind to understand the behaviour and treating mental illness. Freud believes that the mind is topographical and dynamic and has three divisions which are always moving and interacting with one another, produce the personality. The three divisions of human mind are the conscious, subconscious and unconscious which are interlinked with Id, Ego and Super Ego produce behavioural characteristics. The three important components of personality are given below.

The ID : The id is the immoral basic stuff of a man's personality that is hidden in the deep layers of his unconscious mind. It is guided by the pleasure-seeking principle and has no values, knows no laws and rules. It does not recognize right or wrong and cannot differentiate bad and good. The Id impulses are primitive, blind, irrational and demand immediate gratification. But the id cannot be allowed to dominate because the organism must cope with the realities of the external world and so a second system operates.

The Ego : It functions as a policeman to check the unlawful activities of Id. It distinguishes between subjective reality and things in the external environment. It operates on the principle of reality. The ego formulates a plan for the satisfaction of the need keeping into consideration of reality principle. It brings a compromise between the instinct desire and the external world and take decision what appetites have to be satisfied and in which way they may be satisfied.

The Super Ego : The third concept is the Super ego. It is ethical or moral arm of the personality. It is idealistic and a decision-making entity which decides what is good or bad to the social norms. It works in accordance with the moral standards authorised by the agents of society. Thus personality is the composite view of the functioning of id, ego and super ego.

In addition to the above structure of personality, Freud tried to provide an explanation of the development of human personality through his ideas about sex. He advocated that sex is a life energy. The sexual needs of the individual are basic needs which have to be satisfied for a balanced growth of the personality. He will be an adjusted or maladjusted personality depending on the extent to which his sexual needs are satisfied. He mentioned the five different psycho-sexual stages for the development of personality, namely, oral, anal phallic, latency and genital. According to Freud, the persons experiences at each stage leave some characteristic impressions and imprints that influence his future personality development.

Advantages :

(i) It is a holistic approach to understand human personality.
(ii) This theory recognizes the importance of unconscious motivation in the development of behaviour patterns.

Disadvantages:

(i) The data of psycho-analysis is not validated against any criterion.
(ii) Psycho-analysis is an interpretation of behaviour rather than explanation of behaviour.
(iii) Sex as a source of human behaviour has been discarded by psychologists.
(iv) Objective verification of data is practically impossible.

D: *Humanistic Approach to Study the Personality*

Humanistic psychology, the socalled third force in psychology (the other two being behaviourism and psycho-analysis) reflects a humanistic trend in dealing with and understanding human behaviour. A number of theories, such as those of Goldstein, Angyal, Rogers and Maslow subscribe to the approach advocated by humanistic psychology. In this book we will only discuss the view points of Carl Rogers and Abraham Maslow.

(i) *Carl Roger's Self Theory*

Carl Rogers developed a quite different approach to understand human personality. He stressed the importance of an individual's self for determining the process of his growth, development, and adjustment to his environment and he is the person who determines his own fate. There are two basic systems underlying his personality theory—The Organism and the Self. The Organism is the centre of all experiences which are taking place within the individual at a particular time. It represents the totality of his experience—both conscious and unconscious. The self as a part of the phenomenal field can perhaps best be thought of as the concept of I, me or myself. What we recognise as the personality of an individual is the product of interaction between the organism and the self. The human beings have inherited the tendency to develop their self in the process of inter personal and social experiences which they acquire in the environment.

An individual's adjustment, happiness, growth and development all depend upon the union and harmony between the image of his self and the organisim, i.e., the experience or situation he meets in his life. Thus the basic drive of the individual is towards self actualization. For explaining the personality development it is very necessary to study individuals inner urge toward growth and wholeness, that leads to the development.

(ii) *The Self-Actualization Theory of Abraham Maslow*

Abraham Maslow, an American Psychologist has been the major theorist adopting the humanistic approach for studying human behaviour and personality. According to this theory, human beings are basically good and there lies in every one an impulse for the fulfilment of one's potentials. The behaviour or personality of a human being thus depends upon his style of striving towards the ultimate goal of self-realization. Thus, the pattern of human behaviour is always governed by the satisfaction of our needs from the lower, base level to the upper, top level. He presented his theory in order of hierarchy such as (1) Physiological needs, (2) Safety needs, (3) Need for belonging-ness and love, (4) Need for self esteem, (5) Need for self-actualization. Thus, the goal for personality development according to Maslow's theory is self actualization, i.e., realisation of one's basic human potential to the maximum extent and as effectively as possible. The theory, thus, presents a very bright picture of human behaviour and personality by setting an ultimate motivating goal of self-actualization (for details see motivation chapter). However, it is criticised on account of its not being objective and scientific in its approach.

E: ***Learning Theories of Personality***

The learning theories of personality depict a new developmental approach quite different from Psychoanalytic and phenomenological theories of personality in the sense that they emphasize the importance of learning and objectivity to understand personality. The notable psychologists like Pavlov, Watson, Guthrie, Thorndike, Skinner, Dollard and Miller and Bandura and Walters, consider the study of personality as a branch of general field of learning. They worked on the problems of behaviour changes through experiences and attempted to integrate those experiences in the development of personality. Here the theories of Dollard and Miller and Bandura and Walters are explained.

(i) *Dollard and Millers Learning Theory of Personality*

This theory emphasizes that what we consider as personality is learned. The child at birth is equipped with two types of basic faculties: reflexes and innate hierarchies of responses and a set of primary drives, which are internal stimuli of great strength and are linked with known physiological processes which impel him to action. Thus impelled by drives one acquires responses to the extent that they reduce the drives. Drive reduction results in reinforcements or rewards which in turn may give birth to many other drives or motives and impel the individual to learn new responses and new behaviour patterns. Thus this theory stressed the development of personality on the basis of the responses and behaviour learnt through the process of motivation and reward.

(ii) *Bandura and Walter's Social Learning Theory*

This theory believes that what an individual presents to the world at large as his personality, is acquired through a continuous process of structuring and restructuring of experiences, gathered by means of social learning and later imitated in corresponding situations. The imitation of the Model's behaviour is further reinforced in the viewer's mind by the recognition or reward the model receives as a result of his actions. An individual thus acquires numerous traits and modes of behaviour from many sources, and all these together contribute to the formation and development of his unique, distinctive personalty.

Role of the Teacher in Personality Development

Personality is the result of heredity and environmental influences. As regards to nature a teacher's role is limited but he can play a vital role to ensure favourable environment to foster the development of good personality of children. As we have mentioned the characteristics of a balanced personality elsewhere in this chapter we can say that the teacher can develop these qualities among the children by projecting these qualities through his own personality, showing selected personalities of eminent persons through audio-visual aids and creating conducive social and emotional climate and environment in the school. The way the teacher behaves and interacts with students can influence the children's ways of living. Thus, the teachers are the harbingers of knowledge and can mould the child according to the needs and requirements of the society which ultimately reflects the personality of the child.

Summary

In laymen point of view personality is considered synonymous with a good appearance and healthy physique. In psychology it means 'style' of an individual's behaviour and refers to his special characteristics and traits. The psychologists have defined personality in many ways like study of behaviour, organisation of traits, stress on aggregate nature and stress on adjustment. Allport gives a comprehensive definition of personality by giving importance on continuous, unique, dynamic and study of the whole individual.

Personality is a sum total of various human qualities. The characteristics of a balanced personalty here also mentioned subsequently to understand the nature of personality.

Development of personality takes place due to the influence of biological and situational factors. Biological or heredity factors in personality are difficult to study though there are few studies to determine unique individual attributes. Similarly social or environmental, psychological and cultural factors also influence the functioning of personality. The way children are treated in a culture, determines the personality patterns. Thus there are different factors which contribute to the shaping of personality.

Similarly the individual behaviour or personality can be measured by means of variety of techniques like observation, situation test, questionnaire, personality inventory, rating scale, interview and projective techniques. Thus through objective, subjective and projective techniques we can assess personalty.

At last personality theories try to explain the structure of personality by adopting various approaches such as type, trait, and developmental approach.

Theories adopting the type approach try to classify people into categories on types according to certain characteristics. Hippocrates, Kretschmer, Sheldon, Jung, Freud, etc., classified people on the basis of body built. Similarly, theories based on the trait approach try to describe people in terms of their unique pattern of traits. They define a trait as a broad reaction tendency or relatively permanent or consistent behaviour patterns which an individual exhibits in different situations. Thirdly Freud's Psychoanalytic theory of personality was explained. He had given emphasis on Id, Ego and Super Ego which are correlated with the conscious, the sub-conscious and the unconscious levels of mind. He also held that sexuality is at the core of all human behaviour.

Similarly the other humanistic theory of Carl Rogers self theory hold that personality to be a function of the interaction between the two systems (the Organism and the Self) of one's world of subjective experience. He linked the personalty with the development and maintenance of the self concept and the effort to achieve the ideal self. The second theory of Maslow was also discussed under humanistic approach. Maslow suggested a hierarchy of needs to be fulfilled to achieve self-actualization in his approach to study the personality.

Dollard and Miller in their learning theory of personality attempted to study the drive reduction, whereas Bandura and Walter's in their theory of social learning emphasized that people acquire personality characteristics by observing and imitating real life as well as symbolic models.

Lastly the role of the teacher in personality development was discussed in this chapter. Here emphasis is given on observation, modelling and imitation techniques of the teacher to develop the balanced personality among students.

Questions

1. What do you mean by personality? Describe characteristics of a balanced personality.
2. Discuss the type and trait approach to study of personality. How can the two approaches be reconciled?
3. Explain the importance of different determinants or factors in the development of personality.
4. Explain the concept and nature of personality. Discuss the various approaches to study of personality.
5. Define personality. Explain how to assess the personality.
6. What is the role of heredity and environment in the development or in shaping the personality of the child? Illustrate your answer with examples.
7. What are the various techniques of assessing personality? Describe the projective technique to assess human personality.
8. Mention the various factors that affect one's personality and discuss any two of them.
9. Bring out the difference between :

   (a) A personality inventory and a rating scale
   (b) A situational test and a projective test

(c) Trait approach and the holistic approach of assessing personality.
(d) Personality and Ego.

10. Explain the meaning and value of an integrated personality. Explain the teachers job in the integration of child's personality.

References

1. Allport, G.W (1948) : *Personality : A Psychological Interpretation*, Henry Holt and Company, New York.
2. Bandura, A. and Walters, R.H. (1963) : *Social Learning and Personality Development*, Holt, New York.
3. Campbell, C.M. (1934) : *Human Personality and the Environment*, The Macmillan Company, New York.
4. Cattell, R.B. (1950) : *An Introduction to Personality Study*, Hutchinson's University Library, London.
5. Dollard, J. and Miller, N.E. (1950) : *Personality and Psychotherapy*, McGraw Hill, New York.
6. Eysenck, H.J. (1971) : *The Structure of Human Personality*, Methuen and Co. (3rd ed.), New York.
7. Freud, S. (1953) : *An Outline of Psychoanalysis*, Hogarth Press, London
8. Fredenburgh, F.A. (1971) : T*he Psychology of Personality and Adjustment*, Commings Pub Co., California.
9. Hurlock, E.B. (1974) : *Personality Development*, Tata McGraw Hill Co., New Delhi.
10. Hall, C.S. and Lindzey, G. (1970) : *Theories of Personality*, John Wiley, New York.
10. Kundu, C.L. (1989) : *Personality Development : A Critique of Indian Studies*, Sterling Pub, New Delhi.
11. Pervin, L.A. (1984) : *Personality : Theory and Research*, (4th ed.), John Wiley, New York.
12. Stagner, R. (1961) : *Psychology of Personality*, McGraw Hill, New York.
13. Sherman, M. (1979) : *Personality, Pergamon Press*, New York.

MOTIVATION IN SCHOOL LEARNING

Introduction

There is very little school learning without mental activity on the part of the learner. The most effective learning takes place when there is a maximum of mental activity. Maximum mental activity is best attained through strong motivation.

Motivation is a super highway to learning. The major problem of the curriculum-maker and the classroom teacher is in knowing and applying the science and art of motivation. How do children learn "in doing what comes naturally"? Can such situation be artfully created? If so, how? What is the best technique for utilising this knowledge in motivating school learning?

Anderson said "Learning will proceed best if motivated". Melton said "Motivation is an essential condition of learning". Haris said "The problem of motivation is central both to educational psychology and to the classroom procedure". Gates said "The problem of motivation lies at the very heart of a sound educational programme in a free society or motivation is indispensable to learning". Kelly said "Motivation is the central factor in the efficient management of the process of learning". McClelland said "All motives are learned". Bernard said "Motivation is the basic problem of psychology in education. Thus it can be said that motivation is a golden road to learning although there is no sure method or procedure to guarantee the desired results.

Meaning and Definition of Motivation

Historically, the word motivation comes from the Latin root 'movers' which means to move. It means motivation is the process of arousing movement in the organism which is produced and regulated through the release of energy within the tissues. Thus motivation is an interval process. The following are the definition of motivation:

1. McDonald defined Motivation is an energy change within the person characterized by affective arousal and anticipatory goal reactions. It has three aspects:

   — begins in some energy change in the person characterized by affective arousal, i.e., some sort of psychological tension

   — characterized by anticipatory goal reactions, i.e., helps the individual to sustain his efforts leading towards realization of his/her goal.

2. Dececco defined "Motivation is those factors which tend to increase or decrease the virus in an individual. It determines level of activity in him/her and directs the activity".
3. Johnson defined "Motivation is the influence of general pattern of activities indicating and directing the behaviour of the organism".
4. Guilford defined "A motive is a particular internal factor or condition that tends to initiate and to sustain activity". Thus motivation includes all those internal conditions which begin an activity or sustain it.
5. Bernard defined "Motivation refers to all those phenomena which are involved in the stimulation of action towards particular objectives where previously there was little or no movement towards those goals".
6. Atkinson defined "Motivation is the arousal of tendency to act or to produce one or more effects".
7. More and Max defined "Motivation is characterised as a complex integration of internal processes which arouse, sustain and direct behaviour".
8. Sorenson defined "Motivation is a psychological and physical condition that causes one to expand effort to satisfy needs and wants".

Thus motivation varies in degrees. it may be low, moderate or high/intense. Different degrees of motivation may be required for different levels of complexity of the task.

Functions of Motivation

Motivation has four fundamental functions in learning. These are:

(a) Motivation energizes the behaviour of the organism (the child) and arouse him/her for action (initiates the activity).

(b) Motivation direct and regulate our behaviour (the child's activity).

(c) Motivation controls behaviour and does not allow the child to move in haphazard way.

(d) Motivation directed toward a selective goal (not all the activities) which the individual sets for himself/herself. It provides satisfaction after completion or achievement of goals.

Type of Motivation

Different classifications of motives have been effected from different view points. These are innate or intransic or natural and outward or acquired or extransic or artificial. When motivation arise from within the individual and is not linked with external forces and motivate the individual to perform some task or behave in a manner is called intransic motivation or Motivation is intrinsic when an individual recognises an activity as self-rewarding or derives satisfaction from the activity. Here motives come directly from within the person and no external pressures are necessary.

Similarly when outside forces such as praise/blame, rewards/punishment, and competition/cooperation, etc., compel the individual and provide incentives to achieve the goal is called extrinsic motivation. Or when a child does not perceive the inherent value in an activity and pursues the activity not for its own sake but for the sake of some external reward is called extransic motivation.

Motives : Meaning and Classification

Motives are variously described. They are called urges, drives, will, determination, incentives and the like. Hence there is a great deal of confusion as regards to their meaning. For the purpose of clarity, it is necessary to give the precise meanings of these terms.

1. The Oxford dictionary defines a motive as "that which moves or induces a person to act in a certain way; a desire, fear or other emotion, or a consideration of a reason which influences or tends to influence a person; also often applied to a contemplated result or object the desire of which tends to influence action".
2. McDougall defines it as a condition—physiological and psychological within the individual that disposes it to act in certain ways.
3. Fisher defined "A motive is an inclination or impulsion to action with some degree of direction".

Thus motive is an inner state of mind or an aroused feeling generated through basic needs or drives which compel an individual to respond by creating a kind of tension or urge to act. Motives can be grouped in the following categories:

TYPES OF MOTIVES

Physiological or Biogenic or primary or organic ↓	Socio-psychogenic or psychogenic/ psychological or social or secondary or Acquired ↓	Personal ↓
1. Food/Hunger	1. Social approval	1. Interests
2. Water/Thirst	2. Affection	2. Attitudes
3. Sex	3. Respect/Prestige & Money	3. Values
4. Clothing		4. Goals
5. Shelter and sleep	4. Praise and blame	5. Self-concept
6. Organic (temperature, glandular-excretions, etc.)	5. Aggressiveness 6. Gregariousness	
7. Emotion/fear/angry	7. Imitation	
8. Urge to escape	8. Sympathy	
9. Curiosity	9. Affiliation and	
10. Humour	10. Reward and Punishment	
11. Maternal behaviour &		
12. Combative role.		

Difference between Needs, Drives or Urge, Incentives, Goal Instincts, and Motives

1. *Need* : Needs are general wants or desires of a person. Need indicates a lack of something which is useful or desired. Every human being has to strive for the satisfaction of his/her basic needs if he/she

has to maintain or improve or fulfil himself/herself in the world. (Details will be discussed in theory).

2. *Drive or urge*: Drives indicate mental tension aroused by physical needs such as hunger, thirst, etc. The strength of a drive depends upon the strength of the stimuli generated by the related need or drives prompt man to action which should result in the satisfaction of bodily needs. It is an original source of energy that activates the organism or is an intraorganic activity or condition of tissue supplying stimulation for a particular type of behaviour. A drive is because of needs. If there is no need—no drive. The drive directs the behaviour in a definite direction according to the needs.
3. *Incentives*: The elements in the environment which help to satisfy drives are called incentives. Dececco describes incentives as the actual goal objects. Incentive insist, arouse and move to action or activates the activity. Positive incentives include praise, prize, smile, etc., whereas negative incentives are pain, punishment, etc.
4. *Goal* : A goal is that state in an activity whose realization results in the satisfaction of needs of the individual. When the individual seeks some end results of his/her activities and results are referred to as his/her goal. It may be immediate and remote.
5. *Instincts*: An instinct is an innate tendency to behave in a particular manner. It is called unlearned behaviour, because it arises from tendencies which exist in the mind of the individual at birth. it is a natural impulse by which human beings and all animals are guided independently.
6. *Motives*: It is a combination of thought, feeling or condition that causes one to act. According to William Thomas, there are four fundamental motives; (i) desire for security, (ii) desire for response, (iii) desire for recognition and (iv) desire for new experience. (For details see reverse.)

Techniques of Classroom Motivation

Research in child development is providing working generalisations for the class room teacher. Children differ in their rate of growth. Growth is an individual matter and must be appraised from the point of view of the nature of the individual. There can be no common expectancy for achievement when it is conditioned by sex differences, the total maturity of the child, and the family from which he comes. Children as they present themselves in schools have more things in common when viewed broadly than when single attributes are studied in detail. Similarities as well as differences deserve attention in class room.

Any successful school programme will have to take into account the dynamic nature of the child, his/her past experience, his/her total environment plus individual differences, and the manifold needs and wants as they manifest themselves. The following practical suggestions are presented as tool for the classroom teacher for effective handling of the classes and to bring desirable change in the school.

1. *Understanding the Degree of Maturation Required for Learning*

It is useless to attempt motivation in school learning, if the assignment is too difficult or the goals is too remote for the child's readiness or related to his/her maturation. Maturation and motivation must be synchronized. Formal learning can take place only if the learner is physically, mentally, emotionally and culturally mature enough to understand and carry out the assignment.

2. *Bringing Assignments within Child's Experience*

Experience is not only the best teacher—it is only the teacher. There can be no learning apart from experience and every experience can be an education. Quality learning is determined by the quality of experience on the part of the learner. learning is conditioned by past experience. We interpret new experience in the light of the old. Thus Learning based on past experience and tied in with the "total pattern" is more effective in comprehension and speed of learning. It is better integrated and longer retained because it is better organised. It is more functional and therefore meets the objective of all school learning in producing approved conduct through the various satisfactorily desirable experiences of the learner.

3. *Respect for Personality of the Child, Appealing to Ego-Maximization*

Ridicule and sarcasm are far from the best means of

motivating school learning. Children, as well as adult, have their pride and self respect. Any attempt to embarrass or humilate a child, especially in the presence of his/her classmates is likely to end in one of two undesirable results—withdrawal or pugnacity. Shame and embarrassment are not healthy emotions. They tend to disorganise the personality of the child. They produce uncertainty, hesitation, frustration, loss of confidence and self-respect. Sometimes they force a child to complete withdrawal from school activities and setup a mental attitude against all learning. In extreme cases, the child refuses to cooperate at all and will not answer any questions or utter a single word in school. In most cases, the child becomes pugnacious and aggressive, with a hostile attitude towards school and towards society. Thus, disregard for the personal integrity of the child is unwise and a feeling of frustration is the worst psychological atmosphere for motivating school learning.

Similarly it is a fact that we like those people, objects and situations that make us feel important and conversely, we dislike those people, objects, situations that make us feel inferior. Thus, the teacher can accomplish a great deal more in motivating school learning by appealing to ego-maximization than by shaming, ridiculing, and belittling the would-be learner.

4. Securing Attention, Creating Interest and Enthusiasm

The inattentive child is preoccupied and does not hear what is said—Securing attention is, therefore, the primary prerequisite for motivating school learning. It is true that the attention span is very short, especially in young children. The only thing that will bridge the gap is interest and enthusiasm. Interest may exist to some extent on the part of the pupil, if it is artfully created by the teacher. Thus, capitalising on natural interests and cultivating new ones is the hallmark of a good educational programme. The wise teacher explains a subject when the child is an inquiring mind or asks questions. The teacher's own interest and enthusiasm are contagious and will go a long way toward inspiring and maintaining interest on the part of the pupil. The teacher may provide multiple choice situations and numerous incentives suitable to the child's abilities and comprehension.

5. Attitude in Motivation

Attitude is one's set to react in a given way in a particular situation. It is relatively permanent and wider in scope then interest. Attitude limits and channels motives. It is a habitual response to identical or near identical total situations. It also creates the contours of the new experience and sets boundaries. Thus attitude of the teacher towards teaching play a vital role in learning and brings newness in the child.

6. Praise and Reproof in Learning

Experimental studies have proved that both praise and reproof are useful in moderation and may have a bad effect if carried too far or used indiscrminately. Thus reward seeks to influence conduct favourably by associating a pleasant feeling with the desired act and punishment seeks to defer or prevent an undesirable act by associating unpleasant feeling with it. Therefore, reward is pleasant and generate interest and enthusiasm and develop high moral. However, punishments often act as a deterrent and if the child can be made to realise that it is the undesirable act and not himself/herself that is being punished, then generate learning interest in the child.

Similarly, success and failure both help in learning. As the mercury in the thermometer fluctuates with temperature, so the level of aspiration varies with success and failure as determined in the mind of the learner. Thus, success and failure should be so balanced that the child does not lose his/her perspective. In the classroom the teacher can manipulate the situation so that every child will get a taste of success to temper the ill effects of failure. Failure may be considered temporary, with success as the ultimate goal. Thus the ideas of "quitters never win and winners never quit" may be emphasized in learning.

7. Emphasis on Positive Guidance

Experimental studies show that learning with positive guidance is superior to negative guidance. Positive guidance sets up a pattern and tends toward habit formation. The nervous system is so constituted that once a stimulus is received, its force is on-going, even after the original incentive is dropped. The negative approach of telling children what not to do is unfortunate, because it suggests, emphasizes, and keeps "warm" at the focus of consciousness, the undesirable act. The idea takes the form of compulsion and the act becomes inevitable.

8. *Clear Assignments and Definite Goals*

If the pupils possess a clear insight and understanding of the goals and objectives then it acts as a moral boost for him/her to do the work consistently. Frequent testing in the class with clear transparency will motivate the students to do the work with better perception. Thus, the teacher should set the goal very clearly to bring efficiency in the system of school effectiveness.

9. *Encouraging Self Motivation among Children*

Knowledge of results, high aspiration and clear goals are the best preparation and incentive to self-motivation, especially, if the pupil is directed and encouraged to set his/her own goals for themselves by presenting the possible choices and letting them choose. Self-motivation implies a will-to-learn. Thus to develop the will-to-learn, the teacher may demonstrate to the learner by figures and facts that desire for improvement and may be assured that he/she has not yet reached the limit of performance.

10. *Making Unconscious and Semiconscious Needs and Wants Conscious*

One significant means of strengthening the will to learn and improving aspiration to help the pupil make his/her unconscious and semiconscious needs and wants conscious. According to Brill, many of our actions are guided by our unconscious. An appeal to emotion is often more effective than an appeal to reason. Moreover, the unconscious is a truer index of the real innermost wishes and desires, and it never lies. Helping the pupil to clarify his unfelt goals and objectives as well as his pressing immediate needs and wants, gives him a better insight into the reasons for learning.

11. *Development of Self-Appraisal*

Many people live mediocre lives because they do not know "their own strength". On the other hand, the person who overrates his capabilities is constently running into rebuffs and failure for attempting the impossible. Proper appraisal of one's own potentialities is essential to a happy and useful life. The school programme and the class room teacher can do much in aiding the pupil to appraise himself/herself and his/her talents properly.

12. *Developing Values, Ideals and Life Goals*

Values serve as standards, as guiding principles, and place boundaries on behaviour. They delineate character and personality. It is the personality that determines behaviour. Personality develops in response to basic needs and wants. The process begins very early in life. Personality, in turn, even while in the early formative period, serves to regulate conduct. Thus to be effective in character-building, ideals need to be personified. It is much easier to be loyal to a person than to an ideal. Children are highly imaginative and decidedly imitative. They identify themselves with imaginary and real people whom they admire and envy. They are hero-worshippers. When they are encouraged to imitate worthwhile personalities, they unconsciously identify themselves also with traits of their heros.

13. *Setting a Good Example*

The teacher is a very important person in the school child's life. He personifies the democratic ideal and serves as a model. This is why the personality of the teacher is just about the most decisive factor in the success or failure of the school programme. His/her influence as a person far exceeds methods and materials in teaching. Thus, setting of a good example by the teacher play an important role in teaching-learning process.

14. *Emphasis on Group Dynamics*

The teacher, although very important, is not the only influence in a child's life. His/her playmates, parents, siblings, relatives, in short, every person with whom he/she comes into contact influence his/her behaviour directly or indirectly. Thus learning in groups seems to be superior to learning in isolation. Group dynamics are more effective when all members of the group are interested in the problem being studied and where there are vast differences in motives, group dynamics, will be adversely affected. Children are more cooperative, show more initiative, quarrel less, and display less friction and hostility between the members when they work in a group where democratic leadership prevails and it offers the best means available for development of social skills essential for democratic living, better social understanding and preparing the individual member of the group for democratic citizenship.

15. *Competition vs. Cooperation*

Experimental studies show that among very young

children (infants) the cooperative responses are more noticeable than the competitive responses. But excessive use of competition spirit may develop demoralization and frustration and cooperative and friendly rivalry develop team play, community spirit, self-discipline and high morale.

16. *Participation Through Participation*

This could serve as a motto for all schools. Participation is both an ideal method of motivating school learning as well as the most desirable objective in all formal and informal education. Thus activity based teaching-learning can produce better result in learning.

17. *Appealing to as Many Motives as Possible and to the Total Personality*

If appealing to a single motive is effective, the appealing to two or more motives is just that much more effective. This is the basic principle of the transfer of learning. The effectiveness of a given motive in any situation varies directly with the number of cooperating motives or facilitating factors, and inversely with the number of competing motives or inhibiting factors.

18. *Token Economy*

In a token economy, students are given tokens (e.g., check marks by their names on a blackboard), for appropriate (or inappropriate) behaviours, and these tokens can be traded in for prizes or privileges. Weil and Merphy (1982) have suggested three categories of rewards for classroom management. These are :

(a) Social rewards (e.g., smiles, praise, or hugs),
(b) Material rewards (e.g., stickers, stars, and awards), and
(c) Token rewards (e.g., tickets, passes, or check marks on a chart), etc., that can be redeemed for valued prizes or privileges.

Thus as part of the token economy, the teacher praises appropriate behaviour and ignores inappropriate behaviours.

19. *Knowledge of Progress*

This is found to be a strong incentive in learning. A child

who knows about the progress he/she is making, gets much encouragement and motivation from this knowledge. Thus it is a powerful incentive leading to improvement in performance, and elimination of errors.

20. *Effective Repetition and Active Participation*

It is a fact that repetition makes a man perfect and leads to effective learning. Thus the teacher should provide maximum satisfaction to students which ultimately strengthens voluntary repetition of action among them. Similarly pupils tend to do better work when they are active partners in an enterprise. School programmes which do not activise pupils become a one-way affair. Thus, the teacher should encourage the pupil's participation which promotes school learning ultimately.

Theories of Motivation

There are large number of theories of motivation. On the basis of these theories the importance, process and mechanism of motivation in studying human behaviour is explained. The following are some of the theories of motivation:

1. Morgan's Physiological theory of motivation
2. Maslow's theory of self-actualization or Need theory
3. Freud's Psycho-analytic theory of motivation
4. McClleland's theory of achievement motivation
5. Murray's theory of motivation.

Morgan's Physiological Theory of Motivation

This theory of motivation was developed by Clifford T. Morgan. However, the other supporters of this theory are William James, Zangwill, Rutherford, Lashley, Kretschmer and Sheldon, etc. This theory believes that body has to face number of changes and number of reactions every day due to some stimuli. The body of a person will determine his/her attitude and interest towards work or for action and behind all these changes and reactions motivation play a vital role. The concept of Central Motive State (CMS) was developed by him and concluded that all behaviour and activities are due to CMS on the part of the human beings and has a direct relevance in the recent wave of interest in electric stimulation of brain centres to find out the central control of physiological drives.

II. *Maslow's Theory of Self-actualization*

The theory of self-actualization was developed by Abraham Maslow (1954). His approach to understand human personality and motivation is different from other psychologists. He put forth the theory that man's basic needs are arranged in a "hierarchy". The appearance of one need generally depends on the satisfaction of the others. They are closely related to each other and may be arranged from the lowest to the highest development of the personality. The five sets of basic needs is given in hierarchy as follows:

V. Self actualization
IV. Self-esteem needs or independence
III. Belongingness and love needs
II. Safety needs
I. Physiological needs

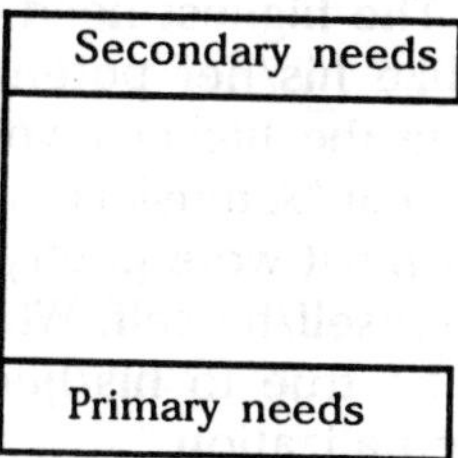

Maslow's Hierarchical Structure of needs

While the physiological needs, i.e., the need for the food or hunger, thirst, sex, etc., are necessary for survival are at the bottom of the structure the psychological needs, i.e., self-actualization are at the top. Starting from the satisfaction of the physiological needs, every individual strives for the satisfaction of the other needs of a higher order and this striving provides motivation for his/her behaviour. In this way the motivational behaviour of a person is always dominated not by his/her satisfied needs but by his/her unsatisfied wants, desires and needs.

When the basic needs are gratified or successfully fulfilled then safety needs become a dominant force in the personality of the individual. It means maintaining order and security and concern about their future safety. Hoarding money, purchase buildings, land and invest in LIC, etc., belongs to safety need and feeling psychologically secure.

When these needs are gratified the third need like belongingness and love need becomes operational. The individual is interested in making intimate relationship with other members of the society, being an accepted member of an organized group and interested to identify with the group life. But in big cities, people living in the same building do not know the next door neighbour and have no social life.

The fourth order of needs are esteem need. It means reputation, self respect, prestige, self-regard, status and social success and fame. One feels hurt when his/her self respect is injured. There are many status symbols in the society which give the feelings of self-esteem as possessing a house, land or bank balance, titles of honour and automobile, etc. Another type of esteem need is the need to feel superior to others. This need is gratified by purchasing of items as good and costly clothes. Maslow believed that suffient gratification of the esteem needs lessens their dominating force in a person's life and enabling him/her to move in the direction of self-actualization.

The highest need is self-actualization. An individual can actualize his/her potentialities as a human being only after fulfilling the higher level needs life love and esteem. Maslow writes that "A musician must make music, an artist must paint, a poet must write poetry, if he/she is to be ultimately at peace with himself/herself. What a man can be, he must be. He/She must be true to his/her own nature. This need we may call self-actualization."

When an individual is creative, non-conformists have sense of humour, keep means and ends distinguishable, democratic outlook, appreciate basic goods of life, high degree of spontaneity and simplicity, detachment, autonomous and accept themselves with others are the characteristics of self-actualizers.

Thus the fulfilment of self-actualization is a must for an individual otherwise he/she will feel discontented and restless unless he/she strives for what he/she is fitted for.

III. *Freud's Psycho-analytic Theory of Motivation*

Freud's theory of motivation is giving emphasis on instincts (sex urge/desire) and unconscious motives in studying human behaviour and emphasised that instincts are the root cause of all activities in human being. Similarly, the unconscious which is 9/10th of one's total mental content and consists of one's desires, repressed sentiments, wishes, ideas and feelings, etc., is responsible for all that we think, feel and do. Thus, the why and how of behaviour lies in the choices made by one's unconscious which are usually the gratification of sex or the seeking of pleasure. (For details see the psycho-analytic theory discussed elsewhere.

IV. *Murray's Theory of Motivation*

This theory comes under need theory and put forward

the concept of need to explain human behaviour. According to him a need is a construct (hypothetical force) which stands for a force which organizes perception, appreciation, intellection, contain and action in such a way as to transform in a certain direction an existing, unsatisfying situation. It means an unsatisfied need will force/compel a person to work until it is satisfied. He further classified needs as vicerogenic needs (primary needs) and psychogenic needs (secondary needs) to describe the motivation behind the tension reduction.

V. *McClleland Theory of Achievement Motivation*

The theory of achievement motivation was developed by D.C. McClleland at the Harvard University and John W. Atkinson at the University of Michigan. They are of the view that human behaviour is not intended to reduce tension and reach a state of physiological and psychological equilibrium rather it is the desire to do better, to achieve unique accomplishment, to compare with standard of excellence and to involve oneself with long-term achievement goals.

They are also of the view that achievement motivation refers to the degree to which a student desires to be successful. Within the context of schooling, it refers to the degree to which a student desires to perform well on school tasks or attempts to monitor his or her abilities (Weiner, 1978). Students who have high achievement motivation work hard and perform well on tasks. Thus in learning the teacher should encourage students and success must be reinforced immediately.

The propounder believes that human beings differ from one another in the strength of achievement motive and also in the opinion that all human motives are learned in the environment irrespective of their nature.

Development of Achievement Motive

The home, school and society plays an important role in the development of achievement motive. Early training at home, parental expectation, guidance to the child, social philosophy of the society telling the stories of great men and their achievements, proper environment in the class, teacher attitude, fixing independent responsibility, commitment and social climate, etc., develops achievement motive among students.

Measurement of Achievement Motive

The common measure employed to measure achievement motivation is T.A.T. (Thematic Apperception Test) of Projective tests. In addition to that a method of fantasy production and need for achievement questionnaire of Mehbrabian (1969) can also be used for measurement.

Educational Implications of the Theories of Motivation

Motivation plays a vital role for educational settings. Thompson is of the opinion that motivation is that education by which interest is created in a person, who does not have it. Similarly performance on educational tasks depends both on the students ability and effort. Thus the teacher should try to develop the spirit of co-operation among the students, develop the skills and competence in children which are of value to them, create group feelings among the students and provide the opportunities to students for self-expression.

Summary

Why we behave and how we behave in a particular fashion at a particular movement can be explained in terms of motivation. It is motivation which prompts, compels and energises one to engage in a particular behaviour. Thus, motivation is a super high way or golden road to learning and a central factor in the efficient management of the process of learning. McDonald, Dececco, Johnson, Guilford, Bernard, Atkinson, and many other psychologists have defined motivation according to their own way and suggested different functions of motivation.

The concept of intransic (when motivation arise from within the individual) and extransic (when outside forces compelled the individual) motivation have been defined. Similarly three types of motives such as physiological, socio-psychogenic and personal, etc., have been classified. Not only this the difference between needs, drives, incentives, goal, instincts and motives have also been given in the body of the chapter.

The techniques of classroom motivation in a practical manner have been given. These are understanding the degree of maturation required for the learning, bringing assignments within child's experience; respect for personality of the child; creating interest and enthusiasm; praise and reproof; positive guidance; clear assignments; encouragement; making unconscious and semiconscious needs and wants conscious; self-appraisal; developing values, ideas and life goals; setting a good example; emphasis on group dynamics; competition and co-operation; participation; token economy; knowledge of results/progress and effective repetition and active participation in learning.

Lastly Morgan's physiological theory, Maslow's self actualisation, Freud psycho-analytic, McClleland theory of achievement motivation and Murray's theory of motivation along with the educational implications for instruction have been given.

Questions

1. What do you mean by motivation? Classify motivation and bring out clearly its importance in the field of education.
2. What is meant by motives? Why some motives be realized and others inhibited?
3. Enumerate the merits and demerits of rewards and punishment in motivation of school learning. Which is more effective? What precautions would you suggest in the use of rewards and punishments in the classroom?
4. Discuss the different techniques in motivating school learning.
5. Define motivation and its role in learning. Differentiate between motives, needs, drives and incentives.
6. Describe Maslow's theory of hierarchy of needs. How is this theory related to the development of motives?
7. Discuss some of the important motives which can be used for learning in the classroom.
8. What motives are likely to be operative in the following activities (a) love of adventure; (b) dancing, (c) a mother's pride in her children; (d) stealing; (e) playing football?
9. What is the importance of motivation in learning? How will you motivate the unwilling pupils to learn?
10. Motivation is the golden road to learning 'Discuss'.
11. What do you mean by achievement motivation? Explain how do you develop achievement motive among students?

12. How will you motivate children in classroom teaching? Illustrate your answer with suitable examples.
13. What are motives? Why are moves considering important for understanding behaviour?
14. What is meant by motivation? Explain its significance in learning.
15. Explain the various devices of increasing motivation in the classroom.
16. Answer in brief :

    (a) Why is intransic motivation preferable to extrinsic motivation?
    (b) Which one would you prefer as a motivational device—reward or punishment ? Why ?
    (c) Differentiate the biogenic and socio-psychogenic needs.
    (d) Dangers of over motivation.
    (e) Sources of motivating force.

References

1. Atkinson, J.W. (1964) : *An Introduction to Motivation*, Princeton NJ: Nostrand.
2. Atkinson, J.W. and Feather, N.T. (1966) : *A Theory of Achievement Motivation* (Ed.) Wiley, New York.
3. Ansubel, D.P. (1968) : *Educational Psychology: A Cognitive View*, Holt, Rinehart and Winston, New York.
4. Bugelski, B.R. (1956) : *Theory of Motivation*, Henry Holt and Company, New York.
5. Bolles, R.C. (1967) : *Theory of Motivation*, Harper and Row, New York.
6. Bindra, D. (1959) : Motivation : *A Systematic Interpretation*, Ronald, New York.
7. Hall, J.F. (1961) : *Psychology of Motivation*, Lippincot, Chicago.
8. Jordan, A.M. (1956) : *Educational Psychology*, Henry Holt and Company, Inc. New York.
9. Kelly, W.A. (1956) : *Educational Psychology*, Bruce Publishing Company, Milwaukee.
10. McClelland, D.C. *et al.* (1953) : *The Achievement Motive*, Appleton Century-Croft, New York.
11. McClelland, D.C. ed. (1955) : *Studies in Motivation*, Appleton-Century-Croft, New York.
12. McDonald, F.J. (1972) : *Educational Psychology*, Wadsworth Publishing Co., California.

13. Maslow, A. (1954) : *Motivation and Personality,* Harper and Row, New York.

14. Petri, H.L. (1985) : *Motivation : Theory and Research*, Wadsworth, Belmont, C.A.

15. Stacey, C.L. and De Martioo, M.E. (Eds.) : *Understanding Human Motivation*, Howard Allen, Clevelands.

16. Stipek, D.J. (1988) : *Motivation is to Learn: From Theory to Practice.* Englewood Cliffs : New Jersey.

17. Valley, F.P. (1988) : *Motivation—Theories and Issues*, Brooks Cole, California.

18. Yong, P.T. (1936) : *Motivation of Behaviour*, John Wiley and Sons, New York.

19. Weiner, B. (1980) : *Human Motivation*, Holt, Rinehart and Winston, New York.

MENTAL HEALTH AND ADJUSTMENT

Introduction

A child is born in a home where he/she remains in the constant company of his/her mother in the formative years of his/her infancy. The impressions and experiences which a child has in these formative years leave permanent impressions on his mind. But it is true that harmonious development of personality in children cannot be developed because most of the parents do not have access to the scientific knowledge of human behaviour. The other problem is that a child at the age of six enters into the school and spends six to seven hours in school. Thus for balanced development not only the mental health of teachers but also the mental health of children are important because both physical and mental health is pre-requisite for self-development and self realisation. Everybody expects in these days that the main objective of the educational institutions are to produce pupils who are physically robust, mentally alert, emotionally stable and culturally acceptable individuals. Thus, this situation demand and provide sufficient ground to have a chapter on mental health and adjustment.

Mental Health: Meaning and Nature

Man is an integrated psychosomatic unit whose behaviour is determined by both physical and mental factors. Mental health is a normal state of well-being and defined as a 'condition and level of social functioning which is socially acceptable and personally satisfying.

1. Johns, Sutton and Webster defined mental health "is a positive but relative quality of life. It is a condition which is characteristic of the average person who meets the demands of life on the basis of his capacities and limitations". By the word 'relative' means the degree of mental health which an individual enjoys at a time is continuously changing.
2. Hadfield defined "Mental health is the full and harmonious functioning of the whole personality". It is a positive and active quality of the individual's daily living.
3. Coleman defined Mental Health "is the ability to balance feelings, desires, ambitions and ideals in one's daily living and to face and accept the realities of life. It is the habits of work and attitude towards people and things that bring maximum satisfaction and happiness to the individual".
4. Bowers defined mental health refers to "such abilities as of making decisions, of assuming responsibilities in accordance with one's capacities, of finding satisfaction, success and happiness in accomplishment of everyday tasks, of living effectively with others and of showing socially considerate behaviour".
5. Clark defined mental health "as the ability to adjust satisfactorily to the various strains of the environment or various types of situations in one's life".
6. Ottaway defined a mentally healthy individual has adequate self-acceptance, holds a realistic view of himself, enjoys freedom from inner conflicts and anxiety, and possesses adequate self-reliance and self-direction. He is able to express himself adequately in words deeds and thoughts to the best of his ability.

Thus a mentally healthy person enjoys the harmony of the "internal with external" and maintains a balance between his needs and the enviornmental factors that influence the satisfaction of these needs. He lives a fuller, happier, harmonious and effective life and accepts himself and accepts others. Thus, mental health has both individual and social aspects. The individual aspect connotes that the individual is internally adjusted and free from internal conflicts and tensions or inconsistencies and skilful enough to be able to adopt to new situations. But he achieves this internal adjustment in a social set up although society is constantly moving and changing. If a person maintains equilibrium and adjusts to the changing situation and is acceptable as a member of his society it is defined as mental health.

Mental Hygiene: Its Meaning and Nature

Mental hygiene is concerned with realisation and maintenance of the mind's health and efficiency or it deals with healthfulness of mind.

1. Crow and Crow defines "Mental hygiene is a science that deals with human welfare and pervades all fields of human relationships".
2. Dictionary of Education pointed out that mental hygiene means "establishment of environmental conditions, emotional attitudes and habits of thinking that will resist an onset of personality maladjustment. It is the study of principles and practices in the promotion of mental health and the prevention of mental disorders".
3. Shaffer has defined mental hygiene is to assist every individual in the attainment of fuller, happier, more harmonious and more effective existence. It deals with the human welfare and pervades all field of human relationships.
4. Boring has defined mental hygiene is to "aid people to achieve more satisfying and more productive lives, through the prevention of anxieties and maladjustment".
5. Wallace-Wallin has defined mental hygiene as "the application of a body of hygienic information and technique called from sciences of psychology, child study, education, sociology, psychiatry, medicine and biology for the purpose of observation and improvement of mental health of the individuals and of the community, (ii) for the prevention and care of minor and major mental diseases and defects and of mental, educational and social maladjustements".

Thus the mental hygiene has three aims (i) preventive, (ii) preservative, and (iii) curative. If we fulfil these three aims we will be having harmonious functioning of our mental health. Mental hygiene gives clue, rules and the laws which help us to establish adjustment and co-ordination with the environment.

Characteristic of a Mentally Healthy Person

(i) A person possessing sound mental health can adjust well to environmental situations and interpersonal relations and has a clear self-concept.

(ii) The well-adjusted person accepts his limitations and does not blame others for his deficiencies and does not run away from challenging situations. He is self-confident.

(iii) The well-adjusted person when meets with a conflict, he tries to resolve it on sound basis. He develops tension-tolerance and does not get disturbed in moments of displeasure.

(iv) He accepts joy and sorrow, success and failure with poise. Hence, mental health becomes synonymous with mental adjustment. He is happy and remains cheerful.

(v) A mentally healthy person knows his abilities, motives and desires, etc., and works accordingly. He has the right perception.

(vi) A mentally healthy person participates in creative and constructive activities and carries on nicely in society.

(vii) He is in touch with reality and his emotions are under his control.

(viii) He has developed a philosophy of life that gives meaning and purpose to his daily activities.

(ix) He has faith in his ability to succeed, he believes that he will do reasonably well whatever he undertakes. He has the capacity to face realities rationally and objectively.

(x) He is able to think clearly and constructively in solving his problems.

(xi) He is adoptable to the changing circumstances of the society, emotionally satisfied, capacity of evaluating his self behaviour, enthusiastic and reasonable and possess good habits and socially awakened.

Thus a mentally healthy person has developed a zest of living that includes a desire for activity which is reflected in an attitude of utilising whatever potentialities he possesses, in productive forms of behaviour.

Need for Mental Health

In fact, the foremost concern of education, today, is to produce mentally healthy persons and thereby well-adjusted personalities because mentally healthy persons are the real assets of the society for the twenty-first century. When something shocking happens, attention is immediately focused on the need for doing something about mental health in our schools. Thus for the development of the society in the scientific competitions age it is the teacher who can teach mental hygiene to the children in the class which in turn can maintain balanced mental health. Thus the mental health of teachers and students are the most important topics of the day because if teachers have mental health problems, they will most certainly affect their students in negative and even in dangerous ways. Therefore, it is essential to give emphasis on mental health of both educator and the educant in the educational institution.

Factors Determining Mental Health

There are different factors which determine the mental health of the individuals. These factors are as follows:

(a) *Heredity*: It is the sum total of the traits which provides the raw materials or the potentialities of the individual. What the individual inherits is the potentialities in relation to growth, appearance, intelligence and the like. Thus heredity sets the limits for his mental health. (For more details see heredity and environment chapter of the book.)

(b) *Physical Factors* : It also contributes to mental health. An individual with a feeling of physical well being ordinarily enjoys a good disposition and is enthusiastic and intellectually alert and reverse in case of sick people. Thus sound physical health causes sound mental health.

(c) *Social Factors*: It is the factors of the society in which the individual lives and moulds his behaviour. The following are the social factors which determine the mental health.

   (i) *The Home*: For enhancement of mental health the home should provide affection and security to her children, atmosphere of happiness and freedom, and harmonious relationship otherwise it may lead to abnormal mental health.

(ii) *The School*: The school can develop a sense of personal worth and social competence if its experiences are satisfying and affectionate in nature. A good school provides a congenial atmosphere and meeting the needs and interest of pupils which in turn develop the sound mental health.

(iii) *The Community*: The community which provides love and affection, a feeling of belongingness and settled the problems of the individuals by providing different welfare measures can facilitate for sound mental health.

(d) *Satisfaction of Basic Needs*: The basic needs like food, clothing and shelter are to be satisfied for development of sound mental health. If the needs are gratified by the individual then it will be a stepping stone for promotion of mental health.

Causes of Abnormal Mental Health

There are many causes of abnormal mental health. Some of the important causes are given below:

(i) *Home Conditions*

There are different conditions at home which causes poor mental health. These are (a) too much of punishment, (b) over protection, (c) unnecessary comparisons, (d) judging the child from one's own adult standards, (e) presence of step father or mother, (f) cruel behaviour, (g) broken home, (h) lack of love, sympathy and insecurity, (i) poverty and illiteracy, and (j) undesirable neighbourhood and uncongenial environment.

(ii) *School Condition*

The following conditions may lead to ill mental health.

These are : (a) frustrated teachers, (b) authoritarian environment, (c) lack of encouragement and harsh attitude of the teacher, (d) staff-students conflicts, and (e) indiscipline and strike.

(iii) *Society*

The following factors lead to poor mental health, i.e., (a) corruption and conflicts, (b) bad companionship, (c) degraded value system, (d) bad films and obscene literature and (e) favouritism, cruelty and injustice.

Thus, when a child gets such an environment he is unable to decide what should he do and what he should not. Accordingly he may loose mental balance and ultimately develop certain tensions which may lead to poor mental health.

Mental Health of Students: Its Restoration

The school is the second line of defense which assumes great responsibility in the process of harmonious development of personality. If teachers are encouraging and understand the child's needs and provide necessary facilities; if their discipline is not too rigid and harsh; if they allow children to behave like children rather than as young adults; if the school provides a number of interesting group activities instead of negative rules adaptations which the child has to make will be facilitated and no complications will arise then mental health of children can be restored. In order to preserve and maintain the mental health of the children the following steps should be taken in the school:

(1) *School Environment*: School environment plays an important role in the development of positive attitudes and promotion of positive mental health if it is free from caste, creed or religious feelings. Thus conducive environment for learning at school should be provided.

(2) *Democratic Administration*: School as an institution should function on democratic lines. School problems should be discussed with teachers and students and decision should be taken up by taking students into confidence.

(3) *Understanding of Potentialities and Weaknesses*: The duty of the teacher is to help the child to develop proper understanding of himself/herself. An exaggerated view of oneself always causes failures and frustrations. Therefore, child should have a realistic view of himself/herself as well as the world around him/her and should be helped to minimise negative factors as far as possible for their development.

(4) *Helping the Student to Reduce Suffering from Inferiority Complex*: The teacher should try to help the students to reduce their suffering from inferiority complex on the basis of engagement in multifarious activities. Once the child has achieved success and

develops self confidence he/she starts thinking about himself/herself and develops positive mental health.

(5) *Provision for Co-curricular Activities*: The school should organize co-curricular activities in such a manner that which will stimulate and encourage the child to participate. The organizational activities of the school may develop mental horizon and restore mental health in children.

(6) *Teacher's Role*: The teacher must be emotionally stable and have positive attitude towards teaching. His/her behaviour with students should be friendly so that he/she can create confidence in his/her students to face the realities of life which will ultimately help him/her towards promotion of mental health.

(7) *Helping the Children Coming from Families with Strained and Broken Relations:* The children who are coming from immoral families, should be given a careful treatment by the teacher. If the teacher tries to sublimate and channelise the thinking of such children and develop positive thinking then the teacher should try to reform themselves and maintain balance mental health.

(8) *Provision of Sex and Moral Education*: Most of the problems of adolescents are concerned with sex and moral conflicts which causes mental disturbances. Thus to develop positive mental health, sex and moral/value education should be made an integral part of regular curriculum.

(9) *Removal of Conflicts*: It is quite natural for the students to quarrel among themselves. It is wrong to criticise, beat or threaten the students in the class. Thus, the teacher should take necessary steps to remove the internal conflicts of the students for restoration of mental health.

(10) *Respect for Individual Differences*: The teacher should mark the individual differences among the children in the class and respect these differences. If freedom of expression and proper guidance can be given to the child in the class then there is every possibility to develop positive mental health.

Mental Health of the Teacher: Its Restoration and Promotion

Teachers' mental health plays an important role in the teaching-learning process. A mentally healthy and well-adjusted teacher plays a vital role in promoting the mental health of school children. If the teacher's mental health is improper he/she can misguide, breed discontentment and dissatisfaction amongst his/her pupils and do incalculable harm to the nation and to the students. The causes of maladjustment and poor mental health of a teacher are given below:

Causes of Poor Mental Health or Factors Affecting Mental Health of the Teacher

1. Personal difficulties sometimes stand intensified by the nature of the professional life.
2. Lack of professional aptitude and devotion to the profession causes poor mental health.
3. Lack of prestige. It is a fact that teachers are the builders of future nation. But the social prestige of the teachers are very low in comparison to other people with equal education. Hence it affects mental status of a teacher.
4. Heavy pressure of work. In schools, load of work is too much. The excessive work develops emotional tensions and mental fatigue which leads to anxiety.
5. Lack of service security causes anxiety in the minds of the teachers which may cause mental disturbances.
6. Poor salary: The salary offered to a teacher is inadequate. In comparison to other persons the salary is low and his/her promotion facilities are limited. Thus the teacher lives with utmost dissatisfaction.
7. Casteism : Sometimes the feelings of casteism become very discouraging for a teacher. He feels himself helpless and develops inferiority complex and may develop maladjustment.
8. Occupational hazards like frequent criticism, restrictions, extra work, high expectations of the members of society and leg pulling among teachers, etc., create conflicts in the mind of the teacher which leads to maladjustment.

9. Autocratic supervision: The supervision and inspection of the teacher's work is autocratic. The higher authority interfere unnecessarily in the work of teachers. They are generally in habit of finding faults only and do not find ways to improve the teaching work which ultimately affect their mental health.
10. Recruitment system: In most of the cases teachers are appointed on the basis of other considerations rather than teaching aptitude and teaching ability. This situation create conflict and jealousy among the teachers which leads to frustration.

Restoration/Improvement of the Mental Health of the Teacher

The following are the procedures/trips for the teachers to adjust with environment and with the profession.

1. Economic conditions of teachers should be improved by increasing salary and providing necessary facilities.
2. A close relationship should be established between teachers and the community. They should be encouraged to participate in community functions to strengthen social status.
3. The service conditions of teacher must be improved. The teacher should be given the minimum facilities to work in the school so that he/she can do new innovations, research and other experiments for professional development.
4. They should provide facilities to exchange their ideas without any fear.
5. Selection of the teacher should be done on the basis of the interest, attitudes, capacity of effective communication and high standards of academic pursuits.
6. Teachers should be allowed to present his/her academic activities in different professional bodies to obtain new ideas and exchange his/her ideas with others. Thus organization of seminar/workshops/ conferences, etc., may be arranged to develop a sense of self-realization and confidence in the teachers.

Meaning of Adjustment

The concept of adjustment is as old as human race on earth. From the very beginning of the period of Darwin the concept was used purely in biological sense. But man as a social animal not only he is to adapt to physical demands but also adjust to social pressures. Thus the concept of adjustment is not simple as adaptation. Psychologists and scholars differ considerably in interpreting its meaning and nature and defined adjustment as follows:

1. According to Coleman adjustment is the "outcome of the individuals attempts to deal with stress and meet his needs to maintain harmonious relationships with the environment".
2. According to Smith, "A good adjustment is one which is both realistic and satisfying. At least in the long run, it reduces to a minimum the frustrations, the tensions and anxieties which a person must endure".
3. According to Gates and Jersild the "term adjustment is a continuous process by which a person varies his behaviour to produce a more harmonious relationship between himself and environment".
4. According to C.V. Good "adjustment is the process of finding and adopting modes of behaviour suitable to the environment or the changes in the environment".
5. According to Shaffer "adjustment is the process by which a living organism maintains a balance between its needs and the circumstances that influence the satisfaction of these needs".
6. According to Arkoff "adjustment is the interaction between a person and his environment. How one adjusts in a particular situation depends upon one's personal characteristics as also the circumstances of the situation. In other words, both personal and environmental factors work side by side in adjustment. An individual is adjusted if he is adjusted to himself and to his environment".

Psychologists have interpreted adjustment from two points of views, i.e., Adjustment as an achievement and Adjustment as a process.

Adjustment as an achievement means how efficiently an individual can perform his duties in different circumstances.

Similarly, adjustment as a process is of major importance for psychologists, teachers and parents and describes the ways and means of an individual's adaptation to himself and his environment without reference to the quality of such adjustment or its outcome in terms of success or failure. It only shows how an individual or a group or groups of people can cope up under changing circumstances otherwise known as adjustment as a process.

Thus we see that adjustment means reaction to the demands and pressures of social environment imposed upon the individual or it is not only the process of fitting oneself into available circumstances but also the process of changing the circumstances to fit one's needs.

Meaning of Maladjustment

Maladjustment refers to the failure of the individual to adjust to the needs of self and demands of the environment. It can be judged from the behaviour of an individual shown in a given situation. Thus the pattern of behaviour is not conformity with the social and cultural patterns or within the range of the culturally permissible patterns at home or in the school or in the community is called maladjusted behaviour. These children are unmanageable in the home, causing difficulties for the parents and siblings. They are problem creators in school, retarded in educational achievements, destructive, quarrelsome and often socially immature. These children are sometimes called emotionally disturbed or socially unacceptable or delinquent or having psychological instability and require special educational treatment in order to develop their personal and educational readjustment. Thus, maladjustment refers to a disharmony between the person and his environment.

Causes of Maladjustment

There are numerous factors in home, society and school which leads to maladjustment in addition to the physical, psychological and psycho-social factors. Let us now discuss the factors contributing to maladjustment.

1. *Physique*

The physique and appearance play an important role in the social development of the child. Inadequacy of the biological structure and nervous system very much influences the adjustment of the individual. Eysenck is of the view that the tendency of maladjustment is to some extent genetically determined. Physical disabilities develop a number of problems resulting in maladjustment.

2. *Long Sickness and Personal Inadequacies*

When a child suffers from long diseases or sickness his/her social development and academic achievement in school suffers a lot. He/She feels perplexed and frustrated. This situation leads to maladjustment. Similarly there are ambitious parents who decide the goals for their children without understanding the mental status and abilities. This may frustrate the child and he/she may commit many mistakes which ultimately affects his stability.

3. *Parental attitude and Broken Home*

Today the parents fail to give the child the love, affection security, acceptance and direction that he/she needs to develop adequately. Besides, there are rapid social and economic changes taking place and the old practices are being replaced by new ones. If the parents are unable to fulfil the needs and show lack of affection then it may lead to maladjustment. Similarly children in broken homes and conflicting family, do not get the affection, security and guidance which affect the mental stability of the children.

4. *Poverty and Illiteracy*

It is true that due to poor home condition the parents cannot fulfil the legitimate needs of their children which may lead to maladjusted behaviour. Similarly, illiterate parents sometimes may not give proper guidance and help to the child which are certainly required for smooth running of his/her life. This may also create confusion and conflict which may lead to maladjusted behaviour.

5. *Acceptance of Social Values*

There exists the reciprocal relationship between a person and the society in which he/she lives. He/She must adhere to the values and norms prescribed by the society. If the social values are maintained, the individual will be given the status of a normal person. But sometimes the individual is unable to cope up with the societal values which may lead to misunderstanding and turn to maladjusted behaviour.

6. *Class Differences and Religious Practices*

In our country it is a fact that there are privileged and underprivileged people living with different beliefs, habits, practices and thinking. Because of these differences, differential treatment are given to the children of different communities which may consequently lead to maladjustment.

7. *Teacher and Curriculum*

Teachers are the pivot in the school. They can either make or mar the nation if they so desire. But it is noticed that most of the teachers in the school are ill-trained and commit blunders in handling children and their problems. Similarly the needs of the children are not met in the present day curriculum effectively and also do not cope up with the changing environment. Thus this situation creates tension and anxiety in children which leads to maladjusted behaviour.

8. *Classroom Climate or Unfavourable Atmosphere in the School*

Classroom climate and unfavourable atmosphere in the school may create emotional tension and problems among the students which may ultimately lead to maladjusted behaviour. In the research study it is found out that authoritarian administration affects the mental health adversely and negatively and develops the feeling of inadequacy and incompetence which ultimately results in maladjusted behaviour.

9. **Rigid Discipline**, adverse report, discrepancy, lack of recognition, present day examination pattern and lack of guidance, etc., also develop the maladjusted behaviour among the children.

10. Unfulfilment of Need

If the needs of the children are not gratified then it may lead to frustration which ultimately affects the pattern of adjustment. This situation may develop, maladjusted behaviour among the children.

Symptoms of Maladjustment

An adjusted individual is able to make appropriate responses to overcome frustrating situations whereas the responses of a maladjusted person is inadequate and inappropriate, unable to resolve his internal conflict, partially successful in reaching his goals, lack of insight and potentialities and leads to abnormal emotional responses. The symptoms of maladjustment are the following:

1. ***Physical Symptoms***: Stuttering, stammering, scratching head, facial twitching, biting nails, rocking feet and restlessness.
2. ***Nervours Disorders*** : Fears—anxiety, phobias, timidity, oversensitivity. Withdrawal—unsociability and solitariness. Depression—brooding and melancholy periods. Excitability—overactivity. Apathy—lethargy, unresponsiveness and no interests.
3. ***Habit Disorders***: Speech—stammering and defect in speech. Sleep—night terrors, walking or talking in sleep; Nail biting, indiscriminate eating, physical symptoms like allergic conditions.
4. ***Behaviour Disorders*** : Unmanageable—defiance disobedience, aggressiveness, destructiveness, cruelty, jealous behaviour, stealing and begging, truancy, violence, hyperactivity, negativism and sex disturbances.
5. ***Emotional Symptoms***—Excessive worry, fear, inferiority, hatred, extreme timidity, persistent anxiety, conflict and tension.
6. ***Educational and Vocational Difficulties***: Unusual response to school discipline, inability to concentrate and inability to keep jobs.

All these symptoms are the signs of maladjustment.

Measurement of Adjustment

There are different techniques through which detection or measurement of adjustment can be possible. These techniques are testing techniques, projective techniques, inventory techniques, sociometric techniques, scaling techniques and observation and interview techniques.

The teacher may use any of the technique to measure adjustment. The important tests and measures of adjustment are Bell's adjustment inventory, Edward's personal preference schedule, Heston personal adjustment inventory and money problem checklist, etc. In addition to that there are various other inventories through which measurement of adjustment can be undertaken.

Characteristics of a Well-adjusted Person

The following are the characteristics of a well adjusted person:

1. Awareness of his own strength and limitation.
2. Respecting himself and others.
3. An adequate level of aspiration, i.e., neither too low nor too high in terms of his own strength and abilities.
4. He feels reasonably secure and maintains his self esteem.
5. He likes people, admires their good qualities and wins their affection and does not have fault finding attitude.
6. Observation is scientific in nature.
7. Accept the views of others and accommodate to changed circumstances.
8. He has the will and the courage to resist and fight odds and the capacity to deal with adverse circumstances.
9. A realistic perception of the world and always plans, thinks and acts pragmatically.
10. He feels satisfied with his surroundings and fits in well in his home, neighbourhood and other social surroundings.
11. A balanced philosophy of life and no stress and strain.
12. He is in touch with reality and not easily frustrated.
13. He is happy at work.
14. He can make and break friendships.
15. He maintains his zeal and enthusiasm despite all odds.

Methods of Adjustment or Defence Mechanisms or Mechanisms of Adjustment

When an individual meets with stress in the form of a conflict, frustration, anxiety or pressure, his immediate reaction is either to be aggressive or to be withdrawal type or play as a neutral role in order to reduce his mental tension and to maintain balance in the society. These common ways which the individual use to defend or escape from conflicts is known as defence or adjustment mechanisms. The defence mechanism helps the individual to preserve him self-concept and to protect him from anxiety. Every individual uses these mental mechanisms or protective devices to some extent or the other to escape from conflict situation.

Any habitual method of overcoming blocks, reaching goals satisfying motives, relieving frustration and maintaining equilibrium is called adjustment mechanism. Thus, in order to lead a healthy, happy and satisfying life one has to learn the various ways of adjustment, i.e., coping with one's environment as effectively as possible. The methods used for keeping and restoring harmony between the individual and his environment can be grouped into two categories, i.e., direct and indirect methods.

Direct Methods of Adjustment Mechanism

This is the method by which the individual makes efforts to reduce/release his tension consciously. These methods are logical and rational in nature and employed intentionally in getting permanent solution of the problem faced by the individual in a particular situation. The following are the direct method of adjustment mechanism:

1. *Removing the Difficulty/Hurdles*

Here the individual tries to either remove or destroy all the barriers and difficulties which comes in his/her way to reach his goals.

2. *Improving Efforts*

When one finds it difficult to remove his/her barriers or solves his/her problems to cope up with the environment he/she may attempt with a new zeal by increasing his/her efforts to overcome the difficulties. This activity develops confidence and improves his/her behaviour.

3. *Change in the Working Pattern*

When the individual sees that he/she is unable to remove or destroy his/her barriers, he/she thinks again about his/her approach and makes necessary changes in the means or path to achieve the goal/destination.

4. *Adopting Compromising Means*

For maintaining harmony between himself/herself and

the environment one may change his/her direction of efforts by changing the original goal or may seek partial substitution of goal or may adopt compromising means to maintain harmony.

5. *Substitution to Other Goals*

In spite of the best attempts, sometimes it is found out that the individual fails to achieve his/her goal. If this situation occurs then the individual substitutes the original goals by some new goals, i.e., the person who could not become I.A.S. Officer, may adopt the profession of teaching.

6. *Withdrawal*

There are many persons who do not like to face the confrontation and take risk in their life. They try to adjust by accepting defeat or withdrawing themselves from the situation to maintain balance in the environment.

7. *Making Proper Choices and Decisions*

When a person is confronted with two or more equally desirable goals he/she adopts the method of problem solving and starts analysing the total situation and tries to decide more rationally and logically the choices and decisions to achieve the goals.

Indirect Methods of Adjustment Mechanism

This is the method by which a person tries to seek temporary adjustment or makes an effort to reduce tension unconsciously. The following are the mental devices/ mechanisms in the process of one's adjustment to one's self and the environment.

1. *Projection*

Putting blame on others for one's failure is called projection. It means to project one's feelings, thoughts, and aspirations on external objects or in which the individual places the blame for his difficulties to others. By this mechanism the individual is able to direct his aggressive feelings towards others rather than towards himself. A student who has been caught in the examination for cheating may satisfy himself that others had also cheated. Similarly an individual who is lazy prefers to justify himself by declaring that he does not work because all others are not working.

2. *Rationalisation*

It means giving justification. This is a process of protecting our feelings of worth or self-esteem by giving desirable but untrue execuses. For example, the person who could not get the grapes, may say that 'grapes are sour' and he does not want to have them. A boy who is late for school finds many execuses, i.e., the clock was slow, breakfast was late or she failed just by two marks because the teacher had a grudge against her. A promotion is not received because the employer is biased.

3. *Repression*

It is a mechanism in which painful experiences, conflicts and unfulfilled desires are pushed down into our unconscious. In this way one unconsciously tries to forget the things that might make him anxious or uncomfortable. One tries to get temporary relief from the tension or anxiety by believing that the tension producing does not exist. A person who hates his father and a person who wished her mother dead, cannot express their feelings as they cause pain, shame or guilt. Such repressed desire or thoughts however do not remain hidden or permanently inhibited. They crop up nightmares, anxiety, reactions, stuttering and other nervous manifestations. Through repression a person conveniently forgets the things that might make him uncomfortable.

4. *Suppression*

In suppression we consciously decide to exclude an idea from our thoughts, our action and conversation whereas in repression painful and anxiety producing experiences are unconsciously and automatically excluded from the conscious thought process. Suppression is the wilful evasion of an irritating conflict, the conscious rejection of a painful experience or a deliberate attempt to forget a distasteful event.

5. *Simple Denial*

The easiest way of maintaining the balance of personality development is to deny the facts which could create conflict in the mind. When children are busy in play activities, if parents call them, the children will say they heard nothing. Adults are also not always prepared to admit their fault/failures frankly in their daily life. Denial helps to postpone facing a problem or a failure.

Note: The above five mechanisms are called mechanism of Denial. In using these mechanisms the individual is unaware of the existence of the stress situation and explains away the facts by giving excuses.

6. *Compensation*

This is a mechanism by which an individual tries to balance or cover up his deficiency in one field by exhibiting his strength in another field or try to overcome a failure or deficiency in one area through achieving recognition in another area. For example, an academically weak student may work hard and show his abilities in dramatics and compensate his failure, i.e., the boy who is weak in English compensates in math. Thus this is a mechanism which provides an individual with substitute satisfaction, when his actual needs are thwarted.

7. *Sublimation*

It is a mechanism of substitution by which an individual directs his energies and drives away from activities which are socially or morally unacceptable, towards those which are approved in order to satisfy a need. It is usually related to the sex drive, an individual who is unable to satisfy his sex needs would make up by reading romantic books, drawing romantic pictures or writing romantic poems. It is the mechanism in which all divisions of the psychic, i.e., the id, ego, and the super-ego work in concert with each other. An unmarried woman interested in children may give expression to her repressed marital urge by engaging herself in orphanage work or in any child welfare institution.

8. *Identification*

It is an adjustment mechanism which enables one to achieve satisfaction from the success of other people, groups or organisations. An adolescent who accepts a film star as his ideal tries to appear and act in the manner he has seen the star acting and students often identify themselves with their favourite teachers. As a result of this we adopt the mannerisms and habits of our favourite artists, teachers, friends and filmstars, in dress, in speech and in other styles of living.

9. *Displacement*

This is a defence mechanism, whereby the individual expresses his feelings indirectly to an object because he is unable to express his feelings directly to the object of frustration. When a person is rebuked by his boss in the office he comes home and angrily shouts at his wife and children for no apparent reason to retaliate or to reduce stress. This displacement is usually an indirect form of aggression reduction.

(*Note*: An individual at times faces a stress situation which very often gives no scope for escape or denial. Then substitution (above mechanism) are used as a form of defence mechanism. Here the individual does not runaway from reality, nor does he deny the existence of a challenge to his self-concept, instead he recognises his incapacities and tries to do something about it and improve himself in the areas where he can improve. These mechanisms are therefore more realistic and useful).

10. *Seclusiveness on Shyness*

This is the most common form of escape. For example, an inexperienced person in a discussion group would merely watch the proceedings without participating in it. This attitude protects him from doing anything that will be considered as wrong by the group. In using this mechanism an individual tends to withdraw himself from the situation that causes frustration or failure.

11. *Regression*

It means going backward or returning to the past. Very often we tell older children 'not to act like a two year old kid'. It is a device to escape a stress situation by reverting to infantile or earlier modes of behaviour. A five year old child may regress when a sibling is born or he feels neglected, unloved and depressed.

12. *Fantasy or Day-dreaming*

It is a kind of mechanism of withdrawal or escape to reduce frustrations. Sometimes when an individual is unable to solve his/her problems in a realistic manner he/she can satisfy and gratifies his/her desires in fantasy achievements or through imagination or day-dreaming. For example, an ambitious individual may imagine himself/herself winning everything and climbing the ladder of success in every sphere. It is a fact that many of the day dreaming arise from the individual's own environment or are borrowed from movies.

novels and adventure stories. If a person who has never entered the finals in any of the athletic meets imagines himself/ herself running at the Olympics and returning home with a gold medal is known as fantasy.

13. *Alcoholism and Drug Addiction*

When alcohol or drugs is taken by an individual it may give a sadistic feeling of pleasure for the time being and temporarily although he is not free from real life problems. Once a person is addicted to either of them, not only the individual deteriorates physically and mentally but also he will be a failure in the society. Thus it is advised that one should not use the above mechanism to reduce his/her stress in life.

(*Note*: In using these mechanisms of denial the individual is unaware of the existence of the stress situation and feels comfortable by giving excuses. Hence the mechanisms of denial may be avoided as far as possible.

Summary

Adjustment is not a simple term like adaptation or accommodation. It is a condition or state of mind and behaviour in which one feels that one's needs have been gratified. A well adjusted child is able to satisfy a good proportion of his needs and is able to deal with frustrating situations successfully. As long as this situation happens, the individual remains adjusted, failing which, he may drift towards maladjustment or mental illness.

While the normal behaviour is integrative and adaptive and maintain balance between inner needs and perceived opportunities the abnormal behaviour is non integrative. Symptoms of maladjustment include nervous disorders such as fears, unsociability, depression, apathy, disorders of speech, sleep and behaviour disorders.

It is a fact that mental health is the full and harmonious functioning of the whole personality and the ability to adjust satisfactorily to the various strains of the environment. He/ She is the person who develops tension-tolerance habits, accepts his/her limitations, and possess the right perception in life. But there are different factors like home, school, society and the community which affect the mental health of both students and the teacher and accordingly different suggestions have been given to overcome from the above situations and improve the functioning of the teacher.

The concept of adjustment is related to the concept of mental health. A mentally healthy individual has adequate self-acceptance, a realistic view of himself and the world around him and free from conflicts. He maintains his zeal and enthusiasm despite of all odds. But sometimes situation demands to adopt the mechanisms of adjustment to maintain the equilibrium. These are called defence mechanisms although it is used by the individual temporarily for his/her adjustment.

Questions

1. "Mental health of school depends greatly on the basic personality pattern and professional traits of the teacher", Discuss.
2. Describe the concept of mental health and mental hygiene. What are the characteristics of a mentally healthy individual?
3. Define adjustment and its main characteristics. How will you detect maladjustment?
4. How is mental health related to adjustment? Discuss the steps that should be taken to improve mental health of the child.
5. How is adjustment of the child influenced by the behaviour of the teacher? How does teacher's maladjustment affect pupil's adjustment?
6. Explain the term defence mechanism. How are they classified? Why does an individual use these mechanisms?
7. What methods and practices used in the school do you think have an unfavourable effect on the mental health of the pupils?
8. What is adjustment process ? What are the causes of maladjustment and how will you remove them?
9. How can the school help in preventing the mental ill-health of children? Explain.
10. What are the factors responsible for maladjustment of teachers? Suggest some concrete measures to improve the mental health of teachers.

References

Arkoff, A. (1968) : *Adjustment and Mental Health,* McGraw Hill, New York.

Bernard, H.W. (1952) : *Mental Health for Classroom Teachers*, McGraw Hill Book Co., New York.

Bonney, M.E. (1960) : *Mental Health in Education*, Allyn and Bacon, Boston.

Brown, J.F. (1940) : *The Psychodynamics of Abnormal Behaviour*, McGraw Hill Book Co., New York.

Carrol, H.A. (1951) : *Mental Hygiene*, Prentice Hall, New York.

Crow, L.D. and Alice, C. (1956) : *Understanding our Behaviour*, Alfred A. Knoff, New York.

Fenton, N. (1943) : *Mental Hygiene in School Practice*, Stanford University Press, Stanford.

Gates, A.S. and Jersild, A.T. (1970) : *Educational Psychology*, Macmillan, New York.

Klein, D.B. (1956) : *Mental Hygiene*, Henry Holt and Company, New York.

Kaplan, L. (1959) : *Mental Health and Human Relations in Education*, Harper and Row, New York.

Lazarus, R.S. (1976) : *Patterns of Adjustment*, McGraw Hill, Tokyo.

Lindgren, H.C. (1954) : *Mental Health in Education*, Henry Holt and Co., New York.

Maslow, A.H. (1941) : *Principles of Abnormal Psychology*, Harper and Row, New York.

McKinney, F. (1961) *Psychology of Personal Adjustment*, John Wiley, New York.

Patty, W.L. and Johnson, L.S. (1963) : *Personality and Adjustment*, McGraw Hill, New York.

Rivlin, L. (1963) : *Education for Adjustment*, Appleton Century, New York.

Sawrey, J.M. and Telford, C.W. (1963) : *Dynamics of Mental Health : The Psychology of Adjustment*, Allyn and Bacon, Boston.

Shaffer, L.F. (1936) : *The Psychology of Adjustment*, Houghton Mifflin, Boston.

Symonds, P.H.(1946): The Dynamics of Human Adjustment, Appleton Century, New York.

Wall, H.D. (1955) : *Education and Mental Health*, UNESCO, Paris.

William, C. (1971) : *Challenges of Personal Adjustment*, Mcmillan, New York.

Young, K. (1947) : *Personality and Problems of Adjustment*, Routledge and Kegan Paul, London.

EDUCATION OF GIFTED AND BACKWARD OR SLOW LEARNING EXCEPTIONAL CHILDREN

Introduction : Meaning and Definition of Exceptional Children

The term exceptional children has been defined in many ways by different authors. Some psychologists use this term only to refer to bright and talented children, whereas others use it for physically handicapped, socially handicapped, emotionally handicapped and in case of the children of mentally deviant cases. Thus, the term exceptional children would include both the intellectually gifted and the severely retarded children and carries a very wide connotation. The following are the definitions:

(i) Kirk defines "the exceptional child is that child who deviates from the average or normal child in mental, physical or social characteristics to such an extent that he requires a modification of school practices or a special educational services in order to develop to his maximum capacity".

(ii) Cruichshank defines "an exceptional child is he who deviates physically, intellectually, emotionally and socially so markedly from normal growth and development that he cannot be benefited from a regular class-room programme and needs special treatment in school".

(iii) Telford and Sawrey defines "the term exceptional children refers to those children who deviate from the normal in physical, mental, emotional or social characteristics to such a degree that they require special social and educational services to develop their maximum capacity.

Types of Exceptional Children

The above definition clearly indicates that the exceptional children are those children who deviate from the normal or average students to either side. The following are the division of exceptional children:

1. Intellectually Exceptional:	(a) The gifted and the creative, (b) The slow learner, and (c) mentally retarded.
2. Physically Exceptional :	(a) The crippled, (b) Orthopaedically handicapped, (c) The hard of hearing and the deaf, (d) the dumb. (e) The Blind or the Partially sighted.
3. Emotionally Exceptional :	Delinquents.
4. Socially Exceptional :	Juvenile delinquents.
5. Multi-Exceptional :	The children with more then one defect.

Meaning and Definition of Gifted Children

Giftedness is a complex concept. It covers a wide range of abilities and traits. A child who achieves far beyond the level of his or her average peers may be subjected to criticism or social isolation by other children or their parents. Studies conducted by Terman, Hollingworth, Geselt and others have highlighted that a child with high intellectual level and possessing special abilities and talents is regarded as gifted. Even the terminology of giftedness can become rather confusing. Besides, the word "gifted" a variety of other terms have been used to describe individuals who are superior in some way, i.e., "talented or bright", "creative", "genius", and "precocious", etc. The word precocity refers to remarkably early development whereas genius indicates a particular aptitude or capacity in any area or extremely rare intellectual powers; creativity refers to the ability to express novel and useful ideas, and the word talent or bright indicate a special ability, aptitude or accomplishment. Thus the following are the definition of gifted children.

(1) Renzulli defines "Giftedness refers to cognitive (i.e., intellectual) superiority (not necessarily of genius calibre), creativity and motivation in combination and of sufficient magnitude to set the child apart from the vast majority of his age-mates and make it possible for him to contribute something of particular value to society".

(2) Terman traditionally, if a person scored above a particular level (140 IQ) in Binet or WISC scale is called gifted.

(3) Tyler defines "the gifted child is one who is exceptional in the amount of his production, rate and quality of his production".

(4) Paul witty defines "gifted children are those children whose performance is consistently remarkable in music, art, social leadership and other forms of expression".

(5) Havinghurst defines that "the talented or gifted child is one who shows consistently remarkable performance in anyworth while line of endeavour".

(6) Lucito defines "the gifted are those children whose potential, intellectual powers at such as high ideational level in both productive and evaluative thinking that it can be reasonably assumed that they could be future problem solvers, innovators and evaluators of the culture if adequate educational experiences are provided to them".

(7) Marland report indicates "the gifted are those who possess outstanding abilities or potential in the area of general intellectual capacity, specific academic aptitude, creative or productive thinking, leadership ability, visual or performing arts and psycho-motor activity and must be identified as performing in the top 3% to 5% of the school-aged population.

(8) Congressional Record, USA (1978) it is mentioned that gifted and talented children means children, and whenever applicable, youth, who are identified at the pre-school, elementary, or secondary level as possessing demonstrated or potential abilities that give evidence of high performance capacity in areas such as intellectual, creative, specific, academic or leadership ability, or in the performing and visual arts, and who by reason thereof require services or activities not ordinarily provided by the school".

(9) National Society for the study of education reports that "a talented or gifted child is one who shows consistently remarkable performance in any worthwhile line of

endeavour. It indicates not only the intellectual abilities but also promise in music, arts, creative writing, dramatic, mechanical skills and social leadership".

(10) Sumption and Lucking defines "those who possess a superior central nervous system characterised by the potential to perform tasks requiring a comparatively high degree of intellectual abstraction or creative imagination or both is called gifted children".

(11) Guilford defines giftedness in terms of two concepts like "Convergent thinking" and "divergent thinking".

Thus from the above definitions, it is evident that giftedness is a wide term and covers many abilities and if he receives proper attention and opportunity for self expression and development, the gifted child can make a noteworthy contribution to the welfare of society, the nation and humanity at large.

Characteristics of Gifted Children

The following are the characteristics of gifted children.

(1) *Physical Characteristics*

Gifted children as a group are taller, heavier, stronger, more energetic and healthier. Good in their physic and growth, good co-ordination and muscular control, and better than their average age mates in physical stature and health.

(2) *Intellectual Characteristics*

The gifted children have better ability to organise, analyse, memorize, synthesize, reason out things, extensive rapidity in learning, clear self-expression, good comprehension, good insight, unusual ideas, imagination, better understanding, rich vocabulary, good span of attention, varied interests, logical, concentrate well, good memory, fund of general knowledge, better in generalization, and are alert, keen, observant and react quickly.

(3) *Educational and Occupational Characteristics*

Gifted children tend to be far ahead of average children in academic achievement, learn to read easily, more advanced in reading and like school and superior than their classmates. They enter occupations demanding greater than average intellectual ability, creativity and motivation work.

(4) *Social and Emotional Characteristics*

Gifted children tend to be happy and well liked by their peers both gifted and non-gifted. Many are social leaders at school. Socially, they get along well with others, good sense of humour and initiate action and are eager to co-operate. They are more trustworthy and sincere.

They are emotionally stable, display emotional maturity and minimum conflicts with others and self-sufficient and less prone to neurotic and psychotic disorders.

(5) *Moral and Ethical Characteristics*

The gifted children possess moral attributes such as fairness, honesty, compassion and justice. They do the right and see the right more quickly and profoundly than the average person. Most studies show that the gifted to be superior to average individuals in connection with moral and ethical issues and in moral behaviour.

(6) *Personal Characteristics Like Interests, Character and Personality etc.*

Gifted children are persistent, confident and very curious to know things, happy disposition and flexibility to adopt themselves, read a great deal and have interest in abstract things and varied. Various personality characteristics like better planning, ability to adjust, generous, sincere and dutiful, and the ability to analyse and synthesize things.

In addition to that the following are the positive and negative characteristics of gifted children.

Positive	*Negative or Not so Positive*
1. Expresses ideas and feelings well	1. May be grib, making fluent statements without understanding.
2. Can move at a rapid pace.	2. May be impatient to proceed to next level or task.
3. Work conscientiously	3. May struggle against rules, regulations,
4. Wants to learn, explore and seek more information	4. May lead discussions "off the track".
5. Develops broad knowledge and an extensive store of vicarious experiences.	5. May be frustrated by the daily routine work.
6. Sensitive to the felings and right of others and dominate class discussions.	6. May use humour to manipulate.
7. Makes steady progress high curiosity.	7. May loose interest quickly.
8. Makes original and stimulating contributions to discussions	8. May be restless, inattentive and disturbing.

(Cont.).............

9. Sees relationship easily	9. May be indifferent to class work.
10. Learns materials quickly.	10. May be outspoken egoistic and jealous.
11. Is able to use reading skills to obtain new information.	
12. Contributes to enjoyment of life for self and others, stable and socially accepted.	
13. Complete assigned tasks and attentive	
14. Requires little drill for learning	
15. Capable of handling personal problems.	

Screening, Identification and Measuring Brightness or Gifted

The measurement of giftedness is a complicated matter. It is a collective effort of parents, teachers, psychologists and social workers to help in the early identification of such model children at the early stage so that they can develop their special potential to make a unique and valuable contribution to society. Thus it is important that good methods of screening and measurement be used.

Pegnato and Birch (1959) have suggested two criterion for evaluating screening techniques, i.e., effectiveness and efficiency. These can be done on the basis of teacher judgement, creative ability in art and music, superiority in mathematics, intelligence tests and group achievement tests. No single index or procedure will identify the gifted or talented. Identification usually involves a combination of procedures. These include :

(1) Intelligence scores/tests
(2) Creativity measures
(3) Achievement measures/tests
(4) Teacher nomination/judgement/rating
(5) Parent nomination
(6) Self nomination/analysis
(7) Peers nomination, opionions and reports
(8) Careful observation and socio-metric techniques
(9) Aptitude tests
(10) Interest inventory
(11) Anecdotal records
(12) Behavioural assessment through personality tests.
(13) Communicative record card.

A wise and expert teacher should, therefore, try to put

in an all round effort to detect and recognize the specific abilities and talents of these children. So that they may be given appropriate help to achieve success in their specific fields.

Education of the Gifted Children

Teaching a gifted child demands special attention from the teacher. His quest for fresh knowledge and development of his talents should be considered a matter of high priority. Society will be best served if the talents of its most capable problem solvers are cultivated. The gifted are the most precious natural resource for solving the future problems of society. Thus, there is an urgent need for a well thoughtout programme or scheme of special education for the gifted children. The following are the educational considerations for the gifted for Gallaghar (1966):

(1) Administrative programmes (make changes in the child's environment).
(2) Instructional programmes (involve alternations in the content of the subject matter presented and/or the style in which it is presented).
(3) Adjunctive programmes (are special services such as, counselling or tutoring which extend the usual school programme).

Getzels and Dillon (1973) explained the following specific programmes for gifted.

(1) Summar Institutes (ii) Non-graded primary schools (iii) Early admission in school (iv) College level courses for high school students (v) college credit for high school courses. (vi) special classes in a particular subject matter in the students curriculm (vii) Ability grouping and Saturday seminars (viii) Enrichment in regular classrooms (ix) Adding a course to the students normal course load (x) clubs and extra curricular projects for the gifted (xi) field trips and special televised courses (xii) Half-day regular and half day enriched programme (xiii) Acceleration and special schools for gifted children (xiv) Individual tutoring a counselling for the gifted (xv) Advance placement and student exchange (xvi) Honour's programmes and new curriculum.

The three most common types of educational provision for the gifted are enrichment, segregation (ability grouping) and acceleration (double promotion).

1. *Enrichment*

The term enrichment means to those activities which give the gifted pupil an opportunity to study a subject more deeply and more broadly than the average child in the class. It means providing special activities or additional educational opportunities needed to develop their talents such as special assignments (within or outside the syllabus), work on independent projects, preparation of reports and participation in panel discussions, independent library reading, visit to the sites to obtain first-hand information, construction of models, aid and improvised apparatus, participation in the organisation of co-curricular activities and experimentation and independent research.

II. *Acceleration*

Acceleration means providing learning experiences that are usually given to older children or usually known as double promotion and the gifted child is allowed accelerated progress. Approaches to acceleration include early admission to school, grade skipping (promoted to the next higher grade in midsession) without completing the prescribed course, and advance placement and giving opportunity to move through a particular subject grade according to their own rate.

III. *Segregation*

It means ability grouping or practice of placing students into special "tracks" according to their abilities. This gives emphasis on homogeneous grouping. Here a given grade/class is divided into different section on the basis of ability. The opponents argue that it is undemocratic, involves huge expenditure and fosters an intellectual elite but no guarantee of development.

Teachers of the Gifted

Does the teacher have to be gifted in order to teach gifted children effectively? The answer is not necessarily in the sense that teachers should be gifted in different ways to teach different children. Teachers of the gifted do not need to be gifted in the usual sense, but they need to have some particular qualities.

Teachers of the gifted should :

1. Be willing to accept unusual and diverse questions, answers and projects
2. Be intellectually curious
3. Be sympathetic and business like
4. Have a variety of interests
5. Appreciate achievement
6. Be well prepared in instructional techniques
7. Be well-prepared in content area
8. Interested to teach the gifted and feel comfortable

Backward Children or Slow Learning Child

One of the problems of every teacher is to handle the children who lag behind other children in their school work. These children are called backward child or slow learners and differ from person to person. These children show inability to progress normally in school work and need special care at the hands of school authorities, parents and others. Thus the problem of dealing with and educating such a child has bothered the teacher too much and it is essential to know the procedure of handling them.

Meaning

Backwardness had been defined by different authors and investigators. The following are some of the well known definitions:

1. C. Burt—"A backward child is one who is unable to do the work of the class next below that which is normal for his age". He defines on the basis of attainment and if the child's educational age drops below 85 per cent of his own age, he should be regarded as backward. A backward child is a slow learner and whose I.Q is between 70 to 90.
2. Burton Hart—"Backwardness in general is applied to cases where their educational attainments are lower than what they are capable of". The backward child has backwardness or weak either in all the subjects of school curriculum (general) or in a particular subject (specific).

   "Dull children are those children who have I.Q. between 70 to 85. Thus dullness may be one of the causes of backwardness in intelligence but all backwardness is not the outcome of dullness".

3. Barton Hall—"Backwardness in general is applied to cases where their educational attainment falls below the level of their natural abilities.
4. Schonell—Backward pupil is one who, compared with other pupils of the same chronological age, show marked educational deficiency.

Thus a backward child falls far behind other children of his age in matters of study and failure in the academic field. Therefore, backward child should not be misunderstood and labelled as mentally retarded or dull. They may be said as slow learner, if his attainment falls below his natural ability. Truly speaking, any child who does not progress at a rate corresponding to his/her abilities may be said to be backward.

Characteristics of Backward Children

The following are the general characteristics of backward children.

1. Poor muscular co-ordination.
2. Defects in eyes, nose and serious speech defects.
3. Lesser capacity of abstract thinking.
4. Lack in reasoning ability.
5. Lack the so-called common sense.
6. Unable to handle symbolic material and directions for assignments.
7. Unable to understand complex rules.
8. Slow in all areas, i.e., academic, social, emotional and physical.
9. Develop undesirable social traits.
10. Unable to work independently.
11. Really confused and short span of interest and attention.
12. Unable to concentrate voluntarily.

Identification of Backward Children

The backward children may be identified with the help of following measures.

(1) Observation in the class and outside the class by the teachers and parents.

(2) Teachers rating.
(3) Administration of intelligence test achievement test, and personality inventory.
(4) Cumulative Record Card.
(5) Collection of family history and conducting physical test.

Causes of Factors of Backwardness

There can be no simple cause of backwardness. It is a phenomenon of multiple causation. Let us understand the various causes or factors of backwardness.

(1) *Physical Factors*

It has been found that some children are born with an inherited lack of vitality or a weak development impulse which causes them to grow slowly. Physical diseases and defects (defective eye sight, deaf, dumb, headache, cough and stomach trouble, etc.), and postural defects, etc., lead to lack of concentration and promote scholastic backwardness.

(2) *Intellectual Factors*

Lack of general intelligence is the primary cause of backwardness. Burt found out that 75% backwardness is due to low intelligence or I.Q. Some children are born with some inherent defects in their brain system or with intellectual subnormality.

(3) *Environmental Factors*

Apart from the innate factors, environmental forces, i.e., home, neighbourhood and school atmosphere significantly influence the educational attainment of an individual.

(a) Home Factors

Poor home condition such as economic condition, poverty, over-crowding, lack of amenities, parental partiality, unhygienic living conditions, malnutrition, illiterate parents, negative attitude towards education, improper behaviour, step-mother and divorced parents, parental attitudes, indulge in bad activities and lack of love, affection and guidance from family may develop educational subnormality.

(b) School Factors

Similarly poor attendance at school, poor administration, frequent transfers from one school to another, teaching of basic skills at premature age, unsympathetic teachers, lack of individualized attention, lack of regular and intensive drill in skill subjects, ineffective methods of teaching, defective examination, teachers negative attitude towards teaching, unhygienic conditions in school, defective timetable, irregular home assignments, lack of interest in the subject and long absence due to illness, etc., are responsible for backwardness.

(c) The Neighbourhood Factor

The influence of neighbourhood and other social agencies also contribute to the problem of backwardness in children. The neighbourhood where the child lives, the company with whom he plays, the members of the society he comes in contact with, the social places where he visits, the philosophy of life and work habits, etc., contribute to the problem of slow in learning.

4. ***Emotional Disturbance***

Emotional shocks, interpersonal relationships at home or in school, lack of moral standards, insecurity, carelessness, evasion, dishonest and anxieties, etc., have an important influence on the child's educational progress.

Education for Backward Children or Treatment of Backwardness

In order to help educationally backward child, it is necessary to find out the causes and accordingly we should plan an integrated course of action with a view to educating him. The following are some suggestions for guiding a backward child.

(1) Children who are backward owing to low I.Q. need to be grouped into special classes and taught in a detailed and practical manner.

(2) Children who are backward in one subject need individual teaching and special attention in the school or at home.

(3) Size of the class for educationally slow learners should be small.

(4) School conditions should be adopted more closely to their needs and limitations.

(5) Provision of special curriculum, methods of teaching and teachers initation, etc., must be commensurate with the requirement of the backward child.

(6) Verbal instruction should be reduced and educational excursions, play activities and activity based methodology should be followed.

(7) The teacher most develop their self-confidence, stimulate them and have great patience.

(8) Regular medical check-up and necessary treatment, time table, parental education or parent-teacher associations, child guidance clinic and remedial teaching, etc., can also help the backward child for improvement.

(9) The teaching-materials must be prepared by looking into the requirements and level of the children.

(10) There should be a friendly approach, protected/ rich environment, reinforcement in learning and proper motivation, etc., can also offer opportunities for their development.

(11) Provision of truancy (long absence from school) and non-attendance, diversified courses, maintenance of proper progress record card, taking the help of experienced psychologists, and controlling negative environmental factors, etc., rectify the causes of backwardness.

Summary

The term exceptional children includes all children who deviate from the normal child in various dimensions of their personality to the extent of requiring special attention and education for their upbringing, welfare and adjustment.

In spite of the fact that the gifted children are an asset to the society although very little attention has been given to their education. Gifted children have an I.Q. of 140 or above and superior in all areas and demonstrate outstanding praiseworthy and remarkable performance in any worthwhile field of human endeavour. However the giftedness needs to be identified and there are ways and means to do so. They possess special characteristics. For their education the techniques like enrichment, segregation and acceleration, etc., can be used,

Similarly backward children are slow learners whose educational attainment falls below their natural abilities. They are considered failures in their field of accomplishment. They are not mentally retarded or dull. The causes of backwardness are environmental, physical and psychological. For their education specially trained teachers, teaching materials and integrated approach is essential.

Note : Slow learning is that child whose achievement is low primarily because of native intellectual endowment. In fact he is a dull child. Children whose I.Q. is 75-80 is called slow learners but it is otherwise known as backward child.

Questions

1. Define giftedness. What educational provisions will you make for them in your school?
2. Define backwardness. What are the causes? Describe the educational provision for backward children.
3. Who are the gifted children? What are the characteristics ? How can the gifted be located?
4. How do gifted children differ from ordinary children? What arrangements should be made for their proper education?
5. Who are gifted? How can they be identified? Suggest programme of education most suitable to them?
6. Discuss some important suggestions which can be taken up as a task of education for a backward child?
7. Who is a backward child? What can be done for backward children to bring them back to their normal level of attainment?
8. Write a Critical note on the slow learners/backward children?

References

Barbe, W.B. (1965) : "A study of the family background of gifted", *Jo. of Educational Psychology*, 47, 302-09.

Barbe, W.B. and Renzulli, J.C. (1975) : *Psychology and Education of the Gifted,* Irvington Publishers, New York.

Burt, C (1950) : *The Backward Child,* Uni: of London Press, London.

Gallagher, J.J. (1975) : *Teaching the Gifted Child* 2nd Ed., Allyn and Sons, New York.

Newland, T.E. (1976) : *The gifted in socio-cultural perspective,* Prentice Hall, Englewood and Cliffs.

Hallahan, D.P. and Kauffman, J.M. (1973) : *Introduction to Special Education,* C.E. Merrill, Columbias.

Heck, A.O. (1953) : ***The Education of Exceptional Children***, McGraw Hill, New York.

Heward, W.L. and Orlansky, M.D. (1958) : ***Exceptional Children***, Charles E. Merril Pub., Columbus, Ohio.

Highfield, M.E. (1951) : ***The Education of Backward Children***, Harrap and Co, London.

Kirk, S.A. (1970) ***Educating Exceptional Children***, Oxford I.B.H. Pub. Company, Calcutta.

Sumption, M.R. and Lucking, E.M. (1960) : ***Education of the Gifted***, Ronald Press, New York.

Schonell, F.J. (1949) : ***Backwardness in Basic School Subjects***, Oliver and Boye, Edinburgh.

●●●

INDEX